Dretske and His Critics

Dretske and His Critics

Edited by
Brian P. McLaughlin

Basil Blackwell

First published 1991

Basil Blackwell, Inc.
3 Cambridge Center
Cambridge, Massachusetts 02142, USA

Basil Blackwell Ltd
108 Cowley Road, Oxford, OX4 1JF, UK

Library of Congress Cataloging in Publication Data

Dretske and his critics/edited by Brian McLaughlin.
     p.   cm.
  Includes bibliographical references and index.
  ISBN 1557-86198-6
  1. Dretske, Fred I.   2. Knowledge, Theory of—History—20th
century.   3. Content (Psychology)—History—20th century.
4. Psychology—Philosophy—History—20th century.   5. Visual
perception—History—20th century.   I. McLaughlin, Brian P.
B945.D744D74   1991
121'.092—dc20   90-46083
                                                        CIP

British Library Cataloguing in Publication Data

A CIP catalogue record for this book is available from the British Library.

Typeset in 10 on 11 pt Times
by Graphicraft Typesetters Ltd., Hong Kong.
Printed in Great Britain by Billing & Sons Ltd, Worcester

Contents

Notes on Contributors

John Heil is Professor of Philosophy at Davidson College. He is author of *Perception and Cognition*, articles in epistemology and the philosophy of mind, and editor of *Cause, Mind, and Reality: Essays Honoring C. B. Martin*.

Stewart Cohen Assistant Professor of Philosophy at Arizona State. He has published numerous articles in epistemology.

David H. Sanford is Professor of Philosophy at Duke University. He is author of *Conditionals*, and articles in metaphysics, epistemology, and philosophical logic.

Jaegwon Kim is William Herbert Perry Faunce Professor of Philosophy at Brown University. He is author of numerous articles in metaphysics and epistemology.

Robert Cummins is Professor of Philosophy at the University of Arizona. He is author of *The Nature of Psychological Explanation* and *Meaning and Mental Representation*.

Terence Horgan is Professor of Philosophy at Memphis State University. He has published widely in metaphysics and philosophy of mind, and philosophy of language. He and John Tienson are now completing *Connectionism and the Philosophy of Psychology*.

Daniel C. Dennett is Distinguished Arts and Sciences Professor at Tufts University and author of *Content and Consciousness, Brainstorms, Elbow Room, The International Stance*, and numerous articles.

Frederick Adams is Associate Professor of Philosophy and Chair of Philosophy at Central Michigan University. He has published in the areas of cognitive psychology, epistemology, nonmonotonic logic, and philosophy of mind.

Brian P. McLaughlin is Associate Professor of Philosophy at Rutgers University and is author of articles in metaphysics and the philosophy of mind, and is co-editor with Ernest LePore of *Actions and Events: Perspectives on the Philosophy of Donald Davidson* and co-editor with Amelie Rorty of *Perspectives on Self-Deception*.

Introduction

The papers in this volume discuss Dretske's views on the following issues: the nature of seeing, the possibility of knowledge, the nature of content or meaning, the nature of behavior, and the role of content in the causal explanation of behavior. I will briefly summarize the main points of the papers, but I will make no attempt to summarize Dretske's fine responses to these papers or to adjudicate any of the disputes between Dretske and his critics. My purpose is just to introduce the issues addressed in the volume.

I

In *Seeing and Knowing* (London, Routledge and Kegan Paul, 1968), Dretske argued that there is a relational sense of seeing according to which, if one sees X, then X exists (or occurs); and if one sees X, and X = Y, then one sees Y. He carefully contrasted seeing in this relational sense with seeing that something is the case, and with seeing what or where something is. Seeing an object (or event) in the relational sense, he claimed, is not constituted by, nor does it require, having beliefs about that object (or event). It is non-epistemic seeing; in contrast, seeing that something is the case and seeing what or where something is require belief and are cases of epistemic seeing. Dretske acknowledged, however, that seeing an object requires undergoing a certain sort of mental event, namely a visual experience. What one sees must look some way to one, and its so doing consists in one's undergoing a visual experience of it. Having a visual experience of an object, however, is not constituted by, nor does it require, having a belief about the object. In the first paper in this volume, "Perceptual Experience," John Heil makes a case for the view that seeing an object requires having beliefs about it. Moreover, he challenges the claim that seeing requires visual experience and even calls into question the very notion of visual experience itself.

The next two papers, Stewart Cohen's "Skepticism, Relevance, and Relativity" and David H. Sanford's "Proper Knowledge," discuss

Dretske's views on the possibility of knowledge. I will first briefly present the views of Dretske's that they focus on and then summarize the papers in turn.

Dretske is largely responsible for the relevant alternatives response to skepticism about knowledge (see note 1 of Cohen's paper for references). According to Dretske, it is not required in order to know that p that one's evidence eliminate all alternatives to p (that is, all propositions incompatible with p); rather, what is required is that one's evidence eliminate all *relevant* alternatives to p, and not all alternatives are relevant. Dretske claims that in arguing that we cannot know the sorts of things we ordinarily claim to know, the skeptic appeals to irrelevant alternatives. Dretske rejects the following principle that is often invoked in skeptical arguments:

> *Closure Principle*: If S knows that p, and S knows that p implies not-q, then S knows that not-q.

Even if S knows that p implies not-q, it is not thereby required that S know that not-q in order to know that p. For while q is an alternative to p, it may fail to be a relevant alternative to p, even when S knows that p implies not-q. What alternatives, then, are relevant? Dretske claims that the range of relevant alternatives is determined by contextual factors. Knowledge is, he holds, a relatively absolute notion. It is absolute in that the evidence possessed by someone who knows that p must exclude *all* relevant alternatives. But it is relative in that what alternatives count as relevant is relative to a context; an alternative that counts as relevant in one context may count as irrelevant in another.

Stewart Cohen distinguishes two notions of the contextual relativity of knowledge. One notion is this: whether someone knows that p can depend on factors that do not supervene on the person's evidential situation. Cohen points out that knowledge is surely context-relative in this sense if one's evidential situation is compatible with not-p; and he mentions additional factors that may be contextually relevant in this sense. The other notion of contextual relativity is a notion of indexicality. According to Cohen, knowledge attributions contain an implicit indexical component that refers to a standard or criterion of relevance. Contexts of attribution thus set the standard by which a range of alternatives counts as relevant. Cohen claims that this second sort of context relativity – viz., indexicality – explains the intuitive appeal of skeptical arguments. He adds, however, that once we appreciate the indexicality of knowledge claims we can see that skeptical arguments need cast no doubt on them. For the standard of relevance referred to by the skeptic in her denials of knowledge is just not the sort of standard typically referred to in ordinary knowledge attributions. When, in an ordinary context, one says, for example, that David knows that Fred is at the bar, one need not be in disagreement with the skeptic who says that it is not the case that David knows that Fred is at the bar. For the proposition that one asserts may not, despite appearances, be the proposition that the skeptic denies. The standard of relevance referred to by the implicit indexical component of each claim may be different. Thus, the skeptic and anti-skeptic are often at cross-purposes. Cohen says that "by supposing that attributions of knowledge are sensitive to context in this way, we do justice both to our strong inclination in everyday life to say we know things and the persisting and undiminished appeal of skeptical arguments" (p. 28 below). We are often right in saying we know certain things, and the skeptic is right in denying that we know those things. For what we assert is not what the skeptic denies. Cohen also claims that once one appreciates the indexicality of knowledge, one can see that one need not follow Dretske in rejecting the principle that knowledge is closed under known implication, that is, the closure principle. For knowledge is closed under known implication relative to a standard of relevance.

David H. Sanford argues that (1) all alternatives to p are relevant to the *proper* knowledge that p, (2) that all knowledge is proper knowledge, and (3) that deductive closure under known implication is a valid epistemic principle. He claims, however, that while we properly know less than we typically say we know, we nevertheless know a lot that the skeptic denies we know. One might claim to know that p, when what one properly knows is something conditional in nature. One properly knows that if C, then p, where C defines a range of relevant alternatives from which our evidence selects p. Espying Fred Dretske, someone one knows well, at a philosophy convention one might say that one knows that that is Fred Dretske. What one properly knows, however, might be, rather, that if that is a member of the usual philosophical crowd, and not someone in disguise, then that is Fred Dretske. Sanford says that when we assert something of the form "S knows that p" we often intend to claim that S knows that if C, then p (where C is understood to be, or to imply, some range of relevant alternatives). And he says: "A correct claim of proper knowledge typically has smaller scope than the original as broadly interpreted. Having smaller scope, it exposes less flank to skeptical attack" (pp. 50-1, below). Finally, Sanford argues that the Closure Principle is true since all knowledge is proper knowledge, and if one properly knows that p, then one knows everything one knows p to entail.

II

The remaining papers in the volume are concerned with Dretske's account of content, his account of behavior, and his account of the role of content in the causal explanation of behavior. I will first briefly present each of these accounts and then turn to the papers of contributors.

In the preface of *Knowledge and the Flow of Information* (Cambridge, MIT Press, 1981) Dretske said "The entire project can be viewed as an exercise in naturalism – or, if you prefer, materialistic metaphysics. Can you bake a mental cake using only physical yeast and flour? The argument is that you can" (ibid., p. xi). Dretske then proceeded to develop an information-theoretic account of believing that p (for at least some values of p). He was concerned to solve what Jerry Fodor has called "Brentano's Problem." This is the problem of specifying a (broadly) physical condition the satisfaction of which makes it the case that a state is an intentional state with a certain content. In *Explaining Behavior*, Dretske refined and developed his earlier solution to Brentano's Problem, and in what follows, I will focus on his account as presented there. My reason is two-fold: first, it is his most recent and most developed statement of his account, and second it is the one contributors focus on. I should note that in presenting Dretske's solution to Brentano's Problem, I will omit many of its details.

To begin, Dretske holds that an internal physical state of type C (e.g., a neural type) of an organism O counts as a belief that F (e.g., water) is present *if* in O, C has the natural function of indicating that F is present. Moreover, Dretske holds that a state type C has in O the natural function of indicating that F is present if C acquired a control duty in O because C indicated the presence of F. For C to have a control duty in O is for tokens of C to have a certain kind of causal role in O, one that is specifiable in (broadly) physical terms. The notion of indication is, essentially, the Gricean notion of natural meaning. So, tokens of C indicate that F is present if and only if they naturally mean that F is present. (In *Knowledge and the Flow of Information*, Dretske offered a probabilistic account of natural meaning, calling natural meaning "information content." But his solution to Brentano's Problem in *Explaining Behavior* does not depend on this feature of the earlier account.) Dretske describes how, through a process of operant learning, an internal state can acquire a control duty because of its indication of the presence of a certain environmental feature. But the details of this need not concern us here.

Now indication (natural meaning) does not admit of misindication: If a token of C indicates that F is present, then F is present. Beliefs, however, can be false: One can believe that F is present, even when it is not. Here is how Dretske accommodates this fact: He maintains that C can have the natural function of indicating that F is present (and so count as a belief that F is present) even when it fails to indicate that F is present. Indicator function admits of malfunction. And this, claims Dretske, explains the possibility of false belief. Tokens of C may cease to indicate F's presence due to some change in O's environment. Even if such a change occurs, however, state type C will retain the function of indicating that F is present so long as it retains a control duty and does not do so because of its indicating anything else. (If it retains a control duty because of indicating something else, something other than F, then, claims Dretske, its natural indicator function will change.) And this can happen even if tokens of C cease to indicate that F is present. For the environmental changes that result in tokens of C ceasing to indicate that F is present may have no effect on C's control duty in O. Since C can retain the natural function of indicating that F is present whilst its tokens no longer indicate that F is present, tokens of C can fail to discharge their natural indicator function qua Cs. When this happens, the tokens can be false beliefs that F is present. This, in a nutshell, is Dretske's naturalized account of believing that F is present.

Turn now to Dretske's account of behavior. It receives its most complete and detailed expression in *Explaining Behavior*. There Dretske contrasts product views of behavior with process views of behavior. On the *product* view, behavior is bodily movement that has a certain etiology. Dretske eschews product views of behavior. He argues that they conflate behaviors with one of the components of behavior. Bodily movement is a part of behavior, but it itself is not behavior. Dretske argues for a *process* view according to which behaviors are certain sorts of causal processes, namely (roughly), processes consisting of an appropriate internal state's causing bodily movements (and/or external affairs resulting from bodily movements). A behavior will thus contain an internal state as a component and a bodily movement as a component. And the behavior will be the process consisting of the internal state's causing the movement. This, then, is Dretske's process view of behavior.

In *Explaining Behavior*, Dretske also provides his most complete and detailed account of the role of content in the causal explanation of behavior. When we explain behavior by citing beliefs and desires, the contents of the beliefs and desires have an explanatory role. It is in virtue of the belief's being a belief that p and the desire's being a desire for r that the belief and desire explain the behavior. Dretske claims that this explanatory role is a causal-explanatory role, that having a certain content is a causally relevant feature of a belief *vis-à-vis* the behavior it explains. Dretske acknowledges, however, that this claim is problematic. The content of a belief state will not supervene on intrinsic properties of the organism in the belief state. Two individuals can be exactly alike in all intrinsic physical respects, and yet occupy states with different contents. So, the problem arises as to how the content property can be causally relevant. This problem was first raised by Stephen Stich, so, following Cummins, let us call this "Stich's Problem." Stich's own response to the problem is to deny that content-properties are causally relevant. He maintains that their failing to supervene on "what's in the head" excludes them from being so. Dretske, however, attempts to show that this does not exclude them from being causally relevant. He attempts to explain how a state's having a certain content can be a causally relevant feature of the state *vis-à-vis* some behavior it explains despite the fact that the content-property will not supervene on "what's in the agent's head."

Dretske's explanation invokes a distinction between triggering causes and structuring causes of behavior. A behavior, recall, is a causal process that consists of an internal state C's causing a movement M. A triggering cause of a behavior is a cause of C's causing M now, rather than some other time or not at all. A structuring cause of C's causing M is a cause of C's causing an M, rather than some other movement or no movement at all. Subtleties aside, Dretske maintains that C's having a content-property is a structuring cause of C's causing M. And he explains how this is consistent with the content-property's failing to supervene on what's in the agent's head.

In "Dretske on How Reasons Explain Behavior," Jaegwon Kim distinguishes three problems of psychophysical causation, and then presents Dretske's solutions to two of them. Kim points out that Dretske is primarily concerned with the problem of explaining how content-properties can be a causally relevant features of states even though they do not supervene on intrinsic properties of the individual in the state. (This, of course, is Stich's Problem.) Kim provides an elegant account of Dretske's explanation and then raises some difficulties for it. He goes on to suggest how Dretske might avail himself of Kim's own notion of supervenient causation to resolve the difficulties. Kim claims that Dretske's account also implies a solution to another problem of psychophysical causation, the problem of explanatory exclusion. In this context of psychophysical causation, this is the problem of explaining how a phenomenon can have both a physical explanation and a psychological explanation. Kim claims that on Dretske's account, this is unproblematic since the mental states cited in the psychological explanation will reduce to physical states.

In "Actions, Reasons, and the Explanatory Role of Content," Terence Horgan examines Dretske's account of the role of content in the causal explanation of behavior and presents three problems for it. The first arises because of Dretske's process view of behavior. Since reasons, certain belief–desire pairs, are components of behavior, they cannot be causes of behavior. So, on this process view, the beliefs and desires that explain a behavior are not causes of the behavior. But this is a problem, claims Horgan, since the beliefs and desires that explain a behavior are causes of the behavior. The second problem arises because of Dretske's account of how a state acquires content as a result of an organism's undergoing a process of operant learning. This implies that content is a historical-relational property; but, Horgan claims, this is highly unintuitive. Third, and he says most importantly, we have a firm intuition that contents are here-and-now explanatorily relevant, while on Dretske's view they are past-operative structuring causes. Horgan claims post-operative structuring causes are features that explain how the organism became "wired up" in such a way that Cs cause Ms. On Dretske's account, content-properties only explain why the agent's nervous system got configured in a certain way, why an internal state of a certain sort came to cause movements of a certain sort, rather than movements of other sorts or no movements at all. Hence, it does not explain why the particular behavior in question occurs now. Horgan thinks that having a certain content should be relevant to a mental state's being a triggering cause of behavior or action. And he goes on to provide his own solution to the problem of the causal relevance of content, a solution which invokes the notion of a pattern of counterfactual dependencies.

In "The Role of Mental Meaning in Psychological Explanation,"

Robert Cummins characterizes Dretske's account of the causal role of content as an attempt to solve Stich's Problem. Dretske's solution and his account of content, according to Cummins, have certain "unattractive consequences." The unattractive consequences of his account of content are, argues Cummins, first that it is incompatible with the claim that much learning is dependent on innate knowledge; and second, that it is incompatible with the claim that cognitive states can be synchronically specified (since, on Dretske's view, a state will count as a cognitive state in virtue of an historical property). An unattractive consequent of Dretske's solution to Stich's Problem, argues Cummins, is that it is incompatible with the widespread claim that it is current representations and their current semantic contents that (in part) explain current behavior. Dretske's solution has this consquence, says Cummins, because on his account it is an aspect of the natural meaning of an internal state during the learning period that explains why Cs cause Ms. Once the organism becomes so structured that in it Cs cause Ms, a token C will, *ceteris paribus*, cause an M regardless of what the token means or indicates. Cummins also launches a more fundamental attack, arguing that the very assumptions that motivate Dretske's projects are "on the wrong track." He identifies the assumptions as these: (A1) semantic content cannot have a serious explanatory role to play in psychology unless it has a causal role to play; and (A2) the role of semantic content in folk psychological explanation just is, or is our best line on, the explanatory role of semantic content in scientific cognitive psychology. Cummins rejects these assumptions. He maintains that the notion of representation that is to be found in scientific cognitive psychology is a notion of simulation, what he calls S-representation, for which neither of these assumptions holds.

In "Ways of Establishing Harmony," Daniel Dennett characterizes one of Dretske's central projects as explaining how there could be a reliable correlation between the semantics of internal states and internal processes in which those states participate, given that the semantic properties of the states do not supervene on properties in virtue of which the states participate in the processes. Dennett characterizes this as the problem of explaining how there could be a pre-established harmony between the content of an internal state and its causal powers. The problem is to coordinate the meaning or content of an internal state with its causal role. One wants to explain why there is a correspondence between a state's content and what it does, a correspondence that we can exploit to use content to predict effects. Dennett thinks that there are three plausible, and compatible, ways we can try to explain this correspondence: by appeal to natural selection, by appeal to individual learning, and by appeal to deliberate design. Dennett claims that Dretske accepts only the second way. In the body of the paper, Dennett says why Dretske should also accept the third. And in a postscript to the paper, he says why Dretske should also accept the first. He says on Dretske's learning account it is the fact that previous tokenings of C, those that occurred during learning, naturally meant (or indicated) F that explains why this (present) token of C causes M. Hence, learning is no better than natural selection in its demonstration of the efficacy of meaning. It is always, both in learning and in natural selection, the meaning of indicational properties of earlier instances of the structure type that figure in the explanation of why present tokens of this type have the effects they do.

In "Causal Contents," Frederick Adams explains and defends Dretske's account of the role of content in the causal explanation of behavior. He provides a detailed account first of Dretske's naturalized account of content (his solution to Brentano's Problem) and then of the explanatory role of content (his solution to Stich's Problem). Adams argues in the process that Dretske's account of the explanatory role of content need not commit him to a component view of behavior, that even someone who holds a product view can accept the account. Adams then attempts to adjudicate two disputes. The first is between Dretske and Dennett. Dretske distinguishes intrinsic or original intentionality and derived intentionality. Derived intentionality depends on original intentionality; and the latter can, Dretske claims, be accounted for in naturalistic terms. Dennett denies that there is any such thing as original intentionality. Adams offers a defense of Dretske's position that there is original intentionality against Dennett's objections. The second dispute Adams attempts to adjudicate is one between Dretske and Fodor. Dretske offers an account of the role of *wide* content (content that does not supervene on what is in the believer's head) in the causal explanation of behavior. Fodor maintains that only narrow content is causally relevant (content that supervenes on what is in the head). Adams marshalls a defense of Dretske's position.

The final paper, by Brian McLaughlin, entitled "Belief Individuation and Dretske on Naturalizing Content" first poses a dilemma for Dretske's solution to Brentano's Problem and then suggests a way between the horns of the dilemma. The following nonduplication principle for beliefs is fairly widely held:

> *The Content Principle*: No two belief (state types) can be exactly alike in their content.

McLaughlin argues that if this principle is correct, then either natural indicator function does not suffice for belief content or Dretske's account of how natural indicator function is determined by operant learning fails. McLaughlin suggests that Dretske deny the content principle and instead assert the following nonduplication principle for beliefs:

> *The Encoded Content Principle*: No two beliefs (state types) can be exactly alike in their content and in the manner in which they encode their content.

McLaughlin then proceeds to try to undermine the content principle and to offer a plausibilty argument in favor of the encoded content principle.

(McLaughlin leaves open, however, the empirical issue of how belief contents are encoded, of whether they are linguistically encoded, or encoded in units in connectionist networks, or encoded in some other way.)

Acknowledgments

I am deeply indebted to Fred Dretske and Fred Adams for much help, both editorial and philosophical. I would also like to thank Stephan Chambers and Ernest LePore for their help in bringing this volume to publication. Finally, I am grateful for financial aid from Rutgers University Research and Sponsored Programs, which helped enormously with mailing and copying costs.

Brian P. McLaughlin
Rutgers University

1

Perceptual Experience

John Heil

Percepts Without Concepts

Philosophers cut their teeth on talk about perceptual experiences. Seeing, hearing, tasting, smelling, and touching things is, we are taught, a matter of our having *experiences* of those things. Experiences differ from one another *qualitatively*. *Seeing* a bell toll and *hearing* it are not at all the same. Experiences are *nondoxastic*. An experience may *give rise* to belief, but experience is not *reducible* to belief. More generally, experiences are noncognitive, nonpropositional. An experience may be propositionally *characterized*, perhaps, but the content of an experience is not itself a proposition. Experiences are of objects and events, particulars and particular goings-on, not facts. And experiences are, or often are, in some degree, *conscious*.

That we have perceptual experiences with these characteristics is widely assumed, hence rarely defended. The attitude is one inherited from Locke:

> What [perceptual experience] is every one will know better by reflecting on what he does himself when he sees, hears, feels, etc. ... than by any discourse of mine. Whoever reflects on what passes in his own mind cannot miss it: and if he does not reflect, all the words in the world cannot make him have any notion of it. (Locke [1690] 1979, book II, chapter 9, section 2, p. 143)

Indeed in considering the matter, one may feel a certain sense of foreboding. Like time, perceptual experience is something we have a grip on so long as we postpone thinking about it. It is only after we trouble to reflect on the topic that it loses its obviousness. We regard perceptual experience in the way we might regard income from a distant but disreputable source: we make use of it gladly, while preferring not to reflect on its origins.

The epistemological role of experiences is controversial. Philosophers disagree, for instance, on whether experiences play a part in warranting or undermining the warrant of beliefs, whether they are *epistemic*, or whether only doxastic states – beliefs based on experiences, perhaps – are relevant epistemologically. Suppose, for instance, that beliefs I now hold support the proposition p, but that my experiences are inapposite. I have sufficient evidence – where having evidence is a matter of having beliefs – that there is a cat on the mat, no evidence to the contrary. I have an experience of Tabby being nudged aside and displaced by Spot, a large Dalmatian. I do not, however, form the belief that Tabby has been displaced. I do not change any of my beliefs at all about the mat's occupant. Is my belief that there is a cat on the mat (still) warranted?

The example may seem in some way impossible. So long as we uphold a distinction between the having of experiences and the forming of beliefs, however, this is unlikely. Given the distinction, then, what is to be said about the case? On the one hand, it seems patent that I should *not* be justified in believing that there is a cat on the mat given the content of my experiences. On the other hand, my having no beliefs at all about Tabby's giving way to Spot makes it difficult to see how my experience *could* be thought to undermine the warrant I have for the proposition that there is a cat on the mat, any more than would my idly forming an image of Spot's routing Tabby. Perhaps our ambivalence about the case stems from our appreciation of a powerful albeit contingent psychological fact about human beings: on the whole, beliefs are tailored to experiences. The move from the one to the other is a move we are conditioned to make spontaneously and unselfconsciously in childhood.

Although philosophers help themselves to features of perceptual experiences in various ways, it is rare that anyone takes the trouble to scrutinize the role they might be thought to play in our mental lives. Fred Dretske is a notable exception. Indeed, Dretske's defense of "nonepistemic" or "simple" perceiving is perhaps best appreciated as an account of the category of perceptual experience.[1] The idea is admirably straightforward. In perceiving, we register our surroundings in a certain way. The process can be broken down into distinct components. It begins with sub-perceptual sensory events elicited by a stimulus, passes into perception, and culminates in judgment (and, often enough, an appropriate response; see figure 1.1a).

Consider visual perception. As I gaze about the world, photons bombard my retina. When conditions are right, when there are *enough* photons, sensations are produced. Sensations, the constituents of perceptual experience, incorporate information about distal objects and events, those objects and events, namely, structuring the light reaching my retina, hence, indirectly, the pattern of responses occurring there. My visual system, in this way, captures incoming information about my surroundings.

The mere capturing or registering of information by sensory organs, however, cannot, according to Dretske, be counted perception. Information thus picked up must be available to the system as a whole, to the

Figure 1.1a The psychological place of perceptual experience.

Figure 1.1b Perception as an information-processing stage.

perceiver. Incoming light might carry information about the chemical composition of the surface reflecting it, for instance, and this information might be registered somehow by retinal cells. Unless the larger system is equipped to extract it, however, unless that information can be *passed along* up the informational chain of command, it is perceptually irrelevant. We may think of a perceptual episode as culminating in a *percept*, a perceptual state incorporating information registered by the senses and made available to the perceiver's cognitive centers. Typically, a percept will contain far more information than we could hope to extract cognitively. A percept is worth a thousand beliefs.

Dretske worries that psychologists and philosophers have tended to conflate perceiving with cognizing. If one supposes that perception involves an *appreciation* of what is perceived, he suggests, one is confusing a judgmental operation following on the heels of perception with perception itself. The mistake is easily made. We may decide what an agent perceives by asking him or by observing his nonverbal behavior. Descriptions supplied, however, and deeds, are a function not merely of what is perceived, but also of beliefs formed on the basis of what is perceived. The point is implicit in figure 1.1b. Dretske concedes that psychologists and philosophers nowadays use the expression "visual perception" to refer to cognitive – belief-like – states that succeed perceiving proper. The practice is encouraged by a tendency to regard perceiving in a functional light. In going to bat for simple perceiving, his aim is to persuade us that this is a mistake, that there is a useful and important distinction to be made between perceiving and cognizing.

Seeing *Tout Court*

In one respect the psychological account of perceptual processes as depicted in figure 1.1b is uncontroversial. One who accepts a causal theory of perception, for instance, might assign a functional role to a Dretske-style percept, while insisting that *perceiving* occurs only at some later stage of the process. Showing that this is wrong requires showing that perceiving and conceiving (or cognizing) are *conceptually* distinct. Ordinarily a demonstration of this point might proceed by invoking either a bottom-up or a top-down strategy, that is, either by providing clear-cut instances of simple perceiving or by generating an explanatorily satisfying theory that independently motivated appeals to some such notion. In this case, however, the latter route is blocked. One could accept the psychological picture Dretske sketches without conceding the notion that perceiving, in some ordinary, pretheoretical sense, is what he says it is. This would be so if, as in the cases above, one thought that Dretske had characterized in an interesting way an intelligent perceptual system but misidentified the *place* in that system occupied by perception.[2]

We are, then, obliged to consider *instances* of perceiving that might be thought to have the properties required by Dretske's view. As we noted at the outset, the instances in question are most naturally appreciated as corresponding to what philosophers have learned to call *experiences*. To focus discussion, let us follow Dretske and concentrate on *visual* experiences, Dretske's *simple seeing*, what I shall call seeing *tout court*. Such seeing is to be distinguished from seeing *that* something is so or seeing a thing *as* a such and such. Dretske's contention is that seeing (*tout court* – the qualification will be presumed in what follows) is to be identified with the having of distinctive nonconceptualized, nonepistemic experiences. My seeing the cat on the mat is a matter of my being in a certain state, one the character of which in no way depends upon my conceptual resources. Dretske does not deny that we often, even typically, form beliefs about what we see. Simple, nonepistemic seeing is not something that occurs only in isolation from judgment or belief, but something that in no way *depends* on judgment or belief. Seeing a thing is like stepping on it. In stepping on Tabby, I may form many beliefs including, perhaps, the belief that it is Tabby I am stepping on. But my *stepping on* Tabby is conceptually independent of these beliefs. I might have stepped on Tabby without recognizing that I had done so, without having any beliefs at all about my circumstances.

Simple seeing, then, is not an eccentric or primitive form of seeing, not something that we grow out of or that occurs only in infants and creatures lacking our conceptual sophistication, not something we might induce by putting ourselves in a special frame of mind. If there is seeing at all, visual perceiving, there is simple seeing: seeing *is* simple seeing. More generally, perceiving is the having of unconceptualized, nonepistemic perceptual experiences. Judgment, belief, and the rest commonly *accompany* perception, at least in noninfant human beings, but remain conceptually distinct from it.

How is seeing, on Dretske's view, related to *conscious awareness*? Are percepts *conscious* states? In addressing this question caution must be exercised. It is, in the first place, a notable feature of the flow chart set

Figure 1.2   Ambiguous figures.

out in figure 1.1b that there is no obvious need for conscious awareness at the perceptual stage. Is it, then, merely a contingent fact that seeing, in the case of human beings, involves consciousness? The very same question might be raised about the philosopher's category of experience. Experiences are invariably described as conscious states, but it is by no means obvious that their being conscious is required for them to play the role they are most often thought to play.

Second, care must be taken not to confuse simple seeing with *noticing* or *attending*. On Dretske's view, what we see, for the most part, far outstrips what we attend to or notice. Noticing requires a focusing of attention. In so doing, the visual field comes to be organized into figure and ground. When our attention is attracted by something, its surroundings recede. When we shift attention, the relationship is altered, even reversed. The phenomenon is most easily appreciated in the case of ambiguous figures (see figure 1.2). I may fail to notice the likeness of a rabbit or a white cross on a black ground. Nevertheless, these seem to be included in my visual experience of the figures. (How could they *fail* to be included given that their boundaries are congruent?) Dretske might say that they are *seen* by me, despite my failing to appreciate or recognize their presence.[3]

I may, then, see much that I never notice, much that I fail to appreciate. It is on this feature of seeing *tout court* that Dretske has most wanted to focus. I gaze at a flag and *see* 50 stars, though I have no clue as to how many there are. You *see* Garbo ducking into a taxi, though you are entirely ignorant that it is Garbo you see.[4] In each case, according to Dretske, what each of us *sees*, what we visually experience, exceeds our *grasp* of what we see, the beliefs we may chance to form on the basis of our respective visual experiences. And this will be so even for what we *notice*. I notice the stars on the flag, yet fail to *appreciate* their number; you notice Garbo, yet fail to *recognize* her.

Dretske finds further confirmation for his view in the experimental work of Sperling and others (see, e.g., Sperling 1960; Neisser 1967, chapter 2). Typical experiments involve the tachistoscopic presentation of arrays of elements (nine letters of the alphabet, for instance, arranged in three rows) to subjects for brief durations (50 milliseconds). The duration

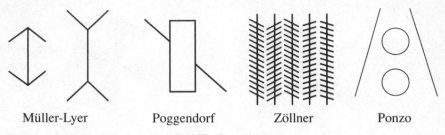

| Müller-Lyer | Poggendorf | Zöllner | Ponzo |

Figure 1.3   Some common "optical illusions."

is such that subjects are unable to identify more than three or four of the letters after exposure to the stimulus. *Which* letters subjects identify, however, can be manipulated by visual prompts occurring *after* the removal of the stimulus. Experiments of this sort have encouraged the postulation of visual *icons*, fleeting, after-image-like replicas of stimuli. During the momentary persistence of an icon, subjects seem capable of adjusting their attention in the way they might were the stimulus still available. What is preserved in the icon, though only for an instant, might be thought of as something close to the original visual experience in all its fullness.

The character and even existence of icons is a matter of some controversy (see, e.g., Neisser 1976, pp. 46ff). Nevertheless, we may agree with Dretske that it is possible to regard the underlying phenomenon in a way that fits nicely with his notion of seeing *tout court*. Iconic memory seems to capture something at least close to what is simply seen, a visual experience *naked*, prior to any cognitive manipulation.

Another sort of case, a sort that Dretske does not discuss, but one that might be thought to support his position is provided by familiar perceptual illusions (see figure 1.3). These call attention to a familiar distinction between the way things *look* or *appear* to us and our beliefs about them. A visual experience that we should describe as an object's looking a certain way is possible even when there is no such object. An oar may *look* bent to me, I may have the visual *experience* of a bent oar, without coming to believe that there *is* a bent oar. If I am a naive perceiver, an infant say, I may know nothing whatever of oars. If I am sophisticated, I may know that ordinary oars immersed in water will *look* bent without *being* bent.

This will be true as well for ordinary optical illusions.[5] One line may continue to *look* longer than another even after I assure myself that this is not so. These facts, long recognized, seem to support the notion that seeing is fundamentally a matter of having visual experiences, of coming to be in perceptual states that are themselves unaffected by judgments we may make about what is seen. Cases in which lines *look* unequal, oars *look* bent, are to be explained by reference to features of my experiences.

The apparent inequality and bentness are features of my visual experience, properties of *me*, not properties of the objects outside me.

Although Dretske holds that his conception of seeing *tout court* accommodates what we have in mind in speaking of the look of things, there is no reason to think that he would be sympathetic to such arguments. There are at least two reasons for this, one quite general, one attaching to Dretske's information-theoretic perspective on perception. The general point is a familiar one. It seems unpromising to explain how it is that X can appear to have some property, P, by reference to a second, posited item, Y, distinct from X, that actually possesses P. Applied to the case of lines looking of unequal length, for instance, we should have to posit something – an image, perhaps – containing lines that *really are* unequal. The move offends a number of sensibilities.

Consider a case in which you examine the Müller-Lyer lines in figure 1.3 and take them to be of different lengths. A companion tells you that this is not so. Skeptical, you measure them against one another by marking off their end points on a scrap of paper. You gaze at the lines and at the scrap of paper. Can what you encounter in so doing coherently be described in terms of the continued presence of an item (an image, sense datum, percept, or whatever) that includes lines of unequal length? However we elect to explain the possibility of things appearing to have properties they lack, it is surely wrong to do so by conjuring up *other* things actually possessing those properties.

A second reason Dretske would be reluctant to appeal in this way to illusory figures to bolster the case for seeing *tout court* is related to the information-theoretic character of the doctrine he advances. Perceptual states contain information that is accessible to various higher cognitive centers. When I look at the Müller-Lyer figure, however, the resulting perceptual state could not contain the information that its lines are of unequal length for the simplest of reasons: the lines are *not* unequal in length.[6] What might occur, instead, is the formation of a percept that would, normally perhaps, carry information that the lines differ in length but which, on this occasion, does not.

These points pose no special difficulties for Dretske. Even if a satisfactory explanation of such cases turned out to be a problem for his view, it remains a problem, as well, for competing views. For the moment I want merely to put aside a line of argument that has traditionally been used to defend accounts of perception that identify perceiving with the having of experiences.

Evidence for Seeing *Tout court*

I have likened Dretske's conception of simple perceiving, perceiving *tout court*, to the philosophical notion of perceptual experience. Although philosophers, on the whole, regard the latter as uncontroversial, not everyone has been persuaded by Dretske's arguments. This might be due to Dretske's simply getting it wrong; perhaps there is some better, more winning account of perceptual experience available. Or it might be that what Dretske has in mind when he speaks of percepts and simple perception has nothing at all to do with what everyone else has in mind in speaking of perceptual experiences. Both possibilities seem to me unlikely. The concept of perceptual experience – as commonly deployed by philosophers – appears innocent only so long as it is not scrutinized. When we set out to make the notion explicit, when we inspect it more closely, it loses much of its initial charm. In this section, and in the next, I shall advance reasons for doubting that perceiving *is* simple perceiving and for doubting, as well, the innocence of the philosophical category of perceptual experience. Dretske has done more than anyone else, perhaps, to capture and motivate that category, and we can learn much from uncovering respects in which his conception goes awry. There is, as well, a larger moral to be drawn, one pertaining to the legitimacy of philosophical appeals to experiences.

Do the sorts of case Dretske regards as relevant for the establishment of the concept of simple seeing require what he contends they require? Let us first consider those cases, then examine a possibility that seems at odds with Dretske's account.

I look at a flag featuring 50 stars, see *all* the stars, yet fail to realize that there are 50 of them. It is not merely that my seeing something, X, that possesses a certain property, P, does not require that I in any sense *recognize* or *take* X to be P. That is altogether unremarkable. Objects have countless properties, and we may come to know a great deal about an object without coming to know about all of these. I may recognize that a flag has *stars*, for instance, without recognizing that it has 50 stars, just as I may recognize you without recognizing that you are n centimeters tall. Dretske, however, advances a conception of seeing according to which X can be seen without being taken to possess any properties whatever.[7] On this conception, my recognizing X to be P is based on X's possessing P being seen by me. It is not enough in such cases merely that X be seen. Dretske's thesis is that X's *being P* is part of what is seen and entirely distinct from my seeing *that X is P*, my *taking* X to be P, and the like.

It is difficult to know what to say about the possibility of episodes of this sort. On the one hand, it is easy to imagine cases in which, for any given property, P, possessed by X, S sees X without *taking* X to have P. And we might describe such cases as ones in which S fails to see X under a certain aspect. On the other hand, the plausibility of these cases may well rest at least in part on the tacit assumption that X, if not seen under *this* aspect, is seen under some *other* aspect, if not taken to have P, then taken to have some other property, P'. Dretske's notion of seeing *tout court* requires that there be cases in which S encounters X perceptually, but does not take X in any way at all. It is far from clear, however, that there are any such cases, or that, even if there are, they are in any way illuminating.[8]

When I see the flag, according to Dretske, I see its 50 stars, *each* of them, though I do not (thereby) form the belief that there are 50 stars, much less 50 distinct beliefs, one for each star. If I see each of the 50 stars, however, and *this* star is one of the 50, then I see *this* star without forming any beliefs about it at all, without taking it to have any property whatever. But how apt is this description of the case? I scan a televised image of a football crowd taken from a blimp. You are somewhere in that crowd. Do I see you? Do I *see* you, the man in the red hat seated next to you, the hotdog vendor with a tattoo on his left forearm standing in the aisle? This seems wrong just as it seems wrong to say that I see individual hairs on your head, when I see you walk beneath my window. When I set foot on the beach, I step on 20,000 grains of sand. Do I step on *each* grain? Putting it thus is bound to mislead.

Such considerations do not, I think, establish that Dretske is wrong about visual perception. Indeed, they may, if anything, incline one to suppose that the dispute between Dretske and those who regard perceiving as essentially cognitive or belief-like is merely terminological, one that boils down to a dispute over what labels belong in which boxes in figure 1.1b. Do I see you in the football crowd; each of the 50 stars on the flag? Well, someone might say, *yes and no*; it depends on what you mean by *seeing* in each case.

There are, however, reasons to doubt the appropriateness of Dretske's terminology. I shall suggest below a way of accounting for the locutions favored by Dretske for describing these cases, one that does not require that we embrace his conception of simple seeing. Then, in a concluding section, I shall offer what appear to be counterexamples to that conception. My argument, then, will be that we *need* not regard perception as Dretske would have us regard it, and that we *ought* not to so regard it.

Seeing Without Believing

It is true, certainly, that we have occasion to say that someone sees things that fall outside his ken. You see Garbo ducking into a taxi without an inkling that it is *Garbo* you see; indeed you may never have *heard* of Garbo. This may be less a feature of your sensory state, however, than a feature of our ordinary ways of *describing* such states. I may describe your perception either by reference to its *content* or by reference to its *object*. You notice an elderly woman hailing a taxi. This, it might be said, constitutes the *content* of your perception. The elderly woman in question is, as it happens, Garbo. The *object* of your perception, then, the elderly woman, is Garbo. When reporting what you saw, I may mention either the content or the object of this state. Reference to the former is called for in circumstances in which the focus is on *you*, on what you are likely to do or say, for instance. Mention of the latter is appropriate in circumstances in which attention is focused, not on you, but on the object. In these circumstances, the way *you* take what you see, the properties *you* recognize it to have, are mostly irrelevant. My describing the object of your perception in this way, however, *seems* to require your having a perception with a particular content. That is, my aptly characterizing your seeing by reference to the object seen, might be thought to depend on my taking you to have come to be in a perceptual state with a particular content.

The plausibility of the cases Dretske describes, then, seems to rest on our accepting the uncontroversial notion that the object of one's perception can have properties one does not take it to have, not on our accepting the less obvious notion that one might perceive *this* object despite one's not taking it to be anything at all. One cannot, at any rate, conclude from the fact that, for any property, P, possessed by X, it is possible to perceive X without taking X to possess P, that it is possible to perceive X without taking X to possess any property whatsoever.[9]

The point need not be thought to depend on a theory of mental content according to which reference is fixed internally – by one's beliefs, for instance (see Dretske 1979, p. 8). My beliefs about a given perceptual object, X, maybe largely false, or they may hold for some other object, Y. *What* I perceive, what counts as a perceptual object for me, could turn out to be fixed *causally*. I now see Polly, not her twin Holly, because I am causally interacting in a certain way with Polly, not Holly, even though some of my beliefs about what I am seeing maybe true of Holly, not Polly.

Even if we suppose that the content of perceptual states is fixed at least in part causally, however, we need not imagine that seeing has the character Dretske takes it to have. More particularly, it is possible to accept the notion that perceptual *objects* are not (or not *exclusively*) determined by belief-*contents*, without conceding that perceptual states are belief-independent or nonepistemic. A theory that identified perceiving with the having of certain sorts of belief, for instance, might well incorporate a causal component (theories of this sort are discussed in Armstrong 1973, and in Heil 1983). That the content of a given mental state is, or might be, at least in part, externally fixed, then, is perfectly consistent with that state's being essentially cognitive and epistemic.

What *Are* Perceptual Experiences?

We must conclude, I think, that Dretske has offered no compelling reasons for supposing that seeing is essentially noncognitive, nonepistemic. Even so, we may continue to feel that there is something importantly right about the conception he defends. It certainly seems, for instance, that in gazing about our surroundings, we are, in some sense, *aware* of far more than we recognize or bother to identify. And it seems, as well, that the *constituents* of this awareness are not, or need not be, cognized, brought under concepts, judged to be this or that. The constituents of an infant's visual awareness might be identical to those of an adult, though the adult, owing to a degree of conceptual sophistication, is able to extract more from those constituents than the infant.

This *seems* right. But what are we to make of it? A standard philosophical move is to launch into a discussion of perceptual experiences. In this way, entities and properties that naive perceivers take to be external, public features of the world are moved inside, made into features of perceivers. My visual field is thus populated not by tables, trees, and clouds, but by *images* of these, *sensations*, sensory *qualia*. These elements are part of *me*, constituents of a particular sort of mental state, the having of which is an experience. The occurrence of experiences in me is a fundamental aspect of perceiving.

Dretske's view is usefully seen as falling squarely into this tradition, or so I have contended. His notion of simple perceiving is readily identifiable as an updated version of the classical empiricist notion of bare experience, what Locke and Hume, respectively, identified as the having of *ideas* and *impressions*. So long as we focus solely on functional aspects of such views, the point is apt to be missed. We have noted already that the notion that perceivers might be regarded as incorporating functional states with the properties Dretske attributes to percepts is something that any causal theorist could accept. The rub comes in Dretske's making these, in a certain way, central: seeing just *is* the having of such states. To convince us of this, Dretske is obliged to move beyond a purely functional or theory-driven perspective on perceiving to a consideration of instances. The implicit aim in this is to encourage the identification of certain functional states with the having of perceptual experiences, and, in turn, an identification of the having of perceptual experiences with perceiving *tout court*.

If we are to abandon such a view, then, we shall want to show either that perceiving is more than (or perhaps distinct from) the having of nonepistemic, unconceptualized experiences, or show that there is something objectionable about the notion of experiences thus conceived. We have seen already that the examples Dretske provides do not establilsh his point. This way of putting it suggests that he bears the burden of proof: the notion that perceiving is simple, nonepistemic is presumed false until proven true. Perhaps this is unfair. What reasons might there be for thinking Dretske *wrong*? Let us consider the matter in this light, and examine evidence suggesting both that it is a mistake to identify perceiving with the having of noncognitive states and that the identification of perceptual states with experiences is misguided.

First, let us pretend that the notion of visual experience is entirely unproblematic. A visual experience is an internal episode phenomenologically and informationally characterizable. If this is unclear, the reader is directed to the passage from Locke quoted at the outset. Experiences are, we may suppose, produced causally, the products of agents' interactions with their surroundings. The properties of experiences, and indeed experiences themselves, depend not merely on external causes that give rise to them but also, and crucially, on properties of agents in whom they occur. An agent lacking a certain piece of equipment, photosensitive receptors in the retina, for instance, will lack the capacity for certain sorts of experience, what we should call *visual* experience. A perceiver with damaged or maladjusted equipment may enjoy experiences that differ qualitatively from those had by normal perceivers. If certain cells in my retina are deficient, I will experience colors differently than you do, or perhaps altogether lack the capacity to experience colors visually.

Now imagine that we are visited by creatures from a remote galaxy, creatures, in most respects, exactly like us. Eventually we learn to communicate with these visitors, and we set out to investigate their psychology. We discover that they exhibit a range of perceptual abilities comparable to our own. That is, they can describe the colors and shapes of things at a distance providing the illumination is adequate. In the dark they lose this ability. They are sometimes fooled, just as we are, by trick mirrors, and by objects placed under conditions of nonstandard illumination. Thus, so long as we disguise the conditions, they judge white objects under red light to be red. The alien creatures turn out to be comparable to human beings, as well, along the whole range of perceptual aptitudes. Researchers capture this aspect of their psychology be means of the chart in figure 1.1b.

One day an accident befalls one of the visitors, and it dies. Seizing the opportunity, anatomists open it up and explore its biology. A wonderful discovery is made: the aliens lack a capacity for perceptual experiences. Their neural hardware is functionally identical to ours, but the biological components responsible for the having of experiences are entirely lacking. The creatures have mechanisms for processing and storing information. Like human beings, they take in far more information than they could possibly use – a fact already established in the course of ordinary psychological testing and now confirmed. But they evidently lack anything plausibly describable as perceptual experiences. Although they nicely fit the characterization afforded by figure 1.1b, they fail to fit that set out in figure 1.1a.

What are we to conclude about such creatures? Must we say that our original assessment was in error, that their lacking appropriate experiences shows that they cannot (or cannot, *strictly speaking*) perceive? I doubt that anyone without a philosophical axe to grind would be tempted to say this. But if that is so, it seems to follow that, on our ordinary conception, perceiving does not require the having of particular sorts of experience – where *experience* is understood in the philosophical sense set out above. Compare the case with that of another tribe of alien creatures, a tribe psychologically very different from us. The creatures seem intelligent, but they altogether fail at standard visual tasks. We conclude that these aliens cannot see. If one of the creatures dies and, on examination, we discover that it has, after all, almost certainly had experiential visual states identical to ours, it is far from clear that we should be tempted to revise our original assessment.[10]

One might balk at these examples on the grounds that they are, in some way, incoherent. If we suppose, however, that perceptual experiences are states of perceivers of certain particular sorts, then a charge of incoherence is difficult to support. Of course, there may well be something fishy about this notion of perceptual experience. If that were so, however, then there would be something fishy, as well, about the model of perceiving we have been considering.

There may, in fact, be cases in which it seems natural to regard certain unfortunate human beings as resembling alien creatures of the first sort discussed above. I have in mind instances of what is called *blind-sight* (see Heil 1983, chapter 4 for a discussion and further references). Lesions in a particular region of the brain produce apparent blindness in certain regions of the visual field. We might wish to describe these cases as ones in which agents, thus afflicted, *experience* nothing in those regions. Tests however, reveal that, despite this deficit, blind-sighters are adept at regulating their behavior in ways that suggest that they are picking up information available in the blind field. Such agents might be described as *seeing* what is in the blind field despite lacking appropriate visual experiences.[11]

The blind-sight phenomenon may turn out to be otherwise explicable. The point of mentioning it here is only to show that it is not at all obvious that there is a conceptual connection between perceiving and the having of experiential states. To the extent that Dretske's account of perceiving denies this, then, we must be suspicious of it.

Whither Perceptual Experiences?

For the sake of the discussion, we have conformed to the traditional practice of taking these to be uncontroversial sensory givens. If a Dretske-style account of perceiving is objectionable in the ways I have suggested, however, the whole notion that perceiving involves essentially the having of perceptual experiences seems much less compelling. What then might be said about the sort of unconceptualized awareness we all seem to have of our surroundings?

One possibility is that the naive view of perceiving is right: items constituting the content of that awareness are simply objects and events outside us in the world. If asked to describe elements of our visual field, for instance, and then to say where we imagine these elements to reside, most of us will take ourselves to be describing features of the world, not features of ourselves. Only someone in the grip of a philosophical theory is likely to differ. The notion that external objects could not possibly have the properties we perceive them to have – hence that the properties in question must be properties of experiences or sensory episodes, not properties of external objects – is a manifestly philosophical notion, one resting on arguments that ought to arouse suspicion. It is sometimes imagined that the move from what we take to be facts about perceiving to the postulation of specialized mental episodes is motivated by purely empirical considerations. This is a mistake. It is only when we see those empirical considerations in a certain light, only when they are illuminated by a certain philosophical doctrine, that we are tempted to construe them as evidence for impressions or experiences (in the non-ordinary, philosophical senses of these things).

Many of the features philosophers commonly ascribe to phenomenal perceptual states are in fact perfectly objective features of the world. Evidence suggests, for instance, that the visual icon discussed earlier is, if it is anything, a retinal occurrence (see, e.g., Neisser 1976). Many of the differences cited to distinguish the *looks* of things from the things themselves (and thus to the postulation of distinct internal objects or episodes to which these looks can be ascribed) are explicable by reference to the optical properties of ambient illumination (see, e.g., Gibson 1979; Heil 1983). In cases where such explanations are more difficult to find – the optical illusions, for instance – it is not obvious how appeals to mediating sensory objects in any way advance our understanding.

My suggestion is that we should be better off dropping talk about perceptual experiences altogether. Dretske is right: there *is* an important sense in which we enjoy a primitive, noncognitive sort of awareness that far outstrips our capacity to conceptualize or make judgments. But the field of this awareness is not some internal state or process. It comprises, rather, ordinary objects and goings-on in the world outside us. These objects and goings on, of course, do not depend on judgments we make. Mostly they persist independently of our thoughts about them. They are the same for me as for an infant. And they are, often enough, objects of perception. But perceiving such things must be more than their simply being there – as they indisputably are when we open our eyes and gaze about. Perceiving them involves *taking* them in various ways, forming beliefs about them, judging them to be one way rather than another.

Our doing this, perhaps, requires much in the way of sensory machinery. And that machinery may well, as Dretske plausibly contends, supply us with far more information than we should ever want or need. But this fact, if it is a fact, pertains to the mechanisms underlying our capacity to perceive. It does not settle the question of what it is to perceive.

Notes

Work on this paper was supported by a National Endowment for the Humanities fellowship (FB-24078–86). I am indebted to Fred Dretske, Alfred Mele, and Paul Snowdon for their comments on earlier drafts.

 1   See, e.g., Dretske 1969, chapter 2; 1978; 1979; and 1981 chapters 6 and 7. The account of simple seeing, seeing *tout court*, offered here is a hybrid constructed from all of these sources.
 2   Putting it this way suggests that the issue between Dretske and those who take perceiving to be essentially cognitive is, at bottom *verbal*. Even if that were so, however, there might be reasons for preferring one system of labels

to another. And *one* way to motivate a Dretske-style taxonomy would be to show that it nicely accommodates a full-blooded notion of perceptual experience. The aim here is to raise doubts about the philosophical category of perceptual experience and thus, by extension, doubts about Dretske's preference for a non-cognitive account of perceiving.

3 Dretske (1978 p. 110) says that in "the shifting perception of ambiguous figures ... there is a change in the percept without a change in the corresponding stimulus ..." This comes perilously close to identifying percepts – simple, unadulterated seeing, seeing *tout court* – with *seeing as*, however, an identity Dretske is bound to deny. My seeing the figure as a duck, your seeing it as a rabbit, and an infant's seeing it (but *as* nothing at all) are all cases presumably of seeing the *same* figure. The percepts here might differ, but not, I gather, simply because each of us sees the figure *as* something different.

4 Such examples are discussed in Dretske 1978, 1979. See, also, Heil 1982; and 1983, chapter 4.

5 Evidence suggests that the illusions depicted in figure 1.3 are not uniquely visual. In each case, tactual analogues are possible. See Heil 1987 for discussion and references.

6 Notice that these cases differ from those, for instance, in which a white thing, under a red light, looks red to me. Here we may say that light reaching my retina contains infomation that, in certain crucial respects, is identical to that contained in light reflected from a genuinely red thing. The case of an apparently bent oar may be similar. In each instance, however, there is a perfectly objective feature of the world – light radiation of a particular structured sort – to which one might appeal in explaining the looks of the things in question.

7 Which is, of course, not the same as taking it to have no properties whatever.

8 Here is a possibility suggested to me by C. B. Martin. S, blind from birth, undergoes an operation that revives his sight. When the bandages are removed and *S* opens his newly restored eyes for the first time, he is sitting in a chair that faces a pale blue wall. *S* sees the blueness of the wall, yet is so awestruck by the experience that he makes nothing whatever of it. If Dretske is right, then all seeing is like this.

9 In the case of infants, it is significant that we begin to speak of their *seeing* this or that only once they begin to manifest signs of *recognition*. It would be, at any rate, misleading to say of a newborn baby gazing aimlessly about that it *sees its mother* solely on the grounds that its eyes are open and functioning properly, and its mother falls somewhere within its visual field.

10 Dretske would perhaps agree on this point. He insists that perceptual states, although themselves noncognitive, must be available to a perceiver's cognitive centers. For him a perceptual state is a functional state with certain additional, nonfunctional properties. We might then wonder about a case in which aliens, psychologically resembling the first group, were discovered to have the appropriate experiential states, but it turned out that these were functionally inert: information for perceptual judgments came from mechanisms entirely unrelated to these states.

11 Paul Snowdon has reminded me that blind-sighters typically manifest surprise that their "guesses" are correct. Does this show that such people lack the corresponding perceptual beliefs? Not at all. Unless one imagines that beliefs are inevitably conscious, it shows, a best, only that blind-sighters do not

believe that they have such beliefs. Indeed, it is altogether natural to ascribe to them first-order perceptual beliefs, on the basis of which they issue "guesses" about their surroundings, together with second-order beliefs, on the basis of which they report that they are merely guessing. See Marcel 1983.

References

Armstrong, D. M. 1973: *Belief, Truth, and Knowledge*. Cambridge: Cambridge University Press.

Dretske, F. I. 1969: *Seeing and Knowing*. London: Routledge and Kegan Paul.

—— 1978. The Role of the Percept in Visual Cognition. In *Perception and Cognition: Issues in the Foundations of Psychology* (Minnesota studies in the philosophy of science, vol. 9), ed. W. Savage, Minneapolis: University of Minnesota Press.

—— 1979. Simple Seeing. In *Body, Mind, and Method*, ed. D. F. Gustafson and B. L. Tapscott, Cambridge: MIT Press/Bradford Books.

Gibson, J. J. 1979: *The Ecological Approach to Visual Perception*. Boston: Houghton Mifflin.

Heil, J. 1982: Seeing is Believing. *American Philosophical Quarterly*, 19, pp. 229–39.

—— 1983: *Perception and Cognition*. Berkeley: University of California Press.

—— 1987: The Molyneux Question. *Journal for the Theory of Social Behaviour*, 17, pp. 227–41.

Locke, J. [1690] 1979: *An Essay Concerning Human Understanding*, ed. P. H. Nidditch, Oxford: Oxford University Press.

Marcel, A. J. 1983: Conscious and Unconscious Perception: An approach to the relations between phenomenal experiences and perceptual processes. *Cognitive Psychology*, 15, pp. 238–300.

Neisser, U. 1967: *Cognitive Psychology*. New York: Appleton-Century-Crofts.

—— 1976: *Cognition and Reality*. San Francisco: W. H. Freeman.

Sperling, G. A. 1960: The Information Available in Brief Perceptual presentation. *Psychological Monographs*, 74, no. 498.

2

Skepticism, Relevance, and Relativity

Stewart Cohen

The relevant alternatives response to skeptical arguments is largely due to the work of Fred Dretske.[1] The primary virtue of this approach is that it can accommodate two opposing strands in our thinking about the concept of knowledge. As Peter Unger has observed, knowledge is an *absolute* concept.[2] On one interpretation, this means that the justification or evidence one must have in order to know must be absolute or conclusive[3] – one's evidence must eliminate all alternatives to what one believes (where an alternative is a proposition incompatible with what one believes). When there is an alternative to what one believes that one's evidence does not eliminate, there is a strong intuitive pull in favor of saying that one does not really know what one believes. This aspect of our thinking about knowledge is precisely what skeptical arguments exploit. Calling our attention to alternatives that our evidence can not eliminate (e.g., hallucinations, dreams) the skeptic shows that this requirement of conclusive reasons is seldom, if ever, satisfied.

This conclusion flies in the face of our deeply entrenched supposition that we do know the truth of many ordinary empirical propositions. Thus, there is a tension between two components in our thinking about knowledge. We believe that knowledge is, in the sense indicated, an absolute concept and yet we also believe that there are many instances of that concept.

There would seem to be two options, each involving the denial of one of the components on the basis of the other. Peter Unger argues from the absolute character of knowledge to a skeptical conclusion, apparently finding absoluteness to be too central a component of our concept of knowledge to be relinquished.[4]

Most philosophers have taken the other course, choosing to respond to the conflict by giving up, perhaps reluctantly, the absoluteness criterion. The so-called fallibilists argue that this is precisely what we need to do, holding as sacrosanct our common-sense belief that we know many things.[5] Each approach is subject to the criticism that it preserves one aspect of our ordinary thinking about knowledge at the expense of denying another.

Dretske's theory of relevant alternatives offers an elegant and ingenious way out of this unsatisfactory situation. It provides a view of
knowledge that respects its absolute character as well as our common-
sense suppositions regarding our epistemic accomplishments. What Dretske proposes is that we qualify, rather than deny, the absolute character of
knowledge. According to Dretske, knowledge is relationally absolute –
"absolute, yes, but relative to a certain standard."[6] In order to know a
proposition to be true, our evidence need not eliminate all the alternatives to that proposition. Instead we can know when our evidence eliminates all the *relevant* alternatives (where the set of relevant alternatives, a
subset of the set of all alternatives, is determined by some standard). As
such, there is no skeptical mileage to be gained from the absolute character of knowledge. The fact that the skeptic can discover alternatives to
the propositions we claim to know, that our evidence cannot eliminate,
does not in itself guarantee a skeptical result. For knowledge, being
relationally absolute, requires that our evidence eliminate only the
relevant alternatives. And the standards for knowledge are such that
skeptical alternatives fail to be relevant.

Dretske motivates this view of the concept of knowledge by noting that
other concepts exhibit the same logical structure. Two of his favored
examples are the concept of empty and the concept of flat. Both appear
to be absolute concepts – a space is empty only if it does not contain
anything and a surface is flat only if it does not have any bumps. However, as Dretske points out, the absolute character of these concepts is
relative to a standard. In the case of flat, there is a standard for what
counts as a bump and in the case of empty there is a standard for what
counts as a thing. We would not deny that a table is flat because a
microscope reveals irregularities in its surface. Nor would we deny that a
warehouse is empty because it contains particles of dust. To be flat is to
be free of any relevant bumps. To be empty is to be devoid of all relevant
things.

Dretske suggests that we use the logical structure of these concepts as a
model for understanding the concept of knowledge. Thus Dretske proposes that to know a proposition is (*inter alia*) to have evidence that
eliminates all relevant alternatives.

I believe that Dretske's view of knowledge is, in most respects,
correct.[7] In particular I am sympathetic to Dretske's claim that the
relational character of knowledge is a kind of contextual relativity or
context sensitivity. I propose to show that if we understand this claim in
the right way, the theory of relevant alternatives provides a powerful
response to the skeptical challenge.

The Skeptical Paradox

Initially one might think that the theory of relevant alternatives begs the
question against skepticism. After all, precisely what the skeptic claims is

that the existence of alternatives our evidence cannot eliminate undermines our claims to know. The relevant-alternatives theorist merely responds that the alternatives the skeptic has invoked are not relevant, i.e.,
do not have to be eliminated in order for us to know. Since this is the
point at issue, doesn't the relevant-alternatives theorist need an argument
in support of this crucial claim?

Although in one sense, the relevant-alternatives theorist does not have
an argument, he is able to appeal to our strong intuition that in many
cases we do know things. And it is not apparent that the skeptic has an
argument that undermines those intuitions.

One might think that there is such an argument available to the skeptic.
The argument emerges once we are precise about what Dretske means
when he refers to our evidence *eliminating* an alternative. According
to Dretske, one's evidence eliminates an alternative just in case one's
evidence against the alternative is good enough for one to know the
alternative is false.[8] But then the skeptic can claim, quite plausibly, that
whatever else we say about the significance of skeptical alternatives,
it is not correct to say that we know they are false. We might think that
we have some reason to believe that we are not deceived in the ways the
skeptics suggest we might be, but it is very hard to hold that we *know* we
are not so deceived. One of Dretske's own examples of this is the
counter-intuitiveness of claiming that when we are viewing zebras at the
zoo, we *know* that we are not in fact seeing cleverly-disguised mules.[9]
While we do have some evidence against the possibility of such a decep-
tion, intuitively it is not strong enough for us to *know* that we are not so
deceived.

At this point the skeptic can appeal to an epistemic closure principle
with considerable intuitive force:

If s knows q, and s knows that q entails not-h, then s knows not-h.[10]

It follows from this principle and the just-cited claim that we fail to know
the falsity of skeptical alternatives, that we fail to know the propositions
we ordinarily claim to know. (Since those propositions trivially entail the
falsity of skeptical alternatives, e.g., "one sees a zebra" entails that "one
does not see a cleverly-disguised mule.")

This argument presupposes that every alternative is relevant. For the
closure principle is just a precise expression of the unqualified claim that
knowledge is absolute (requires the elimination of every alternative). But
Dretske accepts only the claim that knowledge is relationally absolute.
Indeed, Dretske has appealed to the fact that we know ordinary empirical
propositions and the fact that we do not know the falsity of skeptical
alternatives as an argument against the truth of the closure principle.

Moreover, some have agreed with the skeptic, contrary to Dretske,
that the closure principle is true. But, against the skeptic, they use the
closure principle along with the claim that we do have knowledge, to

reject the claim that we do not know the falsity of skeptical alternatives.[11] So is the skeptic begging the question against these other positions?

It is not clear how to assess this situation. I would suggest that what we are confronting here is a paradox – a set of inconsistent propositions each of which has considerable independent plausibility:

1 We know that some ordinary empirical propositions are true.
2 We do not know that skeptical alternatives are false.
3 If s knows q, and s knows that q entails not-h, then s knows not-h.

Because each member of the set has independent plausibility it would seem arbitrary and unsatisfying to appeal to any two members of this inconsistent triad as an argument against the third. Such a strategy does not provide what any successful resolution of a paradox should, viz., an explanation of how the paradox arises in the first place. As such, it is a constraint on any resolution that defends common sense against the skeptic, that it explain the appeal of skeptical arguments. For it is that very appeal that gives rise to the paradox. While initially we think we can claim to know unproblematically, under pressure from skeptical arguments, we begin to worry whether we really do have knowledge. Often we find ourselves vacillating between thinking we have knowledge and worrying that we do not. As Dretske notes, skeptical arguments have a "persisting and undiminished appeal."[12] No successful response to the skeptical paradox can fail to explain that appeal.

Contextualism

Can the theory of relevant alternatives explain the appeal of skeptical arguments? The core idea of the relevant alternatives approach is that knowledge despite its absolute character is still in some sense a relative notion. Dretske tells us that "this absolute notion [knowledge] exhibits a degree of contextual relativity in its ordinary use."[13] What does it mean to say that the relativity of knowledge is *contextual*? For Dretske the idea seems to be this. One knows relative to a set of relevant alternatives – knowledge requires the elimination of all and only relevant alternatives. And the set of relevant alternatives is determined relative to a context. In this way, knowledge is a context-relative or context-sensitive notion.

There is more than one phenomenon that could be referred to by the expression "contextual relativity" and thus more than one phenomenon that could be described by saying that the set of relevant alternatives is determined relative to a context. Whether or not the theory of relevant alternatives can discharge its burden of explaining why we are troubled by skeptical arguments will depend on how we construe Dretske's crucial notion of contextual relativity.

We can begin by examining Dretske's own account of how the theory of relevant alternatives accomplishes this task. He tells us that with the theory,

> we get a better perspective from which to understand the *persisting* and *undiminished* appeal of skeptical arguments. Most philosophers have experienced the futility of trying to convince a devoted skeptic, or just a newly converted freshman, that we do know there are tables and chairs despite the possibility of dreams, hallucinations, cunning demons and diabolical scientists who might be toying with our brain on Alpha Centuri (Nozick's example). Somehow, in the end, we seem reduced to shrugging our shoulders and saying that there are certain possibilities that are just too remote to worry about. Our evidence isn't good enough to eliminate these wilder hypotheses because, of course, these wild hypotheses are carefully manufactured so as to neutralize our evidence. But dismissing such hypotheses as too remote to worry about, as too fanciful to have any impact on our *ordinary use* of the verb "to know," is merely another way of saying that for purposes of assessing someone's knowledge that this is a table, certain alternative possibilities are simply not relevant. We are doing the same thing (or so I submit) as one who dismisses chalk dust as irrelevant, or too insignificant, to worry about in describing a classroom as empty. What it is important to realize, especially in arguments with the skeptic, is that the impatient dismissal of his fanciful hypotheses is not (as he will be quick to suggest) a mere practical intolerance, and refusal to confront, decisive objections to our ordinary way of talking. It is, rather, a half-conscious attempt to exhibit the *relationally* absolute character of our cognitive concepts.[14]

This passage seems not to deliver what it promises. If "our cognitive concepts" are such that "certain possibilities are just too remote to worry about," if these possibilities are "too fanciful to have any impact on our ordinary use of the verb 'to know'" then wherein lies "the persisting and undiminished appeal of skeptical arguments?" Why don't we immediately respond to skeptical arguments by objecting that skeptical alternatives are too remote and fanciful to undermine our knowledge? It is true that we sometimes are inclined to do just that. But the skeptical problem arises precisely because we can not always sustain that attitude. Sometimes we begin to worry that our inability to eliminate these alternatives does threaten our claims to know. Again, often we vacillate. The appeal of skeptical arguments is indeed persisting and often remains undiminished despite our best attempts to rebuff them. But I see nothing in this passage that shows how the theory of relevant alternatives enables us to understand why this is so.

Nonetheless, I believe the theory does have the means to provide such an explanation. It is here that we must exploit the notion of contextual relativity. What is required is that we distinguish between two very different phenomena that could be thought of as the contextual relativity of knowledge.

One characteristic of knowledge that we might think of as contextual relativity is the fact that whether a subject has knowledge depends on certain features of the subject's circumstances beyond the evidence the subject has. This phenomenon has been illustrated by numerous cases in the literature where various factors such as the availability of unpossessed misleading counter-evidence, the evidential beliefs of the members of relevant social groups, and the objective probability of being wrong, undermine the knowledge of a subject who otherwise possesses adequate evidence.[15] Thus, two subjects could possess the same evidence for the truth of a certain proposition, and one of them know the proposition while the other fails to know the proposition. In this sense, whether a subject knows on the basis of certain evidence is determined relative to the context, i.e., relative to the extra-evidential circumstances of the subject. Dretske refers to cases of this kind and claims as a virtue of the relevant-alternatives theory that it can explain them.[16] In essence, he claims that these factors are part of what determines the set of relevant alternatives. For example, in normal circumstances, when one sees a Gadwall duck, the alternative that instead one sees a look-alike Grebe is not relevant – one's evidence does not have to eliminate it in order for one to know that one sees a Gadwall. However, if the circumstances happen to be such that there are look-alike Grebes in the immediate vicinity, then the alternative that one sees such a Grebe is relevant. Thus one subject may know that he sees a Gadwall on the basis of visual evidence while another fails to know on the basis of the same evidence, due to the fact that the extra-evidential circumstances play a role in determining the relevance of alternatives.

This kind of contextual relativity, while in one sense interesting, is in another sense trivial. That knowledge is relative to the extra-evidential circumstances of the subject follows, on most views, from the truth condition for knowledge alone. On any fallibilist view, two subjects in different cases could have equivalent evidence for a proposition and yet only one of them know the proposition merely because in only one case is the proposition true. So to claim that knowledge is context-relative in this sense, is not in itself to make a novel claim. Of course one of the benefits of the extended Gettier controversy is that it has produced a variety of novel types of extra-evidential circumstances besides the truth of the proposition, that play a role in determining whether a subject knows the proposition. What is novel is not that knowledge is, in this sense, context-relative. Rather, what is novel is the myriad of circumstances that have been discovered to be part of this extra-evidential context.

Another characteristic of knowledge that could be referred to as con-textual relativity or context sensitivity is more accurately described as a characteristic of attributions of knowledge, viz., indexicality. To say that attributions of knowledge are indexical is to say that the truth-value of an attribution of knowledge is determined relative to the context *of attribu-*

tion, i.e., relative to the speaker or the conversational context.[17] Applied to the theory of relevant alternatives, the view would be that the purposes, intentions, presuppositions, etc., of attributors of knowledge – speakers and listeners – play a role in setting the standards of relevance.[18] This kind of relativity is quite different from relativity to the extra-evidential circumstances of the subject of the attribution.[19] If attributions of knowledge are context-relative in this sense, then two speakers could simultaneously say of a subject, "S knows p" and it be the case that what one speaker says is true while what the other says is false. Moreover, holding the circumstances of S fixed, one speaker may say "S knows p" while another says "S does not know p" without it being the case that they have contradicted each other. This is because the sentence "S knows p" will have different truth conditions in different contexts of attribution. If "know" is an indexical, then it will express different knowledge relations in different contexts of attribution and thus sentences containing "know" will express different propositions. Applied to the relevant alternatives view, in different contexts of attribution, attributions of knowledge will involve different standards of relevance.

For example, one factor that Dretske suggests will affect the relevance of an alternative is its remoteness.[20] Suppose then that A attributes knowledge to S that S sees a Gadwall.[21] The context of attribution will determine a standard of remoteness, viz., a standard for when an alternative is too remote to be relevant. That attribution involving that standard is then evaluated at the circumstances in which S sees the Gadwall, where here the pertinent factor is the actual remoteness in those circumstances of the alternative that S sees a lookalike Grebe. And this will depend on whether there are look-alike Grebes in the area – their number, frequency, etc. Thus, the truth-value of an attribution of knowledge is determined in part, by whether the circumstances of the subject are such that there are any alternatives which are not too remote, relative to the standard of remoteness yielded by the context of attribution. The truth-value of a knowledge attribution will vary as we vary either the context of attribution that determines the standard of relevance or as we vary the extra-evidential circumstances governed by the standards.

As I read Dretske, he discusses both of these distinct phenomena under the rubric of contextual relativity. However, it is crucial to distinguish between them. It is relativity to the context of attribution (indexicality) that is suggested by Dretske's analogy with words like "flat" and "empty." Moreover, it is this kind of contextual relativity (indexicality) that the relevant alternatives theory requires if it is to provide an explanation of the appeal of skeptical arguments.

Consider Dretske's treatment of "flat":

> For although nothing can be flat if it has *any* bumps and irregularities, what counts as a bump or irregularity depends on the type of surface being described ... a road can be perfectly flat even though one can *feel* and *see* irregularities in its surface, irregularities which,

were they to be found on the surface, say, of a mirror would mean that the mirror's surface was not really flat.[22]

Although, *in general*, I agree with Dretske's remarks, I think the situation is more complicated than he implies. What counts as a bump (the standard of flatness) can vary even with respect to one type of surface. Suppose it is given that what is being described is a road (rather than a mirror). Smith who is from Colorado says "The road is flat." Jones, from Kansas, says "The road is not flat." Their disagreement stems from the different standards they employ in making attributions of flatness. Jones, being from Kansas has much stricter standards than someone from Colorado, like Smith. Now suppose we ask who is right and who is wrong about the road. Surely it would be inappropriate to decide the issue in favor of one against the other. They make their attributions relative to different standards. Relative to its respective standards, each attribution could be correct (or incorrect). There is no contradiction because by their use of different standards they have, in effect, said different things about the road.

The important thing to notice is that there is nothing in the circumstances on the basis of which we could say that either Smith's or Jones's standards are, in some absolute sense, the *correct* standards – the standards that determine the truth-value of the attribution. I do not mean to imply that it is the intentions of the speaker alone that determine which standards are in effect. Factors such as the expectations of the listeners and the presuppositions of the conversation can play a role in the determining the standards.[23] The point is that the standards in effect result from the context of attribution (the intentions, presuppositions, etc., of speakers and listeners) rather than from the circumstances of the subject (in this case a road) in which the attribution is evaluated.

It might seem as if the standards are determined by such circumstances. In particular, one might claim that it is the location of the road that determines which standards are in effect. So in Colorado, looser standards apply than in Kansas. However, if a group of Kansas residents are traveling through Colorado, they might all agree that they have yet to encounter a flat road. Surely we should not insist that they have all agreed on something false. As residents of Kansas, they assess the flatness of a road relative to stricter standards. And why should we evaluate what they say relative to standards other than the ones they as a group share and understand one another to be using? What they say does not contradict what a group of Colorado residents might agree upon if they were to utter the sentence "The road the Kansas residents are on is flat." Relative to the standards that operate in their respective contexts of attribution, both claims can be true (or false).

If the Kansas residents spend enough time in Colorado, they may be led to relax their standards. Were that to happen, they may say truly of a road in Colorado, "That is a flat road." These same standards could continue to govern their attributions (perhaps only among themselves) even if they were to return to Kansas.

A further example shows that it is the context of attribution that determines the standards that apply (rather than the location of the subject of the attribution). Beings that vary enormously in size would most likely differ in the standards of flatness they employ. A giant would differ from us in his attributions of flatness. Surely there is no basis for us to say that his attributions of flatness are incorrect. If we were to claim that his size makes him insensitive to irregularities that really exist, then our own judgments would be subject to the same objection from ant-sized beings. Again the context of attribution will be what selects the standard. This holds true regardless of where the particular road is located.

Dretske's remarks about "empty" suggest that we should view this family of terms as indexical in this way:

> Something is empty (another absolute concept according to Unger) if it has nothing in it, but this does not mean that an abandoned warehouse is not really empty because it has light bulbs or molecules in it. Light bulbs and molecules do not count as *things* when determining the emptiness of warehouses. For purposes of determining the emptiness of a warehouse, molecules (dust, light bulbs, etc.) are irrelevant. This isn't to say that, if we changed the way we used warehouses (e.g., if we started using, or trying to use, warehouses as giant vacuum chambers), they *still* wouldn't count. It is only to say that, given the way they are now used, air molecules (dust particles, etc.) don't count.[24]

So whether a space is empty depends on the purpose for which we use it. That is to say our criteria for determining whether a space is devoid of things, in the relevant sense, depend on our purposes, goals, intentions, etc. And as Dretske notes, these facts about us may vary. We might decide to use a space that we had previously used as a warehouse, as a vacuum chamber. By so deciding, we change the criteria for determining what counts as a thing in the relevant sense and we thus change our criteria for the correctness of attributions of emptiness. As Dretske says in another work, "The concept [emptiness], though absolute, has a built-in plasticity (in the idea of a 'relevant' thing) that is responsive to the interests and purposes of people applying it."[25]

So we could imagine two speakers, one of whom says "The room is empty," since he intends to use it for storage, whereas another speaker says "The room is not empty" since he intends to use it as a vacuum chamber. Ostensibly, the two speakers make conflicting attributions. But since the contexts of attribution involve different standards, their attributions do not really conflict. Both statements could be true.

If this account of the semantics of "flat" and "empty" (or of the concepts of flat and empty) is correct, then one can not determine the truth-value of sentences containing these terms without considering the context of attribution (or utterance), viz., the intentions, goals, interests, etc., of the attributors. That is we must view the use of these terms as involving an indexical reference to standards or criteria.

If our treatment of "flat" and "empty" is to serve as a model for "know" (or if our treatment of the concepts of flat and empty is to serve as a model for the concept of knowledge) then we should view "know" as indexical in this way. Indeed Dretske at times seems to take this view explicitly:

> When a possibility becomes a relevant possibility is an issue that is, in part at least, responsive to the interests, purposes, and yes, values of those with a stake in the communication process. The flow of information, just like the cognitive exploits it makes possible, is a process that exhibits some sensitivity to the variable purposes of those who send and receive this information.[26]

So whether a subject knows depends on the set of relevant alternatives, and the composition of that set is a function of the context of attribution (or, we could say, the context of communication). That is to say, the criteria of relevance will vary as the interest, purposes, etc., of those involved in making knowledge attributions vary.

This observation provides the key to explaining the appeal of skeptical arguments. Recall that Dretske claims that "for the purposes of assessing someone's knowledge that this is a table, [skeptical alternatives] are simply not relevant." I argued that this approach cannot, in itself, explain what Dretske acknowledges to be, the persisting appeal of skeptical arguments. To explain this appeal, we need to exploit Dretske's claims about the contextual relativity of knowledge. Dretske appeals to contextual relativity in an attempt to defuse skeptical arguments, but it appears that he does not clearly distinguish between what I have claimed are two different kinds of contextual relativity:

> One of the ways to prevent this slide into skepticism is to acknowledge that although knowledge requires the evidential elimination of all relevant alternatives (to what is known), there is a shifting, variable set of relevant alternatives. It may be that our birdwatcher does know the bird is a Gadwall under normal conditions (because look-alike grebes are not a relevant alternative), but does not know this if there is a suspicion, however ill-founded it may be, that there exist look-alike grebes within migrating range.[27]

Here, Dretske cites an example of what I have referred to as relativity to the extra-evidential circumstances of the subject – in addition to the strength of the evidence the subject happens to possess, the context (extra-evidential circumstances) in which the subject possesses that evidence can affect whether the subject knows. If the issue concerns whether someone knows that he sees a Gadwall duck, conditions like the actual presence of look-alike Grebes or the mere suspicion of their presence by a nearby ornithologist can affect whether a subject knows, by affecting the relevance of the alternative that he sees a look-alike Grebe. This makes it look as if Dretske's response to the skeptic is to point out that while in rare circumstances, skeptical alternatives such as look-alike Grebes and cleverly disguised mules may be relevant, normally this is not the case. Presumably Dretske would think that circumstances are never such that the more radical skeptical alternatives (e.g., brain-in-a-vat, or Cartesian demon scenarios) are relevant. As he says earlier in the article, "for the purposes of assessing someone's knowledge ... certain alternative possibilies are simply not relevant." Again this response does not explain the persisting appeal of skeptical arguments.

But Dretske goes on to say with respect to this effect of the circumstances of the subject on the relevance of alternatives for knowledge,

> This will (or should) be no more unusual than acknowledging the fact that a refrigerator could truly be described as empty to a person looking for something to eat, but *not* truly described as empty to a person looking for spare refrigerator parts.[28]

Here, however, there is a crucial shift in the phenomenon at issue. The examples concerning attributions of emptiness do not show that the correctness of such attributions depends on the circumstances of the subject of the attribution – in this case a refrigerator. Rather, they show that the correctness of an attribution of emptiness depends on the context of attribution, viz., the intentions, purposes, etc., of the attributor. This is contextual relativity in the sense of indexicality. In this sense, two speakers could simultaneously say of the same refrigerator "It is empty," and it be the case that what one says is true and what the other says is false. This could occur if, as in Dretske's example, one speaker is looking for something to eat, while another is looking for spare refrigerator parts. The two different contexts yield different criteria for when the presence of a certain type of thing is relevant to attributions of emptiness.

It is this latter kind of contextual relativity that allows us to explain the appeal of skeptical arguments. We have noted that simply to say that skeptical alternatives are, in some sense, too remote to be relevant is to fail to do justice to the apparent threat that they present to our knowledge claims. While we often feel that skeptical alternatives are too remote to threaten our knowledge claims, at other times we find them quite troubling. When we think about skepticism, we often vacillate with respect to the relevance of these alternatives, and thus with respect to whether we know. By supposing that the criteria or standards of relevance, e.g., standards of remoteness or probability, are relative to the context of attribution (the intentions, interests, purposes, etc., of attributors), we can explain our tendency to vacillate in this way. (In the same way, by supposing that the standards for flatness are relative to the context of attribution, we can explain why we might vacillate over whether to describe a particular road as flat).

In everyday contexts, our standards are such that, normally, skeptical alternatives are not relevant. In rare circumstances, some skeptical alternatives will be relevant according to everyday standards, e.g., if we are looking at a zebra in an exhibit that actually contains mules cleverly disguised to look like zebras. Our confidence in the truth of our everyday knowledge attributions is explained by the fact that normally, skeptical alternatives will not be relevant according to the standards in effect. However, when we are confronted with skeptical arguments, we may come to consider skeptical alternatives as relevant, thereby shifting our standards. Skeptical arguments are forceful, precisely because they can have this effect on us.[29] In this new context, where the standards for knowledge are stricter, attributions of knowledge which would be true in everyday contexts, are false. But we are not thereby constrained to use skeptical standards for our knowledge attributions. Upon further consideration, we may decide that skeptical alternatives are too remote to count as relevant, thereby shifting the standards once more. Again, sometimes we vacillate between considering skeptical alternatives as relevant and dismissing them as irrelevant. By supposing that attributions of knowledge are sensitive to context in this way, we do justice both to our strong inclination in everyday life to say we know things and the "persisting and undiminished appeal of skeptical arguments."[30]

One might object that the relevant alternatives view understood in the way I have been suggesting does not really constitute a reply to skepticism. For one could respond that what the skeptic denies is that we ever know relative to standards that make every alternative relevant. Thus to argue that we know only relative to standards that limit the set of relevant alternatives is not to address the skeptic at all.[31]

The problem with this objection is that is gets things backwards. If the theory of relevant alternatives is correct, it is the skeptic who does not really address our everyday knowledge attributions. After all, the interesting issue is whether the claims to know that we make in everyday life are true. What is initially startling about skeptical arguments is that they seem to call those claims into question. The theory of relevant alternatives shows how those claims – properly interpreted – are true. We do know relative to the standards that govern our everyday knowledge attributions.

This is not to deny that knowledge attributions involving stricter standards are false. Rather, the point is that those stricter standards do not ordinarily apply to our knowledge attributions.

The Closure Principle

Let us return briefly to the paradox that is the crux of the skeptical problem. Construing the relevant alternatives theory as I have suggested, it remains unclear which member of the inconsistent triad we should deny. Dretske has argued that proposition (1), the closure principle, is false, since we can know a proposition is true without knowing the falsity of certain alternatives.[32] For example, we can know that we see a zebra without knowing that it is not the case that we see a cleverly disguised mule.

However, if attributions, of knowledge are sensitive to the context of attribution, then it is not clear that the theory of relevant alternatives entails the falsity of the closure principle. It has been argued that we must interpret the closure principle as applying within a fixed context of attribution. Moreover, relative to a fixed context, the principle is true.[33] So in contexts where, e.g., we know we see a zebra, we also know that we do not see a cleverly disguised mule, and in contexts where we fail to know that we do not see a cleverly disguised mule, we do not know that we see a zebra.

On this view, we can argue that the skeptical paradox arises because of our failure to pay attention to contextual shifts. The closure principle holds relative to a context, and one of the other two propositions that constitiute the paradox will be false, depending on the standards of the particular context. In no context are they both true.

Of course, I have only given here a sketch of such a view and I certainly have not shown that Dretske is wrong to interpret the relevant alternatives view as entailing the falsity of the closure principle. However, a discussion of the details of this issue would take us too far afield.[34]

A Further Application

I have been arguing that if we construe attributions of knowledge as sensitive (or relative) to the context of attribution, we have available an effective strategy for dealing with skeptical arguments. But the utility of this view goes beyond its application to skeptical puzzles.[35] A further illustration is provided by a puzzle that Dretske discusses. It concerns the role of the importance of what is known in determining the set of relevant alternatives. It is crucial to note that what is at issue is, as Dretske says, the role of the importance of what is known for *speakers and listeners* in determining what alternatives are relevant. Dretske discusses an alleged example of this phenomenon:

> The fuel gauge (and associated mechanism) that suffices for knowing that you still have some gasoline (when driving in the city) is just not good enough for knowing that there is sufficient liquid coolant surrounding the reactor [on Three Mile Island]. This somewhat paradoxical fact (the fact, namely, that a particular instrument should be good enough to give knowledge in one place, not good enough in another) is to be explained, some would say, by the fact that as the stakes go up, the stakes associated with being right about

what one purports to know, so does the size of the relevancy set. There are more possibilities that must be eliminated in the nuclear power plant than must be eliminated in the automobile. In particular, a malfunction in the instrument itself must be guarded against in the dangerous situation. If it isn't, one doesn't know.[36]

Although in this passage, Dretske notes that it is paradoxical "that a particular instrument should be good enough to give knowledge in one place, not good enough in another," he concedes that "there is some appeal to this point. . . .".[37] However, he claims that the point is mistaken.

I see no reason why a standard automobile gauge, transplanted from the automobile to the nuclear power plant, functioning as the only indicator of coolant level, should not, assuming it continues to function reliably (as reliably as it did in the automobile), be able to do precisely what the more expensive instruments do – viz., tell the operators that the coolant is at a safe level.[38]

Since Dretske admits there is some appeal to the point, i.e., some intuitive pull toward treating the two cases in the example differently, if he claims that the point is mistaken, he must provide some explanation for our intuitive response. What Dretske says is that our intuitions are indeed responding to a difference between the two cases. There is an uncertainty that is appropriate in the reactor case that is not appropriate in the automobile case. It is just that the uncertainty concerns not whether the reactor operator knows what the coolant level is, but rather "when (due to gauge malfunction) they *stop* knowing it."[39]

I find Dretske's treatment of this case to be puzzling. Presumably, his reservation about the original point is that, as he says, it is paradoxical to claim that a gauge good enough for knowing in one place is not good enough in another. But then why should it not be equally paradoxical that the same change of location can make a difference in whether we should be uncertain about when a subject who knows, stops knowing. If the source of our intuitive response is as Dretske says, then he must believe (as I do) that we do not have the same uncertainty about when we will stop knowing that we have enough gas on the basis of the gauge in the automobile.

Moreover, the point cannot just concern our uncertainty as to when, due to gauge malfunction, we stop knowing that there is enough coolant. If the reliability of the gauge over time is at issue, then there will come a time at which we should be uncertain over whether we have stopped knowing, i.e., whether we still know. (We can assume for the purposes of this example that there is a significant lag time between when the fuel level drops and when it is detectable by means other than the gauge).[40]

I agree with Dretske that our intuitive responses to examples of this kind can be puzzling. However, we can resolve the puzzle by viewing the knowledge attributions we make as sensitive to the context of attribution. Recall that what is paradoxical about the example is that when we inquire whether a subject knows on the basis of a gauge, our intuitions pull us toward different answers depending on where the gauge is located (an automobile as opposed to a nuclear reactor). But it is paradoxical only on the assumption that we are asking the same question in each case. And if attributions of knowledge involve an indexical reference to a standard, this assumption may be incorrect. In different contexts of attribution, different standards can apply, depending on the intentions, values, etc., of the attributor. This is crucial for our present purposes since the original issue that Dretske raises is whether the importance *for speakers and listeners* of what is known can affect the composition of the relevancy set. If we suppose that the importance of what is known for attributors (speakers and listeners) does affect the standards of relevance that operate in a context, we get an explanation for what is otherwise puzzling. It is not paradoxical that our intuitions may lead us to judge that a subject can know on the basis of a particular instrument in one place even though our intuitions lead us to hesitate in making the same judgment when the instrument is in another place, if our viewing the stakes as higher in the latter case leads us to employ stricter standards. Moreover, this is just what we should expect if as Dretske says, the composition of the relevancy set is "in part at least responsive to the interests, purposes, and ... values of those with a stake in the communication process."[41]

A further example shows that attributors may employ different standards of relevance for the same case, if they diverge in what they consider to be important: Smith is very worried about whether the cruise ship which he and Jones are on will sink. Jones is not at all worried about this, having the utmost confidence in the seaworthiness of the ship. Smith asks Jones if she knows whether there are enough life preservers aboard. Jones replies that she knows there are a sufficient number since the tour guide says that the ship carries at least one life preserver per passenger. Smith, given his concern about the ship going down, may hesitate to agree with Jones that she knows. Because of the increased importance he attaches to the presence of the life preservers, Smith is only willing to attribute knowledge to Jones (or himself) if Jones has actually seen the life preservers on the ship. That is to say, by Smith's standards the possibility of misinformation in the tour guide is a relevant alternative. Jones, because she does not attach much importance to the presence of the life preservers is willing to attribute knowledge to herself on the basis of what the tour guide says. According to her standards, the alternative that the tour guide is misleading is not relevant. And, of course, there is no issue concerning what the correct standards are absolutely, if we take context-sensitivity seriously. Like attributions of flatness and emptiness, the standards that apply for attributions of knowledge will vary with the context.

Criteria of Relevance

What makes an alternative relevant? While philosophers have been able, through the use of examples, to point to some considerations that play a role in determining relevance, it has proven to be very difficult to give precise formulations of general criteria of relevance.

For example, what is frequently discussed as a major consideration is the probability or remoteness of an alternative. Dretske illustrates this phenomenon in his case of the Gadwall ducks and the look-alike Grebes. According to Dretske, if there are no such Grebes or if they exist but because of geographical barriers are confined to a distant area, then the alternative that someone sees such a Grebe is not relevant to whether they know they see a Gadwall. If they do exist and can migrate to the area, then this alternative is relevant. Dretske suggests that the "difference between a relevant and an irrelevant alternative resides ... in the kind of possibilities that actually exist in the objective situation."[43] I am sure Dretske would agree that this is not a very precise formulation. Because there are so many complex and controversial variations in examples like this, it is exceedingly difficult to capture the distinction between relevant and irrelevant alternatives in a precise criterion.[44]

Because of this problem, many philosophers have been led to have grave doubts about the adequacy of the theory of relevant alternatives as a response to skepticism.[45] Dretske, in his own discussion, holds that the anti-skeptical power of the theory of relevant alternatives (as well as other virtues of the theory) "can only be harvested if certain questions [including, "What makes an alternative relevant?"] can be given reasonable answers."[46] Apparently, Dretske either is more sanguine about the prospects for formulating precise criteria of relevance or he believes that something short of precise criteria constitutes a reasonable answer to the question.

I think that the latter option is the correct position to take. While I am not at all sanguine about the prospects for developing precise criteria, I think that the demand for such criteria in order for the theory to provide an adequate response to skepticism, is misguided. We can see this by looking at two ways we might construe the relevant alternatives approach.

One way for the relevant alternative theorist to argue would be to *begin* by appealing to criteria of relevance in the abstract. The claim would have to be that one can see simply by reflecting on the concept of relevance that the proposed criteria capture what it is about alternatives that make them relevant. Having gained assent on the correctness of the proposed criteria, the relevant-alternatives theorist would then proceed by arguing that when we apply these criteria to skeptical alternatives, we get the result that skeptical alternatives are not relevant. If we were to proceed in this way, then of course, the failure to provide a precise statement of the criteria would undermine the wole approach.

But we should not construe the relevant alternatives theorist as employing this argumentative strategy. Even if we did not worry about the precision problem, surely this strategy would be hopeless. We cannot pull criteria of relevance out of thin air. We formulate such criteria by reflecting on the deliverances of our intuition regarding cases. We try to devise criteria that capture those intuitions. We all have intuitions about relevance (the borderline cases notwithstanding). Since "relevance" is defined in terms of knowledge, our intuitions about relevance are at root, intuitions about knowledge.[47] Even the critics of the relevant alternatives approach demonstrate that they have such intuitions when they criticize various proposed criteria for yielding counterintuitive results.

So we should not construe the relevant alternatives theorist as arguing that skeptical alternatives are not relevant because the criteria show it. The irrelevance of skeptical alternatives is a datum provided by our intuitive judgments concerning what we know. It is illuminating to advert to various factors that account for relevance and it would certainly be desirable to have a precise formulation of the criteria of relevance. But surely it does not follow from our inability to provide a precise formulation, that we cannot legitimately apply the concept. Our inability to provide a precise formulation of the criteria of relevance derives from our inability to provide a precise formulation of the criteria of knowledge. If our inability to precisely formulate criteria made it illegitimate to apply a concept, the skeptic could establish his position simply by appealing to the fact that philosophers have been unable to formulate precise criteria of knowledge.

Of course if we want the theory of relevant alternatives to provide an analysis of knowledge in this sense, then the failure to provide precise criteria would constitute a failure of the theory. But this project is quite different from the project of responding to skepticism.

Again one might think that it begs the question against the skeptic to appeal to anti skeptical intuitions about relevance. And there is a sense in which it does. But equally, the skeptic begs the question against common sense by appealing to his skeptical intuitions about relevance. In this sense, it is impossible for either side of the dispute not to beg the question against the other side.

We need to be very clear about the nature of the enterprise in which we are engaged. What we are confronted with is not an argument that forces us to be skeptics. We noted that just as the skeptic can combine the claim that we do not know that skeptical alternatives are false with the closure principle to conclude that we fail to know ordinary empirical propositions, one could combine the same closure principle with the claim that we do know ordinary empirical propositions to conclude that we know that skeptical alternatives are false. Or we could take Dretske's route and argue that the closure principle is false.

What we face is a paradox. We are inclined to accept each member of a set of propositions we know to be inconsistent. What we seek is a theory that rescues common sense from the skeptical worries presented by the paradox. It is not a constraint on such a theory that it appeal to the skeptic. The project is not to demonstrate to the skeptic that we know. Rather it is to demonstrate to ourselves that we can claim to know without paradox.

One way to see that the problem of formulating criteria of relevance does not undermine the theory of relevant alternatives as a response to skepticism is to notice that the same problem ultimately confronts the skeptic. For just as the defender of common sense must explain the appeal of skepticism, the skeptic must explain the fact that we are strongly inclined to say that we know many things. The persistence of these intuitions (even after the skeptic has raised his alternative possibilities) is as problematic for the skeptic as the persisting appeal of skeptical arguments is for the anti-skeptic.

How can the skeptic explain away these intuitions? The most promising strategy is to claim that in cases where we think we know, while it is false that we know, nonetheless it is in some way appropriate or useful for us to say we know.[48] Thus, if there are no look-alike Grebes, although we still fail to know we see a Gadwall, there can be many purposes for which it is useful to distinguish such a case, from cases where there are lots of lookalike Grebes around. So according to the skeptic, our everyday pattern of knowledge attributions marks a distincton between cases where it is appropriate to say we know and cases where it is not. But in all cases, the skeptic maintains, it is literally false that we know.

If the skeptic argues in this way, and it is hard to see how he can avoid it, then he needs criteria of relevance as much as the anti-skeptic does. The only difference is that for the anti-skeptic, the criteria determine when an alternative is relevant to the *truth* of knowledge attributions, whereas for the skeptic, they determine when an alternative is relevant to the *appropriateness* of knowledge attributions. Since the skeptic needs criteria of relevance as much as the anti-skeptic does, our inability to be precise about the criteria should not incline us toward skepticism. If both sides of a dispute share a problem, the existence of the problem cannot favor one side of the dispute against the other.

Notes

Portions of this paper are taken from my paper "How to be a Fallibilist," in *Philosophical Perspectives* vol. 2, ed. James Tomberlin (Ridgeview Publishing, 1988). I would like to thank Jonathan Vogel and Scott Soames for valuable discussion.
 1 See Fred Dretske's "Conclusive Reasons," *Australasian Journal of Philosophy*, 49 (May, 1971), pp. 1–22; "Epistemic Operators," *Journal of Philosophy*, 67 (December, 1970), pp. 1007–23; "The Pragmatic Dimension of Knowledge," *Philosophical Studies*, 40 (October, 1981), pp. 363–78; *Knowledge and the Flow of Information* (Cambridge, Mass.: MIT Press/Bradford Books, 1981); I will focus on "The Pragmatic Dimension of Knowledge." Also see Cohen, "How to be a Fallibilist;" Alvin Goldman, "Discrimination

and Perceptual Knowledge," *Journal of Philosophy*, 78 (1976), pp. 771–91; G. C. Stine, "Skepticism, Relevant Alternatives, and Deductive Closure," *Philosophical Studies*, 29 (1976), pp. 240–560.

2 See Peter Unger, *Ignorance: The Case For Skepticism* (Oxford: Oxford University Press, 1975); Peter Unger, *Philosophical Relativity* (Minneapolis: University of Minnesota Press, 1974).

3 See Dretske, "Conclusive Reasons."

4 See Unger, *Ignorance*; in *Philosophical Relativity*. Unger modifies his view.

5 See Roderick Chisholm, *Theory of Knowledge* (Englewood Cliffs, NJ: Prentice-Hall, 1977); Gilbert Harman, *Thought* (Princeton, 1974); Keith Lehrer, *Knowledge* (Oxford: Oxford University Press, 1974); John Pollock, *Knowledge and Justification* (Princeton, 1974).

6 "Pragmatic Dimension of Knowledge," p. 367.

7 I defend a view of this kind in "How to be a Fallibilist." In "Knowledge and Context," *Journal of Philosophy* (October 1986) and "Knowledge, Context, and Social Standards," *Synthese*, 73 (1987), I argue that this kind of view can be motivated independently of issues concerning skepticism.

8 "Pragmatic Dimension of Knowledge," p. 371.

9 "Epistemic Operators," p. 1016.

10 This closure principle may be subject to certain quibbles. But surely something very close to it is very intuitive. See Robert Nozick, *Philosophical Explanations* (Cambridge, Mass.: Harvard University Press, 1981).

11 See Pollock, *Knowledge and Justification*; Stine, "Skepticism, Relevant Alternatives, and Deductive Closure;" Peter Klein, *Certainty: A Refutation of Skepticism* (Minneapolis: University of Minnesota Press, 1981).

12 "Pragmatic Dimension of Knowledge," p. 368.

13 Ibid., p. 365.

14 Ibid., p. 368.

15 See Goldman, "Discrimination and Perceptual Knowledge;" Harman, *Thought*; Lehrer, *Knowledge*.

16 Dretske says that he doubts whether some of these cases really are such that the subject fails to know. I discuss a case of this kind later in the text.

17 See David Lewis, "Scorekeeping in a Language Game," *Journal of Philosophical Logic*, 8 (1979) pp. 513–43. Cohen, "Knowledge and Context;" Cohen, "Knowledge, Context, and Social Standards;" Cohen, "How to be a Fallibilist;" Dretske, "Epistemic Operators;" Dretske, "The Pragmatic Dimension of Knowledge;" Dretske, *Knowledge and the Flow of Information*; Goldman, 'Discrimination and Perceptual Knowledge;" Stine, "Skepticism, Relevant Alternatives, and Deductive Closure."

18 Exactly how these features of the context determine the standards is a complex and difficult matter. But this is no special problem for the claim that attributions of *knowledge* are context-sensitive. The mechanisms of context-sensitivity (indexicality) are not very well understood in general. Even (relatively) uncontroversial cases of predicates whose application depend on context-sensitive standards face the same difficulty, e.g., flat and empty.

19 In cases of self-attributions of knowledge, we must distinguish between the same person as attributor and as subject of the attribution.

20 "Pragmatic Dimension of Knowledge," p. 371 Of course, "remoteness" is vague. Later in the text, I discuss the problem of our inability to be precise about the criteria of relevance.

21 Strictly speaking, since on the view we are considering, "knowledge" and "know" are indexicals, the discussion should be framed metalinguistically. So

I should say that A says "S knows that he sees a Gadwall" or A says "S has knowledge that he sees a Gadwall." Because the metalinguistic formulations are somewhat cumbersome, I will not always use them. But the reader should not be misled by this.

22   "Pragmatic Dimension of Knowledge," p. 366.
23   For a theory of how this works, see Lewis, "Scorekeeping."
24   "Pragmatic Dimension of Knowledge," p. 366.
25   *Knowledge and the Flow of Information*, p. 133.
26   Ibid., p. 133.
27   "Pragmatic Dimension of Knowledge," p. 370.
28   Ibid., p. 370.
29   For a more detailed account of how this occurs, see Cohen, "How to be a Fallibilist."
30   My point here is not that Dretske is unaware of this view. As we have seen, there are several places in his writings where he appears to endorse this view. (In addition see Dretske, "Epistemic Operators," p. 1022) I don't know whether Dretske would agree that our standards can shift so as to make skeptical alternatives relevant. He does not argue this way in his explanation of the appeal of skeptical arguments. He does say that the set of relevant alternatives will always be a proper subset of the set of alternative (in "Pragmatic Dimension of Knowledge.")
31   See Palle Yourgrau, "Knowledge and Relevant Alternative," *Synthese* (May, 1983), p. 188.
32   See "Epistemic Operators."
33   To defend closure within a relevant-alternatives framework, one cannot define the set of relevant alternatives simply as the set of alternatives that need not be known to be false. See Cohen, "How to be a Fallibilist;" Stine, "Skepticism, Relevant Alternatives, and Deductive Closure."
34   For a discussion of these issues and a defense of closure within a relevant alternatives framework, see Cohen, "How to be a Fallabilist;" Stine, "Skepticism, Relevant Alternatives, and Deductive Closure."
35   In "Knowledge and Context" and "Knowledge, Context, and Social Standards," I argue that the applicability of this view to nonskeptical issues provides an independent motivation for its application to skeptical issues.
36   "Pragmatic Dimension of Knowledge," p. 375.
37   Ibid., p. 375.
38   Ibid., pp. 375–6.
39   Ibid., p. 376.
40   Some may think that the issue is not whether the operator knows, but whether he knows that he knows, cf. David Sanford, "Knowledge and Relevant Alternatives: Comments on Dretske," *Philosophical Studies*, 40 (October, 1981), pp. 000–00. Although I do not agree, it would still follow that attributions of knowledge, second-order or otherwise, can be affected by the importance of what is known.
41   *Knowledge and the Flow of Information*, p. 133.
42   I first heard an example like this from John Pollock.
43   "Pragmatic Dimension of Knowledge." p. 377.
44   For discussions of this problem, see Sanford, "Knowledge and Relevant Alternatives; Dretske, "Pragmatic Dimension of Knowledge;" Goldman, "Discrimination and Perceptual Knowledge."
45   See Ernest Sosa, "On Knowledge and Context," *Journal of Philosophy* (October, 1986); Yourgrau, "Knowledge and Relevant Alternatives."

46 "Pragmatic Dimension of Knowledge," p. 370.
47 Some non-skeptics might have the intuition that all alternatives are relevant,
    but believe that in everyday instances of knowledge, all alternatives can be,
    in some sense, eliminated. The important distinction concerning which we all
    have intuitions, is the one between alternatives that undermine knowledge
    and those that do not. Whether the latter are such that we can eliminate
    them or are such that knowledge does not require that they be eliminated is
    not important in this context. Of course, this issue matters very much for the
    status of epistemic closure principles. For a discussion of this see Cohen,
    "How to be a Fallibilist."
48 See Barry Stroud, *The Significance of Philosophical Skepticism* (Oxford:
    Oxford University Press 1974); Unger, *Philosophical Relativity*.

3

Proper Knowledge

David H. Sanford

Looking for Dretske

Convention time is here again. After a day in an over-heated hotel room, interviewing young philosophers who are all gifted, affable, and tense, I descend at last to the lobby and enter the dim bar, hoping to find Fred Dretske. A stroke of good luck: there he is, sitting at a table near the far end of the room. I can see that it is he. I know that it is Fred Dretske.

If I know that it is Fred Dretske sitting at the table, then I know that it is not Alvin Goldman or Robert Nozick or David Armstrong, who have advanced similar views about the requirements of knowledge. I know that it is not Dennis Stampe or Daniel Hausman or Donald Crawford or any other of Dretske's colleagues at the University of Wisconsin, Madison. I know that it is not Gilbert Harman or Bernard Williams or Stephen Stich or any other lean, wiry philosopher distinct from Dretske.

There are many philosophers at the convention with whom I have never spoken, who have never been identified in my presence, and whose name tag I have never bent over to read. Perhaps Marvin Shaw is such a person (whose name I just lifted from the *Directory of American Philosophers*). Although I am willing to say that I know that the person sitting at the table is not Marvin Shaw, that is not because I have much of an idea what Marvin Shaw looks like. (I assume that Shaw both is and appears to be an adult male who is not a Dretske-double.)

Someone was sitting at the bar when I came in looking for Dretske. Maybe it was Shaw. I glanced at this person, Shaw or whoever, and saw straight away that he was not Dretske. That was because I know what Fred Dretske looks like. "Shaw is not Dretske" and "Dretske is not Shaw" may be equivalent, but the following are not:

I can see that Dretske is not Shaw.
I can see that Shaw is not Dretske.

It may be that I would never mistake Dretske for someone other than Dretske, although I might mistake, or be tempted to mistake, someone other than Dretske for Dretske. It is not obvious to me whether given any relevant alternative A, I must know that Dretske is not A, or would not mistake A for Dretske, or both, in order to know that the man at the table is Fred Dretske. Even if we remain unsure exactly how requirements for knowledge should be formulated in terms of *relevant alternatives*, the notion is important. In the current example, any philosopher who attends, or who might attend, the convention, figures in an alternative to Fred Dretske's sitting at a table at the end of the bar. For any such philosopher X, I must be able to make at least one discrimination between X's sitting at the table and Dretske's sitting at the table.

Relevant alternatives owe their interest and importance to their contrast with irrelevant alternatives. I can see that the person at the table is not Goldman. I can see that he is not Shaw, or at least I would not mistake Shaw for him. But can I see that it is not a professional actor made up to look like Fred Dretske and trained to behave much as Dretske behaves while sitting in a bar? Can I see that it is not Twin-Dretske, on a quick visit from Twin Earth, long accustomed to drinking mixtures of XYZ and C_2X_5ZX and now about to try a little H_2O with C_2H_5OH? Can I see that it is not an elaborate hologram, designed to emit light indistinguishable from the light Dretske and his immediate environment would reflect in normal bar-room conditions? Can I see that my current visual experiences are not the results of direct intervention on my brain or sensory nerves by a mad scientist? Can I see that the Evil Genius itself has not taken over my soul? One constructs these alternatives to ensure negative answers, that is, to be indistinguishable from an object of putative knowledge or recognition. One who classifies them as irrelevant suggests that such indistinguishability does not preclude genuine knowledge or recognition.

Indistinguishable relevant alternatives, on the other hand, do preclude knowledge. If you cannot distinguish Fred Dretske and Sydney Shoemaker in these circumstances, then you cannot see that Dretske is sitting at the table. For all you know, it is Shoemaker.

Distinguishing between relevant and irrelevant alternatives leads one to deny the validity of the following form of argument:

> S knows that P.
> S knows that it is impossible that both P and Q.
> Therefore, S knows that not-Q.

We have already formulated a counterexample. I know that Dretske is sitting at the table. I know that it is impossible that both Dretske sits at the table and, at this same table at the same time, an actor sits impersonating Dretske. It does not follow, according to the view in question, that I know that an actor impersonating Dretske is not sitting at the table.

An epistemological skeptic faced with the distinction between relevant and irrelevant alternatives might undergo a conversion and accept the distinction as showing that skepticism is pointless. Or the skeptic might dismiss the distinction as entirely beside the point. Or the skeptic can steer an intermediate course and provide some more subtle, complicated response. In this essay I shall not promote and referee a round between skeptic and anti-skeptic. I will take for granted that the notion of relevant alternatives is valuable for the theory of knowledge.

A philosopher who agrees that the notion of relevant alternatives is valuable faces certain theoretical questions. What makes an alternative relevant? In our example, what makes Armstrong or Shaw or Shoemaker sitting at the table relevant alternatives, when an actor made up to resemble Dretske is not? Another, closely related, question concerns the the transmission of knowledge through valid inference. When a subject knows an argument to be valid, and also knows all the premises, under what circumstances does the subject thereby know the conclusion?

Fred Dretske attacks the problems of distinguishing relevant from irrelevant alternatives in a theoretically disciplined way in "The Pragmatic Dimension of Knowledge." The first of his several suggestions refers to his earlier research on contrastive focusing:

> (1) The first point has to do with the way we use contrastive focusing to indicate the range of relevant alternatives. I have discussed this phenomenon in another place, so let me give just one example to illustrate the sort of thing I have in mind. Someone claiming to know that Clyde *sold* his typewriter to Alex is not (necessarily) claiming the same thing as one who claims to know that Clyde sold his typewriter to *Alex*. The sentence we use to express what they know is the same, of course, but they reflect, and are designed to reflect, different relevancy sets. A person who knows that Clyde *sold* his typewriter to Alex must be able to rule out the possibility that he *gave* it to him, or that he *loaned* it to him, or (perhaps) that he merely *pretended* to sell it to him. But he needs only a nominal justification, if he needs any justification at all, for thinking it was Alex to whom he sold it. He has to be right about its *being* Alex, of course, but he isn't claiming to have any special justification for thinking it was Alex rather than, say, his twin brother Albert. On the other hand, the person who knows that Clyde sold his typewriter *to Alex* is claiming to know that it wasn't Albert and is, therefore, expected to be in possession of evidence bearing on the identity of the recipient. But, in this second case, the knower needs only a nominal justification for the belief that Clyde *sold* him the typewriter rather than, say, loaned it to him. He certainly needn't be able to exclude the possibility that the entire transaction was a sham designed to fool the IRS. (Ibid., p. 373)

When Dretske delivered "The Pragmatic Dimension of Knowledge" to a Greensboro Symposium in Philosophy, it was my good fortune to be the commentator. In response to the passage just quoted, I said that Dretske's point about contrastive focusing was "important for the theory of knowledge" but "peripheral to the specific project at hand." "Of course," I said:

> the alternatives relevant to the claim that one knows that *P* will depend on the content of *P*. Contrastive focusing ... [will] help make explicit just what is claimed to be known. Once this is made explicit, the project at hand is the determination, and the provision of its theoretical account, of which alternatives are relevant. Constrastive focusing ... so far as I can see, offer[s] no further help with this project.[1]

I hereby repudiate these remarks. Although they are not exactly false, in my opinion they point in the wrong direction – that is, they point away from the direction I want to explore in this essay. I will return to this topic after discussing some aspects of Dretske's research on contrastive focusing and his treatment of increments of knowledge in chapter 3 of *Seeing and Knowing*.

Grishkin is Nice

Her Russian eye is underlined for emphasis. On other nights, her Russian lips are painted red. Sometimes a light shadowing brings out her high cheekbones. One practiced in cosmetic art can proceed in a hundred ways to emphasize different parts, aspects, and relations between the parts of Grishkin's face. In one sense, these results each differ one from the other, for the emphasis of one is never just the same as the emphasis of another. In another sense, however, these results are all the same. They are all Grishkin's face. Her face with underlined eyes may look different from, and may therefore elicit different responses than, her face with darkened hollows under her cheekbones. Nonetheless, it is the same face. There is no theoretical need to distinguish different facial allomorphs or allomorphic faces.

Neither do we feel tempted to regard differently marked up and emphasized maps of Montana as allomorphic maps or cartographic allomorphs. Many maps of Montana convey enormous amounts of information. With a transparent marking pen, one can emphasize certain highways, or rivers, or mountain ranges, or counties, and so forth. One can emphasize a town or city by drawing a circle that includes the area of the map that represents the city and the name of the city. Consider three maps of Montana, otherwise identical, except that on the first there are circles around (the depictions and names of) Butte, Billings, and Bozeman, on the second there are circles around Helena and Anaconda, and on the third there are circles around Whitefish and White Sulpher Springs. In some contexts, these maps will function very differently. "There is an excellent Swedish restaurant in each of the towns indicated on the map." "For a perfect vacation that will not cost a fortune, go here!" Where we go, in search of a perfect vacation, may depend on which map is before us. Each of the three maps nevertheless depicts exactly the same features. The differences in emphasis involve no differences in depiction.

Maps of exactly the same regions and features can function differently because different parts are emphasized. Statements and phrases about exactly the same events, processes, facts, states, or occurrences can function differently for a similar reason. Dretske's "Contrastive Statements" reveals and develops this insight. Within contexts of knowledge, understanding, other intentional attitudes and feelings, explanation, and causal attribution, contrastive stress and emphasis makes a big difference, at least as big as that between truth and falsity:[2]

> Henry was disgusted to find that there were *millipedes* in the linen closet.
> Henry was disgusted to find that there were millipedes in the *linen closet.*
> Burning *dried rose petals* at midnight made the millipedes move next door.
> Burning dried rose petals *at midnight* made the millipedes move next door.
> Sarah can see that a *millipede* is crawling up the spine of a book by McTaggart about Hegel.
> Sarah can see that a millipede is crawling *up* the spine of a book by McTaggart about Hegel.
> Sarah can see that a millipede is crawling up the spine of a book *by McTaggart* about Hegel.
> Sarah can see that a millipede is crawling up the spine of a book by McTaggart *about Hegel.*

Dretske summarizes his article "Referring to Events" as follows: "Propositional allomorphs designate allomorphic events" (p. 97). In the first pair of sentences above, the two propositional allomorphs follow "Henry was disgusted to find that:"

> there were *millipedes* in the linen closet.
> there were millipedes in the *linen closet.*

The corresponding allomorphic events (or states) are something like:

> The creepy-crawly things in the linen closet being millipedes.
> A location of millipedes being in the linen closet.

I intend my examples of Grishkin's face and maps of Montana to express distrust in the notion of an allomorph as a philosophically useful approach to understanding contrastive stress. Although Dretske's research on stress and focusing is widely appreciated and applied, it deserves greater appreciation and applications that are even wider. Dretske's claims about allomorphs are inessential to his central claims about contrastive stress. If qualms about the elusive nature of allomorphs inhibit ongoing investigations about focus and emphasis, then an attempt to purge the discussion of allomorph talk and allomorph diagrams can serve a noble, constructive purpose.

Although allomorph diagrams have retired to a twilight-hued obscurity, I drag them back briefly into public view for the present occasion. One of Dretske's examples in the "The Content of Knowledge" is:

> *Mary* stole the bicycle.
> Mary *stole* the bicycle.
> Mary stole the *bicycle*.

Which of these is embedded in a larger context can significantly affect the meaning and truth conditions of of the resulting claim. The following examples illustrate the familiar point:

> The Dean was very surprised to learn that *Mary* stole the bicycle.
> You tend to overlook the fact that Mary *stole* the bicycle.
> The one thing that still puzzles me is that Mary stole the *bicycle*.

The embedded sentence in these examples conveniently has a three-part subject-verb-object structure. Dretske can represent each component on a separate coordinate axis of a three-dimensional diagram. (We are accustomed to drawing and reading two-dimensional representations of these three-dimensional diagrams in which the three axes are mutually perpendicular.) Mary has one position on the subject axis; Tom, Dick, and Harriet have others. Stealing has one position on the verb or action axis; buying, borrowing, and painting have others. The bicycle has one position on the object axis; the automobile, the motorcycle, and the canoe have others. Positions on all the axes together determine a point that represents the original sentence "Mary stole the bicycle." Dretske's diagramming innovation provides such points with orientations to indicate their allomorphic affinities. Dretske uses opposed arrows; and although one naturally associates arrow heads with orientation and directionality, these arrow heads have only a decorative function. The shafts to which the arrrow heads are attached do all the representational work. A shaft parallel to the subject coordinate axis and passing through the "Mary stole the bicycle" point corresponds to the allomorph "*Mary* stole the bicycle." A shaft passing through the same point but this time parallel to the object coordinate axis corresponds to "Mary stole the *bicycle*."

The scientific appearance of these techniques of representation is an artifact. One who arranges items along a coordinate axis typically orders the items according to some principle, and often has an appropriate metric for determining relative distances between them. When we graph something against inches of rainfall, we do not think twice about putting the point representing three inches of rain *between* the points representing two inches and four inches of rain. When we construct a subject axis for our current example, should Mary be between Tom and Dick? Or should Tom be in the middle? Or Dick? Once they are ordered, should they be spaced evenly or unevenly? These questions have no answers. Although certain principles of ordering and metric-assigning will be useful in particular circumstances, the phenomena of contrastive stress extends much further than our ability to order the relevant alternatives in a non-arbitrary way. To represent "Mary stole a bicycle" in Dretske's three-space, one can pick any point at all to represent it, including the origin, and then make the appropriate assignments to the coordinate axes.

The following alternative method of representation sometimes appears on classroom blackboards. Despite its unscientific appearance, its representational capacities are greater than Dretske's.

Mary stole the bicycle.

This sentence is stretched out so that we can list all the relevant alternatives under each part, as follows:

$$\text{Mary} \quad \text{stole} \quad \text{the} \quad \text{bicycle.}$$
$$\left\{ \begin{array}{l} \text{Tom} \\ \text{Harriet} \\ \text{Dick} \end{array} \right\} \left\{ \begin{array}{l} \text{borrowed} \\ \text{painted} \\ \text{bought} \end{array} \right\} \quad \left\{ \begin{array}{l} \text{automobile} \\ \text{motorcycle} \\ \text{canoe} \end{array} \right\}$$

Instead of orienting a line parallel to a coordinate axis, we can use some device to indicate one or another list of alternatives. Italics and underlining, the devices we have used all along, serve as well as any. Italics and underlining emphasize. The mode of representation before us differs from the standard methods of emphasis only by listing relevant alternatives in a column beneath the word or phrase to which they are alternatives. While it becomes more difficult to envisage mutually perpendicular axes as their number grows greater than three, there is no limit to number of columns on the scheme just proposed. Many sentences can receive emphasis in more than three places. In the following sentence, emphasis of *to* or *in* or *the* would be inappropriate – there are no relevant alternatives – but emphasis of any other word could be appropriate:

Boswell did not mean to kiss your daughter's ear in the bedroom of Lady Duckblood.

We can distinguish vertical from horizontal contrast. Horizontal contrast is so named because we write English horizontally. Boswell did not mean to kiss your *daughter's* ear. This contrasts horizontally with everything else in the sentence that might be emphasized. One directs attention to *daughter's* rather than to *kiss* or *your* of something else. Vertical contrast is with relevant alternatives, which we happen to list vertically. One directs attention to *daughter's* rather than to *sister's* or to *wife's* or to *stepmother's*.

There is a difference between:

I know that *Mary* stole the bicycle,

and

I know that Mary *stole* the bicycle.

The difference is not well explained by reference to event allomorphs as different objects of knowledge. Rather, the scope of "I know that" shifts in extent and varies in location according to how components of an embedded sentence are emphasized. The same phenomenon occurs with explanation, understanding, and causal attribution; but here I will concentrate on knowledge.

Increments in Knowledge

This subtitle comes from "Seeing and Knowing," Chapter 3 of Dretske's *Seeing and Knowing*. I intend to draw more conclusions from its contents than Dretske does himself. At the beginning of Section 2, entitled "Proto-Knowledge," Dretske writes:

> Our acquisition of knowledge by visual means is incremental in character, and it is the purpose of this section to illustrate this extremely important, but apparently overlooked, feature of epistemic seeing. (Ibid., p. 93)

The following brief dialogue is written in close imitation of Dretske:

George: (in the driver's seat) I am pumping the brake. Can you see anything?
Martha: (under the car) Finally! I can see where the brake fluid is leaking out.
George: You can see that brake fluid is leaking out from a certain place?
Martha: Yes!
George: How can you see that it is brake fluid?
Martha: ???

Martha has ample reason to believe that the liquid that has been leaking and that continues to leak as George pumps the brake is brake fluid. She does not claim that she can identify brake fluid or recognize it visually, at least not while lying under an automobile. She can see that brake fluid is leaking *from that line*, although she cannot see that *brake fluid* is leaking from that line. A diagram in the style Dretske draws in Chapter 3 represents the increment in knowledge Martha visually acquires in this example:

This is leaking from this line.

Increment of knowledge
allegedly acquired by
visual means.

This is brake fluid.

We could use this example in an attempt to show the invalidity of the following argument form:

Martha can see that P.
Martha knows that P entails Q.
Therefore, Martha can see that Q.

In his treatment of such examples, however, Dretske narrows the claim to visual knowledge rather than insist that the epistemic operator "Martha can see that" does not penetrate. And in his initial treatment, Dretske says nothing incompatible with the validity of the following argument form:

Martha knows that P.
Martha knows that P entails Q.
Therefore, Martha knows that Q.

In other words, in the terminology of "Epistemic Operators," the epistemic operator "Martha knows that" does penetrate. Consider the following instance:

Martha knows that brake fluid is leaking from that line.
Martha knows that if brake fluid is leaking from that line, then the leaking liquid is brake fluid.
Therefore, Martha knows that the leaking liquid is brake fluid.

This example will not serve to demonstrate that "Martha knows that" does not penetrate. In the presumed setting of late twentieth-century automotive culture, Martha does know that the liquid is brake fluid. She cannot see that it is brake fluid: that is the main point of the example. A valuable epistemological exercise, one I will not attempt here, would be to explain just how we and Martha know such things. Martha's knowledge that the liquid is brake fluid is *proto-knowledge* according to Dretske. Martha can see that the brake fluid is leaking from that line. Her knowledge of the leak's location is visual; this increment in knowledge is acquired by seeing. Her knowledge of the liquid's identity is not visual; it is proto-knowledge acquired by some other means.[3]

Suppose however that Martha does not know that the liquid is brake fluid, not as proto-knowledge, or as visual knowledge, or as any other kind of knowledge. Suppose that Martha believes, with astounding ignorance, that normally only two liquids flow within a modern automobile, gasoline and brake fluid. She can tell that the leaking liquid is not gasoline; so she infers, unsoundly, the true conclusion that it is brake fluid. Is it still true, in this variation, that:

Martha knows that the brake fluid is leaking from that line?

If not, the epistemic operator "Martha knows that" does not penetrate. But it appears that this operator, unsupplemented, indicates only imprecisely the increment in knowledge that Martha has attained. "Martha knows that the brake fluid is leaking *from that line*" is an improvement. Emphasis narrows the knowledge claim. Emphasis in addition appears to be the best device to indicate a precise increment of knowledge so long as we retain all and only the words of the original sentence in their original order. But by using different forms of words, we can achieve even greater precision.

Scope

Philosophers talk about scope more often than about increments, yet the two ways of talking have very similar purposes. There is no standard way to symbolize increments. Dretske intends his elevated-step diagrams in *Seeing and Knowing* to illustrate a point but not to serve as a model for a new notation. Predicate logic, modal logic, deontic logic, and logics with similar syntaxes, on the other hand, serve as established media for drawing scope distinctions.

In "The Content of Knowledge," Dretske argues that scope differences alone cannot draw the relevant distinctions he has noticed. Continuing with our example of Martha and the brake fluid, let us ponder the following formulations:

$(\exists x)$ [(x is the liquid leaking from that line) & Martha knows that x is brake fluid].
$(\exists x)$ [(x is brake fluid) & Martha knows that x is the liquid leaking from that line].

The first does not require that Martha makes any connection between the brake fluid and the liquid that leaked from that line. If Martha knows that some liquid in a glass jar in the basement is brake fluid, and this fluid in fact leaked from the line, then whether or not she is aware of this last fact, we may interpret the first formulation as satisfied. (If we take tense and temporal cross-reference more seriously, we need only construct examples that are correspondingly more complicated.) The second formulation, similarly, does not require that Martha make any connection between the leaking liquid and brake fluid. If Martha knows that a liquid is leaking from that line, and this liquid is in fact brake fluid, then we may interpret the second formulation as satisfied, even if Martha has never heard of brake fluid. While there may be circumstances in which a third-person knowledge attribution uses concepts unavailable to the subject or presupposes truths unknown to the subject, third-person attribution of knowledge often attributes against a background that the subject shares. The attempts above at indicating scope fail to connect the distinguishable components.

The difficulty, I suggest, is due not to some limitation in the notion of scope but rather to our ingrained habits in expressing scope. There are resources we have barely begun to tap. The following formulations have some advantages:

($\exists$x) [(x is brake fluid & x is leaking from that line) & Martha knows liquid x of some kind is leaking and that x is leaking from that line].
($\exists$x) [(x is brake fluid & x is leaking from that line) & Martha knows liquid x of some kind is leaking and that x is brake fluid].

The first clauses are identical and merely state the pertinent facts of the case. The first clauses within the scope of the epistemic operator "Martha knows that" are also identical. They report that Martha has a general – as opposed to specific – understanding of the pertinent situation. The two sentences differ only in their second clauses within the scope of the epistemic operator. These report Martha's specific understanding. The first says she knows the specific location of the leak. The second says she knows what kind of liquid is leaking. As these increments in knowledge are described, Martha cannot have acquired them in isolation. She must have fit them into an understanding, perhaps one that is quite general, of the situation under discussion.

The predicate-logic style of the above formulations is appropriate, but it may suggest a specious rigor. Here is a more colloquial rendering of the first that attributes the same specific increment in knowledge:

Brake fluid is leaking from that line and Martha knows liquid of some kind is leaking and that the liquid is leaking from that line.

Emphasis of components of sentences within the scope of epistemic operators suggests the incremental character of knowledge. But emphasis may be unable to indicate every relevant increment. Sometimes simple sentences have too few components to provide a potential object of emphasis for each relevantly distiguishable aspect of the situation at hand. Someone says that George knows that the cousins are fighting. In fact, George knows that Dexter just kicked Lester. Emphasis applied to "The cousins are fighting" cannot narrow down the proper object of knowledge to Dexter's kicking Lester.

All knowledge is proper knowledge, but not all statements of knowledge are statements of proper knowledge. Indeed, statements of proper knowledge are rare, which should not be surprising, since some pains and innovations are often necessary for their formulation. A statement of proper knowledge indicates, by some appropriate means, exactly what increment is known.

Do careful statements of proper knowledge resist skeptical attack better than more ordinary statements? Consider again the ordinary-sounding claim:

I know that Fred Dretske is sitting at the table.

Although this sentence could be a correct expression of proper knowledge, I want to consider the case, that I assume to be more usual, in which the knowledge increment is quite narrow. I do not claim to know that tables are really present, or that these people are really sitting, or that these are really people, or even that these are really physical objects. The following formulation makes a narrower claim:

Fred Dretske is sitting at the table, and of all the philosophers at the convention (none in disguise or actor's makeup) I know that the one over there, who appears to be sitting at the table, is Fred Dretske.

The cast of characters we considered earlier, the actors, aliens, and hallucinations, no longer figure in irrelevant alternatives; for they figure in no alternatives at all that pertain to the current claim.

Alternatives and Closure

All the alternatives to a claim of proper knowledge are relevant alternatives. This result should not come as a surprise, given the way that I define proper knowledge. *Relevant alternative* and *proper knowledge* are mutually explainable. No neat or simple procedure exactly determines the extent of either. In many actual situations, indeed, there is no exact increment of claimed or attributed knowledge because of an underlying indeterminacy of human intention. What exactly one properly knows, or claims to know, is still at least in part a function of one's beliefs, desires, purposes, and intentions.

Correlative notions serve a theoretical purpose when each connects the other to additional nodes in a theoretical network. The new, narrower category of proper knowledge eliminates the need for the earlier theoretical distinction between relevant and irrelevant alternatives. There are no irrelevant alternatives. Irrelevant hypotheses, suppositions, and situations are not *alternatives* to what is properly known.

Closure is starkly simple in a similar way. If one properly knows that P, then one knows everything one knows P to entail. On this account, I may still not be required to know that the person at the table is not an actor disguised as Dretske. The reason advanced previously was that knowledge is not closed under known entailment. The current reason is that what I *properly* know about the occupants of the hotel bar does not entail that no Dretske impersonator is before me. What I know properly I can express conditionally: if that is a member of the usual philosophical crowd, and not someone in disguise, then it is Fred Dretske.

We should expect neither too much nor too little from this proposal about closure. It is theoretically unsatisfactory simply to reject a closure principle unless one holds that from one's knowing that P and knowing that P entails Q it *never* follows that one knows that Q. An invalid principle can still have plenty of valid instances, and a theorist has the problem of explaining why the valid instances are valid. (They are clearly not valid just because they are instances of the principle, for the principle is invalid.) The problem before us previously was to explain what distinguishes the valid from invalid instances of the transmission of knowledge by known entailment. I claim to have abolished that problem, not by explaining the distinction, but by rejecting it. But still – whines the voice of the dissatisfaction – all you do is take the entailments that you want not to transmit knowledge in a given situation and then in your statement of what is properly known, formulate hedges, qualifications, and conditions specifically to thwart these entailments. I admit that this is I what I do. The notion of proper knowledge by itself will not tell us just what has to be known and what does not have to be known or order to say truly "I know that the man sitting at the table is Fred Dretske." But when we make decisions about the scope of knowledge and become comfortable with the admission that we strictly know less that our normal words suggest, then the notion of proper knowledge helps our theory of knowledge to be neater.[4]

Right now I think I know each of the following: I am looking out my office window at the west side of East Duke Building; I am not looking at a slide show of East Duke Building; I am not driving a cement truck in Bozeman, Montana; neither I nor any essential part of mine now floats in a lake, pool, tank, or vat; I am not thousands of light-years from the Sun traveling in a spaceship. The notions of proper knowledge or relevant alternatives will not rescue these claims from the teeth of skeptical challenges. If rescue comes from somewhere, it will come from elsewhere. The healing light of proper knowledge will not drive all epistemological skepticism underground to lie with the undead. If the notion of proper knowledge does not promise everything, it still promises something. It shows how a great many of our ordinary attributions of knowledge, first-person, second-person, or third-person, are immune from standard skeptical challenge. For what one intends to attribute by these statements is narrower than the original formulation reveals. A correct claim of proper knowledge typically has smaller scope than the original as broadly interpreted. Having smaller scope, it exposes less flank to skeptical attack.

> You see, Hylas, the water of yonder fountain, how it is forced upwards, in a round column, to a certain height; at which it breaks, and falls back into the basin from whence it rose: its ascent, as well as descent, proceeding from the same uniform law or principle of contrastive emphasis. Just so, the same Principles which, at first view, lead to the rejection of deductive closure, pursued to a certain point, bring philosophers back to Common Sense.

I can read the final passage the *Three Dialogues*, here slightly modified, to represent my central contentions. Attention to contrastive emphasis leads us to appreciate increments of knowledge. Understanding the incremental nature of knowledge supports the distinction of relevant from irrelevant alternatives and the rejection of deductive closure. (All these so far are among Dretske's accomplishments.) When we push incremental knowledge even beyond what colloquial emphasis can indicate, however, the even narrower increments that result allow us to reinstate deductive closure as a valid epistemic principle and to eliminate the distinction between relevant and irrelevant alternatives.

Notes

1 "Knowledge and Relevant Alternatives: Comments on Dretske," *Philosophical Studies*, 40 (1981), p. 379.
2 I discuss the importance of Dretske's work on contrastive stress to theories of causation in "Causal Relata," in *Actions and Events: Perspectives on the Philosophy of Donald Davidson*, ed. Ernest LePore and Brian P. McLaughlin (Oxford: Basil Blackwell, 1985), pp. 282–93.
3 Gerald Doppelt critically discusses proto-knowledge in "Dretske's Conception of Perception and Knowledge," *Philosophy of Science*, 40 (1973), pp. 433–46.
4 On this point my view of deductive closure coincides with that of Gail C. Stine in "Skepticism and Relevant Alternatives, and Deductive Closure," *Philosophical Studies*, 29 (1976), pp. 249–61. The routes by which Stine and I reached this point are different, but I think they are compatible.

References to Fred Dretske's Publications

Seeing and Knowing (London: Routledge and Kegan Paul, 1968).
"Epistemic Operators," *Journal of Philosophy*, 47 (1970), pp. 1007–23.
"Contrastive Statements," *Philosophical Review*, 81 (1972), pp. 411–37.
"The Content of Knowledge," In *Forms of Representation*, ed. B. Freed, A Marras, and P. Maynard (American Elsevier, 1975), pp. 77–93.
"Referring to Events," *Midwest Studies in Philosophy*, 2 (1977), pp. 90–9.
"The Pragmatic Dimension of Knowledge," *Philosophical Studies*, 40 (1981), pp. 363–78.

4

Dretske on How Reasons Explain Behavior

Jaegwon Kim

In a series of papers[1] and a recent book,[2] Fred Dretske has been working out an innovative account of how reasons explain behavior. His starting point is what we may call "the causal thesis," often associated with Davidson,[3] that reasons rationalize behavior by being its *cause*. With Davidson, therefore, Dretske takes rationalizing explanations to be a species of causal explanation, explanations that specify the causal antecedents of their explananda. Reasons are beliefs, desires, and other assorted "content-bearing" states, and these are among the paradigmatic instances of intentional mental states. Thus, the problem of explaining how reasons *rationalize* (that is, explain by providing reasons) is, for Dretske, the problem of giving an account of how intentional states can be causes, that is, the problem of *intentional* or *rational causation*. If we further assume, with Dretske, that behavior to be rationalized is, or often involves, bodily events and processes, our problem is seen as a special case of the problem of *psychophysical causation*, that of understanding how mental events or states can enter into causal relations with physical events, as their causes or their effects. There is of course an even broader problem of *mental causation*, the problem of explaining how mental events can enter into any sort of causal relation, either as causes or as effects, whether with physical events or with other mental events.

The reality of the mental is closely tied to the possibility of mental causation, and anyone who takes a realist attitude toward the mental must be prepared with an account of how mental causation is possible. Dretske is a realist about the mental and takes the problem of rational causation seriously. And the project he sets for himself strikes one as just right: he wants to show how reasons, *in virtue of their content*, can be causes of physical behavior. In explaining how reasons can be causes, he does not want to call on the supposed neurobiological properties of beliefs and desires; rather, he wants to vindicate the causal relevance of their representational or semantic properties, the properties that make them the beliefs and desires that they are. To solve the problem of rational causation we must show, Dretske believes, how beliefs and desires – in virtue of their representational content, *not* their neural-physical properties – can cause, and causally explain, behavior and action.

Moreover, it is part of Dretske's program to show that intentional psychology, that is, psychological theory that invokes contentful inner states ("propositional attitudes"), has a special role in the explanation of behavior, over and beyond what neurobiology and other physical theories can provide. He is convinced that "content has an essential and ineliminable role to play in the explanation of behavior," and that this is so not because "we are too ignorant of neurobiology to know what is really in there making the limbs move."[4]

Many interesting questions arise regarding various aspects of Dretske's suggestive proposals. In this paper, however, I will largely confine myself to some broadly metaphysical issues concerning Dretske's program; in particular, I will suggest another way of formulating a Dretskean account that seems better able to handle certain problems. I begin with a review of some current issues concerning mental causation.

Three Problems of Mental Causation

To begin with, why is mental causation thought to be a "problem?" As we would expect, the answer is that there are certain assumptions, which we take to have a legitimate claim on our respect, that make mental causation *prima facie* problematic. One possible response of course is to deny that mental causation ever takes place. However, that cannot be our initial response: mental causation seems like an everyday phenomenon with which all of us are only too familiar. A bee sting causes a sharp pain (physical-to-mental causation), and the pain in turn makes me wince (mental-to-physical causation). The lingering pain leads me to think that I had better call the doctor (mental-to-mental causation), and I go into the kitchen for the telephone (mental-to-physical causation). And so forth. But these everyday instances are not all; there are also seemingly compelling theoretical reasons.

We standardly explain actions by rationalizing them – that is, by providing "reasons for which" we did what we did; and as Davidson has emphasized, it is difficult to evade the conclusion that the explanatory efficacy of reasons derives crucially from their causal efficacy. For there seems in the offing no satisfactory noncausal account of the critical distinction between something merely being a *reason for* an action and its being a *motivating reason*; and only motivating reasons, it seems, can explain why an agent did what was done. If this is right, the vindication of the rationalizing mode of understanding human action requires an account of how reasons can cause actions. To drive this home, the point can be contraposed: if we cannot make sense of mental causation, or its subspecies, rational causation, we would be forced to scrap rationalizing explanations as a way of understanding human behavior; and this pretty much is to scrap the whole framework of intentional psychology. All this seems unavoidable under the causal thesis. Whether we should ultimately adhere to the causal interpretation of rationalization is a question we cannot take up here. However, we can say this much in its favor: if it can be made to work, that would be an excellent way of accounting for the explanatory efficacy of rationalizations. And, in general, there is good reason for thinking that mental realism and the possibility of mental causation stand or fall together: what possible good could causeless and effectless entities do for us?

What then are the assumptions that prompt us to vindicate mental causation? I believe there are three such assumptions currently on the scene each of which makes apparent trouble for mental causation. Two of these are well known; the third is less widely discussed but equally crucial. One is "the anomalism of the mental" ("mental anomalism" hereafter) made famous by Davidson.[5] Another is what I will call "syntacticalism."[6] The third I call "causal-explanatory exclusion." Each of these generates a distinct problem of mental causation, though the problems are to some extent interconnected. A comprehensive theory of mental causation must provide a solution to each problem, a solution that simultaneously satisfies the constraints of all three problems.

Why does mental anomalism pose a difficulty for mental causation? The initial difficulty, as set forth by Davidson, arises when mental anomalism is combined with the widely accepted nomological requirement on causal relations,[7] the condition that events standing in a causal relation must instantiate a causal law. But this seems to make mental causation impossible: mental causation requires mental events to instantiate laws, but mental anomalism says there are no laws about mental events. Davidson's solution to this difficulty is again well known: his "anomalous monism." True, says Davidson, mental events in causal relations must instantiate laws; since there aren't any psychological laws, that could only mean that they instantiate physical laws. This shows that mental events fall under physical event kinds (or have true physical descriptions), from which it further follows, argues Davidson, that they are physical events.

But this elegantly simple solution has not satisfied everyone. On the contrary, there has been a virtual unanimity among Davidson's commentators on just why anomalous monism is less than fully satisfying as an account of mental causation.[8] Take any mental event, m, that stands in a causal relation, say as a cause of event e. According to Davidson, this causal relation obtains in virtue of the fact that m and e instantiate a physical law. Thus, m has a certain physical (presumably, neural) property N, and e has a physical property P, such that an appropriate causal law relates events of kind N with events of kind P. But this shows that the fact that m is a mental event – that it is the kind of mental event it is – is given no role whatever in determining what causal relations it enters into; it seems that what causal relations hold for m is fixed, wholly and exclusively, by the totality of m's physical properties; and there appears in this picture no causal work that m's mental properties can do, or need to do. This seems to consign mental properties to the status of epiphenomena.[9]

Thus, the problem of mental causation arising out of mental anomalism is to answer this question: *How can anomalous properties be causal properties?* A solution to this problem would have to show either that, contrary to Davidson, mental properties are not in reality anomalous, or that being anomalous in Davidson's sense is no barrier to having causal relevance or entering into causal relations.

Although Dretske sometimes motivates his project by reference to Davidson, the problem of anomalous mental properties is not his main worry about mental causation. Rather, his primary concern appears to stem from syntacticalism, and his theory is best viewed as a response to this problem. By "syntacticalism" I mean the doctrine that only "syntactic" properties of internal states, not their "semantic" (or "content" or "representational") properties, are psychologically relevant – in particular, to behavior causation. Given the further assumption that the intentionality of mental states consists in their semantic or representational character (some will take this as a conceptual truth), syntacticalism appears to entail that intentional properties of mental states, those properties in which their mentality consists, are causally irrelevant. But what persuades us to take syntacticalism seriously?

Many people seem to find the following line of consideration plausible, at least at first blush: the internal cause of physical behavior must be supervenient on the total internal physical state of the agent or organism at the time.[10] For it seems a highly plausible assumption that if two organisms are in an identical total internal physical state, they will emit identical motor output. However, semantical properties of internal states are not in general supervenient on their synchronous intrinsic physical properties, for they as a rule involve facts about the organism's history and ecological conditions.[11] Thus, two organisms whose total states at a given time have identical intrinsic physical properties can differ in respect of the semantical properties they instantiate; they can differ in the contents of their beliefs and desires, the extensions of their expressions, etc. Thus, what semantical properties are instantiated by the internal states of an organism is a *relational* fact, a fact that essentially involves the organism's relationships to various environmental and historical factors. This makes semantical properties relational, or extrinsic, whereas we expect causative properties involved in behavior production to be nonrelational, or intrinsic, properties of the organism. If inner states are implicated in behavior causation, it seems that all the causal work is done by their "syntactic" properties,[12] leaving their semantic properties causally idle. The problem of mental causation generated by syntacticalism, therefore, is to answer the following question: *How can extrinsic, relational properties be causally efficacious in behavior production?*

This problem of relational properties stands out vividly in the context of Dretske's informational theory of content.[13] On this theory, what it is for a state s_i to have content F depends ultimately, though in complex ways, on there being a causal-nomological relationship between the occurrence of s_i and the presence of F in the organism's environment. If the same organism had been placed in a different environment, a state that is identical with s_i in intrinsic physical properties (or s_i itself) might have content G rather than F, or no content at all. But the causal potential of s_i for the production of physical behavior must be the same as long as the state retains the same internal physical-physiological properties – or so it seems. So how could the fact that an internal state has content F, rather than content G, make a causal difference to the organism's behavior?

That is the second problem of mental causation, a central problem of Dretske's recent work on intentionality and the explanation of behavior. Let us now turn to our third and final problem: suppose then that we have somehow put together an account of how mental events can be causes of physical events. But these events, *qua* physical events, must have physical causes; it surely would be an anachronistic retrogression to Cartesian interactionism to think that there are physical events that have *only nonphysical* causes. To countenance such events would amount to the rejection of the causal-explanatory closure of the physical domain, a principle that seems minimally required of any serious form of physicalism. Thus, if a belief–desire pair, m, causes bodily movement b, it is highly plausible for a physicalist to suppose that the total physical state of the agent at the time contains a full cause of b. So mental event m causes behavior b; and also a physical event, p, causes b. *What is the relationship between m and p?* If m and p are each countenanced as an independent sufficient cause of b, we would have to conclude that b is *overdetermined*, which seems absurd. Nor does it make sense to say that m and p are each only a *partial cause* and that they *together* make up a sufficient cause of b. Unquestionably, the simplest and most satisfying solution is *identity*: if we could say that m and p are one and the same event, the problem would vanish. That is the classic solution offered by identity materialism: m just is p, and here there is one cause of b, not two.

The identity solution is undoubtedly attractive, and perhaps feasible, when m and p are "token" events or states; however, its availability is in serious doubt if we are worried about the causal powers of mental *properties*. And the causal relevance of mental properties is precisely the problem we are at present concerned with, as may be recalled from our discussion of mental anomalism and syntacticalism. The difficulty is that mental anomalism apparently rules out the identity solution; for the property identity "m = p" entails that the two properties precisely correlate over all possible worlds. And even those who reject Davidson's arguments for mental anomalism, or mental anomalism itself, are likely to view mental and physical property identities as too strong and unwarranted.[14] Acceptance of such identities is often associated these days with mind–body theories commonly thought outmoded and discredited, such as reductionism and type-identity theory. Thus, the solution that m = p is not a real option for most of us; we need to know how the relation between m and p, each as a cause of behavior b, is to be understood.[15]

The foregoing I call the problem of "causal-explanatory exclusion." For the considerations of the sort we have just seen, when generalized, seem to show that there can be *at most* one complete and independent causal explanantion, or one fully sufficient cause, for any single event.[16] It is clear that the phenomenon of causal-explanatory exclusion presents a special problem for mental causation, especially for mental-to-physical causation, if we assume, with most recent writers on mental causation, a broadly physicalist framework. Thus, the core of the exclusion problem is to answer this question: *Given that every physical event has a physical cause, how is a mental cause also possible?*

Any theory of mental causation, even if it is primarily geared to either or both of the first two problems, must be responsive to the problem of exclusion. Having shown that mental properties, in spite of their anomalousness and extrinsicness, can be causal properties, one must further show how they find a place in an essentially physical world, a world whose causal structure is supposed to be defined at bottom by the causal-nomological relations among physical properties.

Dretske's Dual-Explanandum Strategy

Among the recent writers on mental causation, Dretske seems alone in being sensitive to the problem of exclusion, although he does not explicitly formulate it. He writes:

> One doesn't hear anything about beliefs and desires in the neurobiological explanation of the origin, pattern or propagation of those electrical pulses that bring about muscle contractions and, hence, finger and arm movements. Hence, if it were muscle contractions, finger and arm movements, we were trying to explain, it would be hard to see, from *this* standpoint, what role content was supposed to play in this explanatory game. Unless, of course, one is prepared to say, as I am not, that neurobiologists systematically overlook an important causal factor in their explanatory efforts.[17]

The relationship between an intentional and a neurobiological explanation of behavior is just a special case of the exclusion problem. It seems that Dretske is here accepting the essential point of this problem set forth in the preceding section. He is saying that if we take neurobiology to provide a complete causal account of muscle contractions and other bodily movements, it would be difficult to find a causal role for beliefs and desires with respect to these bodily happenings. That is, neurobiological explanations of bodily happenings would exclude these events' being *also* explained by rationalizing causes. Of course, if beliefs and desires were *reducible* to, or *reductively identifiable* with, neural states of the agent or organism, the two types of explanation could stand together, for rationalizations would then be reducible to biological explanations. If that should be the case, intentional states would be implicitly preserved in neurobiology, whether or not we "hear anything about beliefs and desires" in this science, just as thermodynamic properties are implicitly preserved in statistical mechanics.

It seems that Dretske rejects the reduction option because he thinks it is incompatible with his commitment to a relational theory of content; as we saw, content properties on his view are relational properties essentially involving conditions external to the organism, and hence cannot be reduced to, or reductively identified with, internal neurobiological states of the organism. In a revealing passage, he writes:

> I'm a realist about content, and my realism stems from a conviction that content has an essential and ineliminable role to play in the explanation of behavior. We don't describe one another as believing this and desiring that because it is, as it is with certain machines, merely a useful predictive strategy. Nor do we do it because we are too ignorant of neurobiology to know what is really in there making the limbs move. We describe each other in this way because our inner states actually have a content and it is this content that explains why we do what we do.[18]

Here Dretske is doing a number of things: first, he is expressing his realism about the mental and mental causation; second, he sets his project as a defense of an "essential and ineliminable" causal-explanatory role for intentional properties; and third, and this is a related point, he is here apparently ruling out the possibility of reducing beliefs and desires to neurobiological states or processes. He seems to be saying that even if we knew all about the neurobiology of behavior production, there would still be something we would be missing, something concerning the causal fact of the matter, unless we also had a rationalizing explanation of it. It should be obvious that a solution to the exclusion problem that saves all of these claims would be hard to come by.

What then is Dretske's solution to the exclusion problem? The general approach he adopts can be called "the dual-explanandum strategy:" resolve the explanatory rivalry by holding that two explanations do not in reality share the same explanandum. Since the explanations address different explananda, the potential for conflict vanishes. The same strategy has been used before for rationalizing and physical explanations of action: it has been held that rationalizations explain actions in a full-fledged intentional and teleological sense whereas physiological explanations explain "mere" bodily motion such as muscle contractions and limb movement.[19]

Dretske's implementation of the dual-explanandum approach is different and more sophisticated. His point is that rationalizations explain *behavior*, that is, what we *do*, not bodily movements, while these bodily happenings are just what neurobiology and other physical theory explain. Thus, the distinction between behavior, or doings, and bodily movements such as muscle contractions ("motor output") is crucial to Dretske's overall account. And Dretske does not disappoint: an elegant account of behavior is developed in the first two chapters of *Explaining Behavior*. Briefly, Dretske's concept of behavior is, in his own words, that of "endogenously produced movement, movement that has its causal origin *within* the system whose parts are moving."[20] Let M be some bodily movement of organism S and C its cause: for this to be an instance of behavior, it must be the case that C is an internal state of S. Thus, for Wilbur to raise his arm, it must be the case that his arm rises as an effect of some state *within* Wilbur. This contrasts with the case in which his arm rises, as an effect of someone else's grasping the hand and pulling it up. In the latter case, the cause of the motor output is not internal to Wilbur, and this is why it does not count as his *doing* something: there is here no action or behavior on his part.

We must be careful, Dretske tells us, to identify behavior not with motor output M which, as it happens, has an internal cause C, but rather with the relational structure, *C's causing M*. What Wilbur did is to cause his arm to rise, and the behavior consists in *some internal state C of Wilbur causing M*. Thus, to explain what Wilbur did in this case, according to Dretske, is to explain why some internal C in Wilbur caused M. In brief, behaviors are *causings*, and explanations of behavior must explain these causings by providing *causes of causings*. Neurobiology has M, the "product" or "result" of behavior, as its proper explanandum; it can also explain *how*, that is, through what sequence of intervening states, C led to the production of M. However, it is the proper job of rationalizations to explain *why C caused M*, and in order to do this, they must specify events or states that cause C to cause M.

How successful is the dual-explanandum approach in resolving the exclusion issue? Before we examine Dretske's version of this approach, there is an important general point to notice about this strategy: *a successful execution of the strategy requires commitment to dualism*. For the sundering of the explanandum is only the first step; there still is the second, crucial step that must be taken if the exclusion problem is to be solved. This is so because we need yet to rule out the possibility that one or the other of the two explananda that have been distinguished is amenable to both a rationalizing and a physical explanation (where is Dretske's argument to show that behavior as he conceives it isn't also neurobiologically explainable?). As long as this possibility is alive, the exclusion issue remains. To resolve it, friends of this approach must claim, for each of the two explananda, that it is not explainable both rationally and physically. To hold that neither is explainable rationally defeats the whole enterprise of vindicating the causal-explanatory powers of reasons; so that is not an option for the friends of dual explananda. There is only one other choice: to claim that one of the explananda, namely one that is rationally explainable, is not explainable physically. So this leaves us with phenomena in the world which cannot be explained physically; or, to speak in terms of causes, there are phenomena in the world that have nonphysical causes. These things are either physical or nonphysical; if they are nonphysical, we have a dualism of entities, and dual systems of causes and explanations; if they are physical, some physical things have only nonphysical causes, a form of Cartesian causal dualism and a violation of the causal closure of the physical. Either way, we seem stuck with a robust form of mind–body dualism.

Dretske wants to give intentional psychology a special and ineliminable causal-explanatory job to do. The job he assigns to it is to explain a special set of explananda, relational structures of the form *C's causing M*, where C is some internal state of a behaving system S and M is S's motor output. If the explanatory job is to be a genuine and substantive one, which it must be if it is to vindicate intentional psychology, these causings must be regarded as full-fledged entities in our ontology. Are they then physical things or nonphysical things? M is motor output, and Dretske takes C, its cause, as an inner physical state; so it is likely that Dretske would consider these relational structures as physical as well. In any case, if they are nonphysical, we have a dualism of entities; if they are part of the physical domain, Dretske is stuck with mental causes of physical phenomena.

Is this a violation of the causal closure of the physical? As we saw, once we recognize a nonphysical cause of a physical event, the closure principle requires us to recognize a physical cause of it as well; and once we have these two causes of a single event, the only way to make sense of the situation is some form of identity or reduction option. Dretske is a naturalist and physicalist; and we can be confident that he would not tolerate violation of the physical causal closure. So this only leaves the reduction-identity option for him. But isn't this option ruled out by something we noted earlier, namely his apparent rejection of the reductive resolution of the exclusion problem for rationalizing and biological explanation of behavior? And it may seem also inconsistent with something that Dretske clearly holds, namely that content properties are not reducible to biological properties.

The apparent inconsistency can be seen to vanish if we note that different reduction bases may be involved here. Dretske can hold his nonreductive thesis concerning content in relation to the *internal biology* of the organism as the reduction base, while endorsing at the same time the reducibility of content properties to a wider physical base. This wider reduction base would be an appropriate spatiotemporal stretch of physical environment around the organism; it will include all the physical facts and conditions, past and present, upon which the content properties of the organism supervene.

But if this reductive option is accepted, how plausible is it to claim an essential and ineliminable causal role for content properties of intentional states? What our considerations make plain is that if you accept a broadly physicalist framework, there really can be no independent causal job for mental items – that is, independent of, and ineliminable with respect to, physical items. To insist on an irreducible causal role for the mental is destined to lead to forms of dualism. Dretske's project of finding an ineliminable causal role for content properties makes sense only if the ineliminability is understood in relation to the internal biology of the behaving organism. We should note that "ineliminable" is not synomymous with "irreducible" or "independent:" one could plausibly argue that to be reduced is to be conserved, not to be eliminated. If the ineliminability Dretske has in mind for the causal role of reasons is consistent with its reducibility, I have no complaint whatever. The only point I want to make is this: if the causal role of reasons is to be preserved within a physicalist framework, the exclusion problem tells us that it must be physically reduced.

Contentful psychological states, for Dretske, are essentially relational, involving as they do ecological and historical conditions external to the organism. Thus, a psychological explanation invoking such a state necessarily involves a *relational explanans*, which the *internal* biological theory of the organism is unable to supply. Thus, the point is not that these psychological explanantia are nonbiological or nonphysical, but rather that they are relational and hence non-internal-biological and non-internal-physical. The contrast between psychology and biology, therefore, comes to this: biology, being conceived by Dretske to concern only the internal biological-physical properties of the organism, can explain motor outputs of the organism, but is incapable of explaining why internal state C causes a given motor output M (we don't as yet have an argument for this latter claim). To explain this causal-relational structure, we must resort to facts concerning the organism's relationship to its environment, and this is where intentional psychology, in virtue of its representational and semantic character, can have a role.

Our discussion has shown, I believe, that Dretske's distinction between doings and things done, or between behavior and motor output, does not in itself solve the exclusion problem. The reason is that given his commitment to naturalism and physicalism, he cannot go the full distance with the dual-explanandum approach. In fact, the dual-explanandum approach is not the crucial element in his resolution of the exclusion problem; what has the crucial role here is his *reductive account of content*, the program of his *Knowledge and the Flow of Information* and subsequent works. So I am construing Dretske as a reductionist about content: the reduction-identity option is his way out of the exclusion problem. As we saw, however, that option comes into apparent conflict with mental anomalism, and Dretske would have to contend with the usual arguments in support of anomalism and antireductionism. Dretske describes his program on content as the "naturalization" of content; to resolve the exclusion problem, however, naturalization must be understood in the sense of "physicalization," not in the narrower sense which only requires expulsion of the supernatural, the theological, and the essentially normative-evaluative. I will have more to say about the issue of reduction and supervenience in our discussion of the substance of Dretske's proposals.

Dretske's Account of How Reasons Explain

The explanandum of a rationalization, according to Dretske, has the following form: *some internal state C of organism S causes motor output M*. Two aspects of this explanandum can be objects of explanation: *how* does C cause M?, and *why* does C cause M? On Dretske's account, neurobiology is concerned with the how-question; intentional psychology with the why-question. But the second explanatory question can be further subdivided, for it can be construed as asking either: (a) why does C cause M *at this time rather than another*? or (b) why does C cause *output M rather than M*? If we are asking (a), we are asking for a "triggering cause," Dretske says, and it can be answered by providing a specific event that triggered the causal process (C → M) by causing C. (E.g., "Why did the thermostat turn on the furnace now? Because the room temperature dropped below 70 degrees just now.") Question (b), however, asks for a "structuring cause:" to answer it, we must show how C got "hooked up" with the agent's motor output system so the C causes output of type M rather than another kind. (E.g., "Why did the thermostat turn on the furnace rather than the dishwasher? Because its bimetallic element is wired to the furnace, not the dishwasher, in such a way that it functions as a switch for it.") The causal-explanatory job of reasons, according to Dretske, is to serve as the structuring cause of motor output.

Let's look at how this is supposed to work. What needs to be explained is how some internal state of the system, in virtue of its content property, explains why C got hooked up with M. As I understand it, Dretske's story goes like this: Suppose that for some reason it is advantageous to system S to emit motor output M when, and only when, property F is instantiated in its vicinity. How can a reliable connection between F and the production of M be secured? Obviously, S must be equipped with an F-detector or indicator, an appropriate sensory receptor, that registers F just when F is present in its vicinity. When F is detected, the F-detector, we may assume, goes into a certain determinate state. So far we have not been clear as to whether internal state C is a "token" or "type;" we hereby declare C to be a token state.[21] We will think of C as a token state of the F-detector caused by F's presence in S's vicinity at the time; thus the F-detector registers the presence of F by going into state C. But this happens only because C has a certain neurobiological property, N, and *in general* the F-detector registers the presence of F by entering a state with property N. Thus, the registering at t of F by the F-detector consists in the detector's going at t into a token state with property N. Thus, the problem of securing a reliable connection between the presence of F and the emission of motor output M is now reduced to that of securing a reliable connection between occurrences of an internal state with N and emissions of M. Dretske's point is that when the emission of M in the presence of F is advantageous to the organism (e.g., it satisfies some needs of the organism; the organism is rewarded when it emits M in the presence of F, punished when it fails to do so), the N–M connection will often develop, although the biology of how this happens may still be largely unknown. This is nothing other than the process of learning; so Dretske's point is just that familiar associative learning of this kind takes place.

Thus, the fact that property N registers F plays an essential role in N's being causally hooked up with M in system S, so that whenever the organism (or its F-detector) goes into a state of kind N, motor output of kind M is produced. On Dretske's informational account of content, the nomic correlation between F and N implies that token state C carries *informational content* F; and C does this in virtue of being an instance of ✗ ? N, that is, an N-state. And when certain further conditions are met, we may say that C *represents* F, or has the *content property of representing* F; and C comes to have F (or that F is present in the vicinity) as its intentional content. As Dretske emphasizes, the fact that N is "recruited" or "promoted" as a cause of M is essential to the representational character of N itself; it is in virtue of this fact that N acquires the *function of* indicating F, beyond merely *de facto* indicating F. It is this acquisition of function that makes *misrepresentation* possible: if the organism, or its F-detector, goes into an N-state, when no F is present, the organism (or its state) still represents F, although this is a case of misrepresentation. On Dretske's view, an internal state like this, that is, a representational state capable of misrepresentation, exhibits the sort of intentionality appropriate to beliefs.

But where does desire come in? Dretske associates desire with the possibility of learning through reinforcement. The N–M causal hookup can develop only if the organism has a structure of preferences and aversions that make reinforcement possible; this is the assumption we made above when we assumed that the emission of M in the presence of F is "advantageous" to the organism. So both belief and desire play a causal role in the establishment of the N–M causal connection.

This in brief is Dretske's account. He will be the first to admit that the account as summarized here is only a prototypic model that is not capable, without much refinement and enrichment, of handling more complex cases of behavior causation in which intentional states with more complex and abstract content interanimate each other to generate decisions and actions. For example, it isn't obvious how the model will handle even the basic mode of rationalization that proceeds by way of means–end practical reasoning.[22] He will say, though, that the simple model at least shows the possibility of how intentional states, in virtue of their content, can cause, and provide causal understanding of, our behavior.

Dretske's is an original and suggestive account, one that takes the representational character of intentional states seriously; it is in many ways more direct and straightforward as a response to syntacticalism than other available responses, such as what we may call the "narrow explanans" strategy (e.g., Fodor[23]), which attempts to find nonrelational, "narrow" content properties to do the necessary causal-explanatory

work, and the diametrically opposite approach, what may be called the
"wide explanandum" strategy (e.g., Burge[24]), which externalizes the explananda of rationalizations to match their wide, relational explanantia.
Unlike the former Dretske's approach continues to work with wide content properties; unlike the latter, it does not externalize the explananda,
although it does construe them relationally.

A Puzzle

I want to begin by considering exactly how Dretske's account is an
account of the explanatory role of reasons in behavior causation. As may
be recalled, what we want is an account of how question (i) below is, or
can be, correctly answered by (ii).

   (i)   Why did agent (or system) S do A at t?
   (ii) Because S had reason R at t

For S to have reason R, we may suppose, is for S to be in some internal
state with content property R (the property of representing, say, that F is
present). Given this and Dretske's analysis of behavior or "doings," our
problem is to explain how (b) below is an answer to (a):

   (a)   Why did some internal state of S cause M at t?
   (b)   Because S was in internal state C at t, and C had content
         property R

It will be convenient to use locutions of the form "state C's having
property R at t," and think of causal relations, causal relevance, etc., as
holding between items denoted by such expressions. This will facilitate
talk of the causal relevance of properties of token events and states.
Thus, the expression "C's having R at t caused M" is to mean the same as
our earlier expression "C, in virtue of having R, caused M." (M itself can
be similarly expressed, but that won't be necessary.) The use of this
locution does not prevent us from taking token states or events also as
causes: for C to cause M is for there to be some property P such that C's
having P causes M. This shows that the adoption of the locution is not a
mere linguistic decision; it reflects the view that causal relations between
token events hold in virtue of the properties these events have, and that it
makes sense to speak of causal relations between properties.[25]

   In any event, Dretske's project is to give an account of how (b) can be
a correct explanation in response to (a). Now, the heart of his account, as
sketched in the preceding section, is that content properties of inner
states discharge their causal-explanatory role by explaining how the
appropriate hookups between these internal states and motor output were
established. Property R, being a representational property, is a relational
property, and when token state C with R occurs, this is in virtue of C's

having a nonrelational, intrinsic neural property N. N corresponds to things like a specific degree of the thermometric property of a given thermometer (e.g., a specific height of the mercury column) and the specific degree of curvature of the bimetallic element of a thermostat. We may call such an N "an internal indicating property" for the given content property. And it is C's having N at t that causes the occurrence of M at the time (after the N → M structure has been established). Dretske does not explicitly advert to such internal properties with the indicated causal role, but I believe this is because he uses "C," at least sometimes, to denote an event type rather than a token (as we do), so that for him C plays the role of our N; in any case, properties like N must exist.

I think we can think of Dretske's account as proceeding in the following way. First, consider inserting the following between (a) and (b):

(1) Because internal state C of S had N at t, where N is an internal indicating property of R, and N is properly hooked up with M in system S.

We can think of (1) as having the role of bridging the gap between (b) and (a); that is, (b) correctly explains (a) because (b) explains (1), which in turn explains (a). I think we can accept (1) as an explanation of (a). But how, or why, does (b) explain (1), or its crucial component, that N is hooked up with M in S? The reason why this component is crucial should be obvious: for Dretske, rationalizations must account for why M, rather than another type of motor output M*, is produced when S goes into a state with R, and the part of (1) that helps do this is precisely the clause that the N → M causal hookup now exist in S. As I understand it, it is the heart of Dretske's account that content property R figures in a causal explanation of how the N–M causal structure through a process of conditioning and learning came to be established in S. So our question is this: exactly how does the fact that C has content property R explain this?

What puzzles me is this. C is a token state that occurs at t,[26] whereas ✳ the N → M structure that is present in S at t and is causally responsible for the production of M on this occasion has been there all along, having been emplaced before t, perhaps much before t. So how could C, or C's having R *at t*, causally explain why or how the N → M structure came to be in S? On Dretske's theory, the fact that N is an internal indicator property corresponding to content property R is a causally crucial factor in N's being "recruited" as a cause of M. But what explains this recruitment is the past history of instantiations of these properties (i.e., the particular history of reinforcements), along with the general nomic correlation between N and F. So, again, how can C's having R at t bring it ✳ about that C's having N at t causes M?[27]

This difficulty can be somewhat mitigated, I believe, if the story is put, more explicitly and consciously, in terms of explanation rather than causation. For we can imagine saying something like this:

Look at it this way. In trying to explain why C caused M, we invoke
the fact that C has content property R, the property of representing
F. And C represents F in virtue of having neural property N. Of
course, C occurs now, and it now has property R. So I am not
saying that C, or C's now having R, caused the N → M hookup in
the organism. It's rather this: when we say that C has R, or represents F, we are saying a lot more than what's happening now. For
the organism has the capacity now to represent F because it has had
a certain history of learning and conditioning, a history of interactions with its environment and of internal changes caused by such
interactions. In particular, the organism is now in a state that
represents F because it has in the past exercised its capacity to
indicate F and learned to associate F-indications (instances of N)
with certain motor output M. It is this historical background of the
organism's capacity to represent F that grounds the explanatory
power of C's now having R in explaining why C causes M.

This strikes me not altogether implausible as a way of telling the story
Dretske wants to tell about content. In the next section, I will present a
modified Dretskean account that resolves my puzzle and serves as a
framework for the explanatory story just told.

A Modified Drestkean Account

Consider a system S in which the N → M (Dretske's C → M) causal
structure has already been established in the required way. In particular,
the system is now able to represent (not merely indicate) the presence of
F in its vicinity. As we saw, this means that the system represents F at t
just in case it enters at t into an N-state. Having acquired the capacity to
represent F, the system is also capable of *misrepresenting* F: it misrepresents that F is present just in case it represents that F is present when F is
not present. How does the system manage to represent F when F is not
there? By entering an N-state, of course: S misrepresents F just in case S
enters an N-state in the absence of F. Whether S, or an internal state of
S, has at t the content property of representing F does not depend on the
presence at t of F in S's vicinity, nor on any other external condition at t;
it is solely a matter of the occurence of an N-state in S.

Given this, it is natural and plausible to think of S's representing F at t,
or S's being at t in a state that represents F, as supervenient on S's
internal N-state at t. (This isn't to say that the property of representing F
supervenes on N *in general*, for all systems; we are here talking about S
with its particular history and ecology). Considerations of misrepresentation make this plausible: even if F is not present at t outside S, S will
represent that F is present (and hence misrepresent F) as long as an
N-state is realized in S.[28] True, there is a dependence on the history of
learning and conditioning: on Dretske's account, the relationship between

the occurrence of N in S and S's representing F depends on S's learning history that has entrenched the N → M causal structure. But the existence *now* in S of this causal structure is exactly the present repository, so to speak, of the causal powers of S's representing F. The causal role in S of state N consists of two essential components: (1) it is typically caused by the presence of F in S's vicinity, and (2) it causes S to emit motor output M.

It seems to me that the foregoing is consistent with the main components of Dretske's account. Notice, though, that our story makes the content property of representing F supervenient on neural property N. To repeat, I am not saying that this content property in general, in all organisms and systems, supervenes on N, but only that for system S as it now exists, with its history of learning and with the N → M structure already in place, the supervenience holds. Given that the occurrence of this content property supervenes on N, it is appealing to think of the causal role of this content property as itself supervenient on the causal powers of the subvenient property N. Thus, whatever causes a given token N-state also causes it to be a token R-state, and whatever is caused by this state's having R is caused by its having N. In S, the causal powers of R are supervenient on the causal powers of N.

This greatly simplifies the picture: the causal powers of the content state lie in the neural state on which the content state supervenes. We now have a solution to the exclusion problem: content properties have no independent causal powers of their own; their causal powers (hence their explanatory powers) depend wholly on those of the underlying neural properties. As a response to the problem of syntacticalism, our modified account says this: although content properties are relational properties in the sense that an organism's capacity to instantiate them depends on its past history and relationship to external events, the causal power of a given instance of a content property lies wholly in the causal power of the neural state on which it supervenes. The relationality of the content property plays no role in behavior causation; thus, the account is consistent with the supervenience condition stressed by syntacticalism, the requirement that the proximate cause of physical behavior must supervene on the synchronous internal physical state of the organism. However, the account need not be committed to a broader supervenience principle for content properties in general, to the effect that what content properties a given organism instantiates at a time must supervene solely on the concurrent internal physical properties it instantiates; for physically identical organisms with different histories can differ in respect of their capacity for having content properties.[29]

Let us see how this modified account stands in relation to Dretske's. The crucial difference between them is that in the revised picture, content states supervene on the synchronous neural states of the system, whereas Dretske thinks of content states as essentially relational and hence nonsupervenient. I am suggesting that if we push Dretske's account in a certain way it is in fact natural, perhaps inevitable, to think of them as supervenient.[30] But what happens to Dretske's carefully worked out story about the learning and conditioning and its bearing on the establishment of the N → M structure? In the new picture, the story plays a similar role but its "location" is different: its new role is to explain how system S came to have the capacity to represent F, and do so by entering an inner state with N. This in effect is an explanation of how in S the content property of representing F came to supervene on N. The history of learning and conditioning whereby the N → M structure came to be entrenched in S is of course a crucial part of this explanatory story. But the present causal power of this content state is wholly and exclusively dependent on the causal powers of underlying N; it has nothing directly to do with the history of the system – in particular, nothing to do with the entrenchment of the N → M structure in the system. A given instantiation of the content property causes something in virtue of the fact that the instance of N on which it supervenes causes it. This solves "the puzzle" of the preceding section.

Let me conclude with the following summary. In Dretske's account, C's having content property R explains why S emits M (rather than M*) by explaining how an N → M structure (rather than a N → M* structure) came to be present in S. Our puzzle was how C's now having R can explain the emplacement of the N → M structure or its present existence in S. The modified account represents the situation in two stages:

> *Stage 1*:   Why does C's having R at t cause M?
> Because C's having R at t supervenes on C's having N at t, and at t there exists in S an N → M causal structure.

> *Stage 2*:   But why is the N → M structure present in S? How did content property R (i.e., the property of representing F) come to supervene on N in S? And how did S acquire the capacity to represent F?

> Because, in S, N is the internal indicator property of F, and through a process of conditioning and learning the N → M causal structure was established in S; this means also that in S, R came to supervene on N. In the process, N has acquired the function of indicating F, and this is how S came to have the capacity to represent F.

The stage 2 explanation may seem to have three distinct explananda, but that is only an appearance; for Dretske they are interrelated and interdependent components of a single story. The fact that Dretske's original account is broken down into two explanations, each with its own explanandum, is important. This is precisely what allows us to dispel the puzzle; it does this by separating the question of how an intentional state, with the causal power it has, can cause a certain motor output from the question of how it came to have that causal power and how the organism came to have the capacity to be in that intentional state.

Varieties of Intentional Causation

Consider cases in which one intentional state (say, a belief) causes another intentional state (say, another belief). There surely are such cases, but it is not at all clear how Dretske's model of intentional causation, with its essential involvement of motor output, can be adapted for them. However, the idea that underlies our modified account yields the following simple and natural account: Belief b_1 causes belief b_2 in virtue of the fact that b_1 supervenes on N_1, b_2 supervenes on N_2, and N_1 stands in an appropriate causal relation with N_2. This model of "supervenient causation,"[31] in which mental causation is treated as "supervenient causation" dependent on underlying physical-biological causal processes, is applicable to mental causal relations in general, not just to cases involving intentional states and behavior or actions. It applies to cases in which a physical event causes an intentional state (e.g., causation of perceptual beliefs): a physical event cause an intentional state in virtue of its causing another physical state upon which the intentional state supervenes. What I have called "the modified Dretskean account" is simply an application of this model of supervenient causation in a Dretskean environment.

There is another class of intentional causation seemingly untouched by Dretske's account, cases in which an intentional state, *in virtue of its content property*, causes a bodily event which is not motor output in the familiar sense, and, more importantly, which is *not rationalized* by the content property. The thought that your airplane is about to take off makes your muscles tense and your mouth go dry. Certain thoughts, in virtue of their content, can cause all sorts of bodily changes not standardly thought of as doings or actions; your muscles grow tense and your pulse quickens, you blush and perspire, facial tics are set off, tears well up in your eyes, etc. If you insist on calling these responses "behavior," I have no objection; the main point is that there is no obvious or natural way to fit such cases to Dretske's model of learning and reinforcement. These cases are interesting because they are cases in which content properties serve as causal properties, but not as rationalizing properties; it is because my thought is a thought that p that it causes me to blush, but my blushing is not rationalized by the thought. Moreover, such "non-rationalizing intentional causation," as we might call it, can occur, it seems, in instances of mental-to-mental causation as well. Because of the "wiring" in your brain, the thought that p can cause the thought that q, even if p and q have no significant logical or conceptual relationship, and the thought that q is not in any sense rationalized by the thought that p; we know psychological associations occur in all sorts of ways. We are also familiar with cases in which phenomenal mental events ("qualia") cause intentional states (recall Proust's madelaines).

Such cases are handled, routinely and uniformly, by the model of supervenient causation: the thought that p supervenes on a certain neural state, which causes the blushing, the muscle tensing, etc. The model applies uniformly to all cases of mental causation, including causal relations involving nonintentional, phenomenal mental states. In contrast, Dretske's account is expressly constructed to explain a limited subclass of intentional causation, cases in which intentional states are rationalizing causes of bodily behavior, and there seems no obvious or natural way to generalize it. We can also see the attraction of the two-stage account stated at the end of the preceding section. The explanation in stage 1 applies to mental causation in general; the explanation in stage 2 concerns one particular way in which a content property can come to supervene on a neurobiological property. We can think of Dretske's interesting theory chiefly as a contribution to stage 2: it elaborates one important way in which that often comes about – learning and conditioning. But perhaps that need not be the only way. Such supervenience relations might hold because of the genes; and there seems no difficulty in imagining a surgical construction or implantation of the N → M structure in an organism (Dretske would claim that in such cases the organism lacks the capacity to represent F). The point I want to stress is that the provenance of these structures makes no difference to the stage 1 explanations. Dretske allows only learning to generate structures appropriate for rational causation; that might be true – this can certainly be debated. No matter how this debate is resolved, the separation of the two explanatory stages makes us see that questions about how organisms come to have contentful intentional states can be discussed independently of questions about how the metaphysics of mental causation is to be explained.

Crucial to the model of supervenient causation as applied here to intentional causation is the claim that in spite of their relationality with respect to external conditions, content properties can be thought of as supervenient on the internal neural-physical properties of organisms, organisms with certain histories and related in appropriate ways to environmental conditions. The main trick is to isolate these noninternal, relational properties as specifications of the class of systems and organisms to which the supervenience claim is to apply. Thus, we can think of these relational properties as "parameters" that fix a context within which supervenience claims can be formulated rather than as part of such claims. (We may call such supervenience relations "parametric supervenience.") Even if we hold, with Dretske, that content properties, as representational properties, do not in general supervene on the synchronic internal physical properties of organisms, that need not rule out a supervenience thesis restricted by a specified set historical and ecological parameters. But I must leave this idea in the form of a programmatic proposal here; a general account of this concept of supervenience and its application to mental causation needs to be worked out.[32]

Notes

1   "Machines and the Mental," *Proceedings and Addresses of the American Philosophical Association*, 59 (1985), pp. 23–33; "The Explanatory Role of Content" and "Reply to Cummins," in *Contents of Thought* (University of

Arizona Press, Tucson, 1988), ed. Robert Grimm and Daniel Merrill; "Reasons as Causes," "Putting Information to Work," "The Causal Role of Content," presented at various conferences and lectures.

2 *Explaining Behavior: Reasons in a World of Causes* (Cambridge, Mass.: MIT Press, 1988).

3 Donald Davidson, "Actions, Reasons, and Causes," reprinted in Davidson, *Essays on Actions and Events* (Oxford: Oxford University Press, 1980).

4 "The Explanatory Role of Content," p. 32.

5 Davidson, "Mental Events," in *Essays on Actions and Events*.

6 After Stephen P. Stich's "syntactic theory of the mind" in *From Folk Psychology to Cognitive Science* (Cambridge, Mass.: MIT Press, 1983). This doctrine is related to what Jerry Fodor calls "methodological solipsism;" see his "Methodological Solipsism Considered as a Research Strategy in Cognitive Science," in *Representations* (Cambridge, Mass.: MIT Press, 1981).

7 Not as widely accepted as it used to be; but all known alternatives have their own difficulties, and it seems fair to say that the nomological conception of causation, in its many variants, is still "the received view."

8 See, e.g., Frederick Stoutland, "Oblique Causation and Reasons for Actions," *Synthese*, 43 (1980), pp. 351–67; Ted Honderich, "The Argument for Anomalous Monism," *Analysis*, 42 (1982), pp. 59–64; Ernest Sosa, "Mind–Body Interaction and Supervenient Causation," *Midwest Studies in Philosophy*, 9 (1984), pp. 271–82; Kim, "Self-Understanding and Rationalizing Explanations," *Philosophia Naturalis*, 21 (1984), pp. 309–20.

9 Brian McLaughlin calls this "type epiphenomenalism" in "Type Epiphenomenalism, Type Dualism, and the Causal Priority of the Physical", *Philosophical Perspectives*, vol. 3, ed. E. Tomberlin (Ridgeview Publishing, 1989), pp. 109–35.

10 For a more detailed statement of this argument see Stephen P. Stich, "Autonomous Psychology and the Belief–Desire Thesis," *The Monist*, 61 (1978), pp. 573–91.

11 There are well-known considerations supporting this view; see, e.g., Hilary Putnam, "The Meaning of 'Meaning'" in *Philosophical Papers, Vol. 2: Mind, Language, and Reality* (Cambridge, Cambridge University Press, 1975); Tyler Burge, "Individualism and the Mental," *Midwest Studies in Philosophy*, 4 (1979), pp. 73–121; Stich, "Autonomous Psychology and the Belief–Desire Thesis;" Kim, "Psychophysical Supervenience," *Philosophical Studies*, 41 (1982), pp. 51–70.

12 We may take "syntactic properties" to be physical properties of inner states in terms of which psycho-computational processes are to be defined. This presupposes the computational view of mental processes; if that view is set aside, we may simply talk of physical properties of inner states to generate the second problem of mental causation. It is important to see that what I call the problem of syntacticalism arises even if the computational view is rejected.

13 Dretske's principal work in this vein is *Knowledge and the Flow of Information* (Cambridge, Mass.: MIT Press, 1981); it is continued in *Explaining Behavior*.

14 For example, most of those who take the multiple realizability of mental events seriously would reject psychophysical attribute identities.

15 I have here developed this problem in terms of cause; it can be developed in a parallel way for causal explanations. See my "Mechanism, Purpose, and Explanatory Exclusion," in *Philosophical Perspectives*, 3 ed. James Tomberlin. (Ridgeview Publishing, 1989).

16 For details see my "Mechanism, Purpose, and Explanatory Exclusion."
17 "The Explanatory Role of Content," pp. 33–4.
18 Ibid., p. 32.
19 See Georg von Wright's discussion in *Explanation and Understanding* (Ithaca: Cornell University Press, 1971), chapter 3.
20 *Explaining Behavior*, p. 2.
21 It seems that in *Explaining Behavior*, Dretske uses the letter "C" ambiguously, sometimes to stand for a token state and sometimes for a state type (similarly, "Si" in "The Explanatory Role of Content"). I have disambiguated "C," using "C" for token states and "N" for types (properties) of states.
22 See, however, chapter 6 ("The Interactive Nature of Reasons") of *Explaining Behavior*.
23 See J. A. Fodor, *Psychosemantics* (Cambridge, Mass.: MIT Press, 1987).
24 See Tyler Burge, "Individualism and Psychology," *Philosophical Review*, 95 (1986), pp. 3–45, especially section 1.
25 This is not a new assumption; it underlies the criticism of anomalous monism we saw earlier, and is a presupposition of the first two problems of mental causation.
26 The reader may recall that we earlier chose to take C to be a token state whereas there is some ambiguity as to whether Dretske takes C as a token or type. If C is taken as a state type, the question being raised here can of course be stated in terms of an *instance* of C, that is, a token C-state.
27 This seems related to, but not identical with, a complaint that Robert Cummins makes against Dretske in his commentary on "The Explanatory Role of Content" in *Contents of Thought*, p. 51. Cummins says that Dretske changes the subject by moving from his original project of explaining why C, in virtue of having content property R, causes M into one of explaining how the C–M causal structure was acquired by the system. I am assuming that an explanation of the acquisition of the C–M structure can be a part of an explanation of the original explanandum.
28 Although in time the N-state may acquire a new indicator function and come to underlie S's capacity to represent a property other than F.
29 These remarks by no means settle all the issues raised by syntacticalism; for one thing, the account being sketched needs to be worked out in much greater detail, taking into account the diverse ways in which content can involve external factors. Its relationship to the "narrow content" strategy must be thought through as well.
30 I want to note that I am not myself advocating this form of supervenience thesis for intentional states. A supervenience thesis of this form is committed to physical reductionism concerning intentionality (I earlier argued that Dretske is committed to content reductionism). My claim is conditional: if we want to make sense of intentional causation of physical behavior, the only viable way seems to involve supervenience of intentional states on physical processes.
31 For more details on supervenient causation see my "Causality, Identity, Supervenience in the Mind–Body Problem," *Midwest Studies in Philosophy*, 4 (1979), pp. 31–49; "Epiphenomenal and Supervenient Causation," *Midwest Studies in Philosophy*, 9 (1984), pp. 257–70.
32 My thanks to Ernest Sosa for helpful discussion.

5
Actions, Reasons, and the Explanatory Role of Content

Terence Horgan

Fred Dretske has recently proposed a novel account of how reasons explain actions.[1] In this paper I will first present a hermeneutic exposition of his position; then set forth some objections which convince me that the position is mistaken; and then briefly describe an alternative approach to the philosophical issues he addresses.

The Soprano Problem

There is a *prima facie* problem about whether intentional or semantic properties of an event or state can figure in a genuine causal explanation of the event's effects. In particular, even if actions are caused by reasons, there is a problem about whether a cause's being a reason – and its being the specific reason it is, with its specific propositional content – can have any relevance in explaining the action it produces. Dretske poses the problem very well, as follows. (This and subsequent quotations are numbered for later reference.)

> (1) Something possessing content, or having meaning, can *be* a cause without its possessing that content or having that meaning being at all relevant to its causal powers. A soprano's upper-register supplications may shatter glass, but their meaning is irrelevant to their having this effect. Their effect on the glass would be the same if they meant nothing at all or something entirely different.... [A]lthough reasons may cause us to behave in a certain way, they may not, *so described*, explain the behavior they cause.... McGinn (1979, p. 30) puts it this way: "To defend the thesis that citing reasons can be genuinely explanatory, we need to show that they can explain when described *as reasons*." The fact that they have a content, the fact that have a *semantic* character, must be relevant to the kind of effects they produce. If brain structures possessing meaning affect motor output in the way the soprano's acoustic productions affect glass, then the meaning of these neural structures

is causally inert. Even if it is there, it doesn't *do* anything. If having
a mind is having *this* kind of meaning in the head, one may as well
not have a mind. (EB, pp. 79–80)

This worry, which I shall call the *soprano problem*, is specifically directed
at properties of a cause-event that are semantic, or intentional. I take it
that the soprano problem is the central motivation for Dretske's account
of the explanatory role of reasons. He seeks to show how and why
reasons *qua* reasons, despite their semantic character, are genuinely explanatory rather than being inert like the semantic properties of the
soprano's sounds.

Dretske regards this problem as arising primarily because the semantic
properties of sounds, brain states, and the like are *nonintrinsic*: they do
not supervene either upon the intrinsic properties of the cause-events
themselves, or upon the intrinsic properties of the configuration consisting of the cause-events together with those "background conditions"
which would figure directly in a nonintentional causal explanation of the
events' effects. The importance of nonintrinsicness emerges clearly in
each of the following passages, where Dretske formulates the *prima facie*
case for the contention that the content of reasons is irrelevant to explaining behavior:

> (2) [E]ven if the things that have meaning are in the head, the
> meanings themselves aren't in the head.... [I]t is surely plausible to
> suppose that what something means ... is a matter determined, in
> part at least, by the *relations* that obtain between the elements that
> have this meaning ... and the sorts of situation, the kind of condi-
> tions, the properties or whatever that constitute their meaning.
> Meaning certainly isn't an intrinsic property of meaningful
> things.... But if this is so, then whatever it is in the head that ....
> is responsible for our behaving the way we do (or at least our
> moving the way we do when we behave), is something that will have
> its causal role determined, not by its meaning ... but by whatever
> intrinsic properties it (the stuff in the head) possesses, presumably
> the electrical and chemical properties that neurobiologists study,
> that are capable of making muscles contract and glands secrete....
> Psychological differences which do not manifest themselves as *biolo-*
> *gical* differences are irrelevant to the explanation of motor output.
> But meaning is neither in the head nor does it supervene on the
> stuff that is in the head. Therefore, meaning, or something (in the
> head) having meaning, is irrelevant to the explanation of behavior.
> (RC, pp. 4–5)

> (3) The difference – indeed, the *gulf* – between the semantic and
> the causal properties of a representation can be illustrated by a
> photograph (a familiar type of representation). Consider a picture

of George.... The fact that it is a picture of George, the fact that it has this *representational* aspect, is completely irrelevant to how the picture interacts, causally, with the rest of the world. For as we all know a physically indistinguishable picture – no matter how different it was representationally – would "behave" in exactly the same way.... Such representational differences are obviously irrelevant to the way these pictures interact with other things. Such representational differences do not, as they say, supervene on an object's causal properties.... So it would appear that representational properties are quite independent of causal properties.... If we apply this moral to *internal* representations, those that are supposed to qualify as beliefs, we get the embarrassing result that, if beliefs are internal representations, then *what* we believe doesn't make any difference to what we do. (WTH, pp. 7–9)

Presumably, the reason why the intentional properties of the soprano's supplications are explanatorily irrelevant, relative to the effect of shattering glass, is that they are nonintrinsic. But the intentional properties of internal mental representations are equally nonintrinsic. So *prima facie*, it appears that these properties too are explanatorily irrelevant, relative to the behavioral effects of mental representations.

Yet the claim that reasons, described as such, lack explanatory relevance to behavior is grossly contrary to our deep-seated conception of ourselves as beings who act the way we do *because* of what we believe and desire. For, a statement of the form "He A-ed because he believed such-and such and he desired so-and-so" entails not merely that the pertinent behavior was *caused* by the cited belief and desire, but also that the respective properties, *being a belief that such-and-such* and *being a desire that so-and-so*, are explanatorily relevant to the person's act of A-ing. Dretske sees clearly the conflict between our common-sense conception of human agency and the claim that reasons *qua* reasons are explanatorily inert, and he rightly regards this conflict as philosophically very troubling. His stated objective is "to show how this embarrassment can be avoided within a materialist metaphysics" (EB, p. 80). That is, he seeks to undermine the *prima facie* analogy between the intentional properties of brain structures and those of the soprano's acoustic productions, and to salvage, within the bounds of a thoroughgoing metaphysical materalism, our fundamental idea that we do what we do because of what we want and believe.

There is no guarantee that this goal can be accomplished, but it is certainly worth pursuing. In my view, Dretske has exactly the right methodological attitude toward our common-sense conception of mentality. He says, "I do not hold sacred our ordinary ways of thinking about these matters. But I do think it is a reasonable place to begin. And it is, other things being equal, and assuming a manageable philosophical cost, a desirable place to end" (RC, p. 14).

Dretske's Account

Dretske's proposed account of how reasons explain actions has two principal components. First, he claims that an action should be construed
not as a bodily motion, but rather as a *causal process* that includes the
occurrence of the reason, the subsequent bodily motion (or other bodily
behavior, such as remaining silent or continuing to stand at attention),
and possibly certain subsidiary events as well. An action consists in (i) the
causing, by those concrete mental events which constitute the agent's
reason, of the agent's bodily motion (or other relevant bodily behavior);
and also (ii) those subsequent events in the causal sequence, if any,
whose occurrence was necessary to render the relevant act-description
true of the agent. Suppose, for instance, that Donald flips the switch,
thereby turning on the light, and thereby alerting the burglar. According
to Dretske, Donald's act of flipping the switch is a causal process beginning with the relevant occurrent reason (presumably consisting of an
occurrent desire together with one or more occurrent beliefs), and termi-
nating with the switch's become flipped. His act of turning on the light is
a slightly more extended causal process; it includes the former act as a
proper part, and terminates with the light's coming on. And his act of
alerting the burglar is a slightly more extended process yet; it includes
each of the former acts as proper parts, and terminates with the burglar's
becoming alerted.

Second, Dretske claims that actions, as thus construed, are amenable
to a form of causal explanation that adverts of the content of an action's
constituent reason. The general form of such an explanation, at least in
the simplest cases, is as follows. Let C be an internal state which can
recur in a given creature; let M be a form of bodily motion (or other
bodily behavior); and let F be a feature or circumstance which can recur
in the creature's environment. Suppose that F and C are reliably correlated, and thus that C is in an internal *indicator* of F. Suppose, in
addition, that through a process of reinforcement-driven associative
learning, C gets recruited as a "behavior switch" to produce M in the presence of F. That is, C is harnessed as a cause of M, where this harnessing
is itself a causal process that depends upon the fact that C already is an
indicator of F. C thereby becomes a *representation* of F, as opposed to
being a mere indicator of F. And when there later occurs a concrete
causal process consisting of C causing M in the presence of F, it will be
entirely correct to say that C causes M *because C represents* F. C's being
an F-indicator was causally instrumental in the original recruitment of C
as a switch that causes M in the presence of F; thus, when there later
occurs a causal process consisting of C causing M, C's having representational content F is thereby explanatorily relevant to this subsequent
causal transaction. C's causing of M occurs, at this later time, *because* C
represents F.

Dretske originally studied engineering, and this basic conception of contentful explanation has a distinct engineering flavor. His central example from the realm of engineer-designed artifacts is the thermostat. In order to design a thermostat, an engineer must recruit some physical state C (e.g., the bending of a bimetallic strip) that indicates a drop in temperature F, and must wire it up as a switch that will cause, in the presence of F, an event M consisting of the furnace's coming on. Now according to Dretske, C's being an indicator of F plays no genuine role in explaining why the furnace comes on. Rather, to explain *this* event we cite the drop in temperature as causing the bimetallic stip's bending, the latter as causing the furnace's ignition, and thus the former as the initial "triggering cause" of the furnace's ignition. Although the physical structure of the thermostat is itself a background condition for such a causal explanation, the fact that C indicates F plays no genuine role in the explanation – even though C *happens to be* an F-indicator. However, C's content does become relevant when we ask a different explanatory question: not why the furnace came on, but rather why the drop in room temperature *caused* the furnace to come on. One legitimate answer to this new question, says Dretske, is that C (the bending of the bimetallic strip) was originally recruited as a furnace ignition switch, by the designer of the thermostat, precisely *because* it was an F-indicator.

Design problems are solved by Nature too, although for a good materialist like Dretske the solutions result not from conscious, intelligent planning but rather from the mechanisms of natural selection (for species of creatures) and of reinforcement-driven associative learning (for individual creatures that belong to sufficiently sophisticated species). Here too we must distinguish between (i) asking why a given bodily motion (or other bodily behavior) M occurs, and (ii) asking why an internal state C *causes* M to occur. Although the content of C is irrelevant to question (i), according to Dretske, nevertheless it can indeed be relevant to question (ii). One perfectly legitimate answer to question (ii) might be that C represents F – or, more fully, that C was originally recruited as an M-switch, earlier in the given creature's individual learning history, *because C was an F-indicator*.

One now sees the point of Dretske's claim that an action is not something literally caused by a reason, but rather is a *causal process* which includes the reason itself as the initial component. If actions are construed this way, then explaining an action amounts to answering a question of type (ii), not type (i). The content of an action's constituent reason thereby becomes relevant in explaining the action itself – just as common sense supposes it is. If, on the other hand, an action is construed as an event or processes that is caused by a reason and does not include that reason as a constitutent, then (in Dretske's view) the soprano problem will defy solution: the content of the reason will turn out to be no more relevant in explaining the action than is the content of the soprano's sounds in explaining the glass-shattering.

How exactly does this account of the explanatory role of reasons handle the soprano problem? More specifically, how does the account come to grips with the fact that contentful mental properties – like *being a desire for a beer*, and *being a belief that there is beer in the refrigerator* – do not supervene upon what's in the head? The answer, as I understand it, can be obtained by further elaborating Dretske's position in three stages, as follows.

First, consider the process of reinforcement-driven associative learning, whereby an internal state gets recruited as a behavior switch, It is not known exactly how this process works, at the neural level; presumably it involves changes in synaptic connection-strengths between neurons, or something of the sort. But the crucial fact is that the following schema, which I shall call the *reinforcement principle*, yields true instances for a reasonably wide variety of potential substituends for the capital letters:

> If (i) conditions F are present, (ii) bodily motion M occurs, (iii) M and F together cause beneficial consequences R to occur, and (iv) there is a reliable correlation between conditions F and internal state C, then *ceteris paribus*, internal structural changes will then occur that increase the subsequent degree of causal association between C and M.

C's correlation with F is *semantic*, according to Dretske: it is an *indication* relation. By virtue of the reinforcement principle, this semantic fact has direct explanatory relevance to C's becoming an M-switch in conditions F. (It is what Dretske would call a "structuring cause" of C's becoming linked to M, rather than a "triggering cause.")

Second, consider a subsequent occasion on which causes M in conditions F. If we focus upon C-causing-M itself, rather than upon M, then two different kinds of structuring causes can be cited to explain this process. One kind I shall call *here-and-now* structuring causes; these are features of the creature's present neural organization, in virtue of which C causes M. The other kind I shall call *past-operative* structuring causes; these are (non-momentary) features of C that explain why the creature is currently "wired up" in such a way that C causes M. (Dretske holds, I take it, that in general only causings, and not other kinds of happenings, are legitimately explainable by reference to past-operative structuring causes.) Although C's having content F is not a here-and-now structuring cause of the present C-causing-M process, it is a past-operative structuring cause of that process.

Third, consider the fact that the content of C does not supervene upon what's in the head. This fact prevents C's content from being explanatorily relevant to M itself. It also prevents C's meaning F from being a here-and-now structuring cause of C-causing-M. But it does not prevent C's meaning F from being a *past-operative* structuring cause of this process. So as long as we construe actions properly – viz., as a reason's *causing* something, rather than as something that is itself caused by a reason, then reasons *qua* reasons do indeed matter after all; people really do perform actions *because* of what they want and believe. The soprano problem is thereby solved.

Dretske acknowledges that the model of a thermostat switch is, by itself, too simple to accommodate certain important complexities in the causal nexus in which genuine propositional attitudes figure. For one thing, the bending of the bimetallic strip in a thermostat is an analog of a *belief*, whereas a reason for an action normally is a complex of propositional attitudes involving not only one or more beliefs, but a *desire* as well. But he holds that desires can be naturally accommodated by refining the engineering-based model. The state C is now treated as a *partial* internal cause, and is relabeled B (for "belief"); and another internal state D (for "desire") is introduced which serves as a condition upon which the creature's receptivity to reinforcement depends. He writes:

> (4)   Think of an organism learning to do something in a specific set of conditions: it learns to produce M in conditions F by having the rewards R for producing M contingent on M's production *in F*. . . . [S]uch a process will result in the recruitment of an F-indicator as an internal cause of M. We have relabeled this internal cause B. Since D is the internal state on which R's effectiveness as a reinforcer depends, successful learning also requires the animal to occupy state D when movements M are produced. R will not be effective in promoting the production of M unless the organism is in *both* state B and state D. . . . Since this is so, R will recruit, as a cause of M, both B and D. Or, if you please, the occurrence of R will recruit B as a cause of M only if B is accompanied by D. . . . Hence, this kind of learning results in the recruitment of B and D as *partial* or *contributory* causes of M. (EB, pp. 112–113)

Dretske's model is also too simple in several other ways, as he acknowledges. He classifies these additional complicating factors together under the umbrella phrase "the interactive nature of reasons." First, typically various distinct and potentially competing desires, together with a fairly wide range of relevant beliefs, mix together in the cognitive processing that generates bodily behavior. Second, often the learning process is primarily observational and imitative, rather than associative. Third, mentally complex creatures like humans have the capacity to undergo token beliefs and desires many of which instantiate belief-types and desire-types that were never directly "recruited as behavior switches" in the creature's individual learning history. (In creatures with the capacity for language, for instance, the class of potentially instantable belief-types has a generative structure, as does the class of potentially comprehensible sentences. All it takes to instantiate an unrecruited belief-type is to hear, and believe, a statement whose content you have never before contemplated.) He says rather little about how his model might be refined to take account of such matters, but he does briefly argue that the model provides "basic building blocks" that "can be combined to give a realistic portrait of purposeful, intelligent, behavior" (EB, p. 138).

The Problem of Explanatory Exclusion

The soprano problem should be distinguished from two others that also have figured in recent philosophical discussion of the explanatory role of content. Borrowing terminology from Jaegwon Kim and from Donald Davidson respectively, I shall call these the *explanatory exclusion* problem and the *anomalism* problem.[2]

In its most general form, the problem of explanatory exclusion arises when we assume (i) that every concrete event, state, or process in the world is one that falls within the purview of physics, and (ii) that every event, state, or process within the purview of physics is susceptible, in principle, to a full and complete explanation in terms of the laws and concepts of physics. Under these plausible-looking materialist assumptions, there arises a *prima facie* worry about whether any other kind of putative explanation, over and above physicalistic explanation, could ever be genuine and legitimate. The concern is that basic physical laws and concepts do all the real explanatory work themselves, thereby "screening off" the possibility of any higher-level explanations – for instance, explanations couched in the concepts and generalizations of the various special sciences, or common-sense explanations of actions in terms of the beliefs and desires that constitute reasons.

The explanatory exclusion problem also can be raised in less general terms. For instance, one might assume that neurobiological explanations can co-exist with basic physico-chemical explanations, but then ask whether neurobiological explanations screen off psychological explanations by usurping their erstwhile explanatory role. I shall call this special case the problem of *the explanatory exclusion of psychology* (for short, the EEP problem). Unlike the soprano problem, the EEP problem has nothing specifically to do with the fact that intentional mental properties are typically non-intrinsic. Rather, the problem also arises with respect to the phenomenal or "raw feel" properties of mental states, even though these properties are plausibly viewed as supervenient upon what's in the head.[3] It also arises with respect to intentional mental properties that have so-called "narrow content" – if there are such properties.

The problem of anomalism is as follows. If Davidson is correct in claiming both (i) that two events or states can be related as cause and effect only if they are subsumed by a strict law, and (ii) that there are no strict psychological or psychophysical laws, then there is a *prima facie* worry about whether the mental properties of an event or state could ever be relevant to a causal explanation of its effects. The concern is that mental properties, being non-nomic, are epiphenomenal.

Since Dretske is not a defender of Davidson's "anomalous monism," his readers are not likely to suppose that the issue of anomalism is central to his project. However, one can easily read him as addressing the EEP problem. His book *Explaining Behavior* is especially likely to generate this impression. One reason is that the book contains no remarks like those in passages (2) and (3) above, explicitly linking the central problem to the fact that semantic properties of mental states do not supervene upon what's in the head. (The word "supervenience" does not even occur in the book's index.) Another reason is that numerous passages in the book are just ambiguous between the soprano problem and the EEP problem. This ambiguity is present in passage (1) above, and is even more pronounced in passages like these:

(5) It sometimes seems as though persons and their bodies march to the beats of different drummers.... My reasons, my beliefs, desires, purposes, and intentions, *are* – indeed they must be – the cause of my body's movements.... But does this mean that my thoughts and fears, my plans and hopes, the psychological attitudes and states that explain why I behave the way I do, are to be identified with the structures and processes, the causes of bodily movement, studied by neuroscientists? If so, aren't those scientists, as experts on what causes the body to move the way it does, also the experts on why we persons, behave the way we do? If there is really only one drummer, and hence only one beat, and this is a beat to which the body marches, then one seems driven, inevitably, to the conclusion that in the final analysis, it will be biology rather than psychology that explains why we do the things we do.... It is the business of this book to show how this apparent conflict ... can be resolved. (EB, p. ix)

(6) Materialists ... [claim] that a thought, like anything else, is merely a physical object – presumably (in the case of a thought) a neural state or structure. That may be so, of course, but what about the *meanings* of these physical structures? Are they, like the mass, charge, and velocity of objects, properties that could make a difference, a *causal* difference, to the way these neural structures interact? If meaning, or something's *having* meaning, is to do the kind of work expected of it – if it is to explain *why* we do what we do – it must, it seems, influence the operation of those electrical and chemical mechanisms that control muscles and glands. Just how is this supposed to work? This, obviously, is as much a mystery as the interaction between mind stuff and matter. (EB, p. 80)

Given his persistent ambiguity between the soprano problem and the EEP problem, and given that he nowhere distinguishes these two problems explicitly, there is probably no completely straightforward fact of the matter about whether the underlying motivation for his treatment of reasons and actions is the soprano problem, the EEP problem, or both. But if we interpret his position as addressed at least in part to the EEP problem – as I myself did during my entire first reading of *Explaining Behavior* – then an obvious objection arises. After I had read the book and had repeatedly scribbled this objection in the margins, I encountered a discussion by Jaegwon Kim which also construes Dretske as I had, and which nicely expresses the difficulty. Although Kim acknowledges that Dretske's primary concern is what I what I have here called the soprano problem (Kim calls it the problem of "syntacticalism") he reads into Dretske an implicit concern with explanatory exclusion too. He writes:

> Dretske's solution to the exclusion problem is an instance of what may be called the "two explananda" strategy: rationalizations and biological explanations do not share the same explananda, and therefore there need be no explanatory competition between them, no excluding of explanations of one type by those of the other.... The strategy is appealing: Resolve the explanatory rivalry by splitting the explanandum.... For Dretske, psychology is in charge of actions and doings, causal-relational structures of the form C-causing-M, and neurobiology and other physical sciences are in charge of events simpliciter, such as M. Although Dretske never explicitly mentions the issue of explanatory exclusion, it seems that this would be his answer were the problem put to him.... [But] consider Dretske's causings, the supposed explananda of psychological explanations. We can put the issue in a simple and stark way: Are these causings physical entities or are they not? If they are not, we have an overt dualism. If they are in the physical domain, are they susceptible of physical causal explanations or are they not? If they are, then these explananda, special though they might be, cannot serve to separate psychology from physical theory, and the exclusion problem arises again. If they are not, we would again have a form of psychophysical dualism: there are entities in the physical world for which there in principle are no physical causal explanations but only intentional explanations.... But Dretske is a committed physicalist and naturalist; he will not brook any form of dualism.[4]

Kim's point can be further elaborated as follows. Grant, at least for the sake of argument, that the semantic indication-relation is indeed a matter of correlation, as Dretske maintains. Grant, too, that instances of C-causing-M can be indirectly explained by adverting to past-operative structuring causes. (These indirect explanations, as long as they occupy the same theoretical level as direct ones, are not actually threatened by the problem of explanatory exclusion, because the latter pertains to distinct theoretical levels.) Now, in order to causally explain how C came to be an M-switch, is it really necessary to appeal to the fact that C was correlated with F at the time it became causally linked to M? When one considers the relevant internal structural changes *sub specie physicalis* – i.e., from the perspective of basic physicalistic explanation – it seems that the answer is no. A LaPlacean demon, explaining all of the world's events and processes (under starkly physicalistic descriptions) in terms of the most fundamental concepts and laws of physics, presumably would not need to cite the correlation between C and F.[5] After all, this correlation need not be mentioned in the physicalistic explanation of any *single stage* of the neural alteration process whereby C gets converted into an M-switch – even though F *itself* might get mentioned (under some suitably physicalistic description) in explaining that stage. And presumably the demon could provide a physicalistic explanation for the *complete* alteration process by just conjoining the separate physicalistic explanations of the separate stages; since no conjunct would appeal to the correlation, the conjunctive explanation would not appeal to it either. (Although this explanation might *entail* that C and F (as physicalistically described) are correlated, this correlational fact would not be part of the explanation itself.) Thus, even if the demon may legitimately explain a subsequent instance of C-causing-M by appealing to a past-operative structuring cause, this explanation too will not appeal to the correlation between C and F. A basic physicalistic explanation of C-causing-M will be non-intentional – even if it appeals to some past-operative structuring cause, and even if intentionality can be cashed in terms of correlational facts.

This argument also works, *mutatis mutandis*, with respect to neuro-physiological explanation rather than basic physicalistic explanation. A LaPlaccan physiologist, viewing *sub specie neurologis* the process of C's becoming an M-switch, presumably would not need to appeal to the correlation between C and F in order to explain the relevant alterations in neural structure. Rather, he could confine himself entirely to what happens within the creature's nervous system (including the electrochemical stimulations caused by sensory receptors). So at this explanatory level too, the fact that C means F is irrelevant in explaining later occurrences of C-causing-M.

The moral of these observations, I suggest, is that Dretske's account of rationalizing explanations should not be construed as a putative answer to the EEP problem. If one is a committed materialist like Dretske, then "splitting the explanandum" is the wrong strategy for dealing with this problem. For, as Kim rightly points out, the two resulting explanada both will be susceptible to lower-level explanations, and hence the problem of explanatory exclusion will arise all over again. Rather, Dretske should adopt a "compatibilist" answer to the the explanatory exclusion problem. He should claim that in general, one and the same phenomenon can be susceptible to more than one explanation, at more than one theoretical or conceptual level. And he should claim, on the basis of this general compatibilist perspective, that exclusion *per se* is not a special problem for psychological explanation at all.

It is crucial to realize, however, that the soprano problem still remains to be dealt with – even if we assume that compatibilism is correct *vis-à-vis* the general issue of explanatory exclusion. For, the fact remains that the intentional properties of mental representations do not supervene upon what's in the head. Even under explanatory compatibilism, this nonsupervenience appears to render the intentional properties of mental representations irrelevant to explaining the bodily motions caused by those representations. Herein lies the real point of Dretske's proposal to split the explanandum. For, if we construe an action as the reason's *causing* its effects, rather than as some event or process that is an *effect* of the reason, then the opportunities for explanatory relevance are evidently enhanced. This enhancement is perhaps most clearly expressed as a conditional:

> *If* the content of C is explanatorily relevant to C's original recruitment as an M-switch, *then* C's content thereby becomes explanatorily relevant to subsequent instances of C-causing-M.

Dretske contends that the antecedent of this conditional is true, and hence that the consequent is true too. But this leaves him free to say that the recruitment process, and thus the subsequent causings as well, are also susceptible to lower-level nonintentional explanations.

So his account of the explanatory role of content has point and purpose even under a compatibilist answer to the explanatory exclusion problem. And a compatibilist answer is the kind he ought to favor, I submit, even though he advocates a reductive account of content in terms of statistical/correlational notions of the sort employed in information theory. For as I argued above, when one considers *sub specie physicalis* (or *sub specie neurologis*) the process whereby an inner state C becomes a switch that causes motor output M, it appears that the relevant kind of explanation will not cite the correlation between C and F. Thus, in order for the antecedent of the above conditional to be true, the recruitment process must be susceptible to modes of explanation other than those a LaPlacean demon or a LaPlacean physiologist would employ.

The relevant sort of explanation, I take it, involves the explicit or implicit appeal to something like the reinforcement principle I stated earlier. This is really macrobiological explanation, rather than neurophysiological or ground-level physicalistic explanation. To explain the given process by describing it as "the recruitment of an F-indicator as an M-switch" is to provide an explanation similar to those given by *evolutionary* macrobiology – except that Nature's design problem now gets solved within the individual creature, rather than within the population. At the theoretical level of macrobiology, presumably, the correlation between F and C really does have genuine explanatory relevance. But in principle, the "recruitment" process also is explainable in more fundamental terms, and at lower theoretical levels the correlation will play no explanatory role.

So in effect, Dretske presupposes a compatiblist answer to the general question of explanatory exclusion. From the compatibilist point of view, the issue of exclusion does not, in itself, pose any special problem for psychology. Thus he is best interpreted as addressing only the soprano problem, and not the EEP problem.[6]

Objections

An account of the explanatory role of content in rationalizing explanations should do reasonably well at capturing our pre-theoretic intuitions about why, and how, content matters. These inchoate intuitions might not get completely satisfied, because one reason this issue is philosophically problematic is a certain tension in the intuitions themselves – on the one hand, the intuitive idea that the content of reasons is absolutely central in explaining action; but on the other hand, the idea that any proper explanatory story about behavior must eschew properties that don't supervene upon what's in the head. Still, the goal should be an account that goes a long way toward satisfying the former set of intuitions – while also shedding light on the sources of intuitive tension.

Although Dretske's proposal is ingenious, I think it fares rather poorly at capturing our ordinary understanding of why and how reasons *qua* reasons are explanatorily relevant to action. The problem of intuitive fit is so severe, in fact, that I think it reflects more than a need to modify or supplement his account in certain ways; it reveals instead that the whole approach is fundamentally misguided. In this section I shall set forth three objections the combined impact of which leads me to this pessimistic assessment. I shall discuss them in increasing order of severity; for me the third one is the real clincher.

Reasons as Causes

Consider a statement expressing a rationalizing explanation, say, "Fred went to the fridge because he wanted a beer and he believed there was beer there." As we would ordinarily understand this statement, it is true only if Fred's act of going to the refrigerator was *caused* by the cited belief and the cited desire. Although the existence of such a causal relation presumably is not sufficient for the statement's truth (since the properties *being a desire for a beer* and *being a belief that there's beer in the fridge* also must be explanatorily relevant to the action), it does seem to be at least a *necessary* condition.

Yet Dretske is committed to denying this. For, on his view the action is a causal transaction which includes the reason (i.e., the belief-desire combination) as a component part. Since a causal process cannot be caused by a part of itself, he must maintain that reasons do not in fact cause the actions they rationalize. This goes contrary to our pre-theoretic understanding of the "because" statements that typically express rationalizing explanations.

In reply to this objection, he could claim that under the proper conceptual unpacking of the relevant "because" statements, all they really entail is that the reason, described as a reason, is *causally/explanatorily relevant* to the action (described as an action). Although we ordinarily suppose that this in turn entails that the reason *causes* the action, he could point out that according to his own account, this supposition is mistaken. So if the denial that reasons cause actions were the strongest violation of pre-theoretic intuitions to which he is committed, then the cost might well be tolerable. But the unintuitive consequences of his position get worse.

Reasons without Learning

For Dretske the explanatory role of content rests upon the creature's individual history of associative learning. In such learning, an internal state C that already indicates conditions F gets recruited as a switch for bodily behavior M *because* it indicates F – where the relevant sort of causal explanation appeals to something like the reinforcement principle mentioned earlier.

Recruitment of an internal state as a behavior switch also can occur in the evolutionary history of the species, rather than within the creature's own learning history. This is enough, according to Dretske, for C to count as a *bona fide* representation of F, and not merely as an indicator of F. For, on his account, an inner representation is a state whose *function* is to indicate something; and a state can take on this function via evolution rather than learning. But although internal indicators can be genuine representations even if their function as behavior switches was evolutionarily installed, Dretske maintains that the content of such representations is not explanatorily relevant to a creature's behavior, and thus that they do not qualify as beliefs:

> (7) If we suppose that, through selection, an internal indicator acquired (over many generations) a biological function, the function to indicate something about the animal's surroundings, then we can say that this internal structure *represents* (or *misrepresents*, as the case may be) external affairs. This is ... a representation.... But it is *not* a belief. For to qualify as a belief it is not enough to *be* an internal representation (a map) that is among the causes of output, something that helps us steer. *The fact that it is a map, the fact that it is says* something about external conditions, must be relevantly engaged in the way it steers us through these conditions. (EB, p. 94)

Moths, for instance, are genetically pre-wired to produce evasive wing movements when they detect an approaching bat. But the content of an individual moth's particular internal representation is quite irrelevant, says Dretske, in explaining that moth's current behavior:

> (8) The moth has the kind of nervous system is has, the kind in which an internal representation of an approaching bat causes evasive movements, because it developed from a fertilized egg which contained genetic instructions for this kind of neural circuitry, circuitry *in which* the occurrence of C will cause M. This is a develop-

mental explanation, a causal explanation of why, in today's moths, tokens of type C produce movements of type M.... Even if through a freak of nature (recent enough so that selectional pressures had no time to operate) the occurrence of C in contemporary moths were to signal not the approach of a hungry bat but the arrival of a receptive mate, C would still produce M – would still produce the same evasive wing maneuvers. What C indicates in *today's* moths has nothing to do with the explanation of the movements it helps to produce. And the fact that tokens of C indicated in remote ancestors the approach of hungry bats does not explain – at least not causally (developmentally) – why *this* (or indeed, why *any*) C produces M. Rather, it explains (selectionally) why there are, today, predominantly moths in which C causes M. (EB, p. 93)

Hence the importance of associative learning. Only here, he holds, do we reach a point where the content of a creature's internal state can actually play a causal-explanatory role *vis-à-vis* that creature's own behavior:

(9) It is only when we get to a form of learning whose success depends on the deployment and the use of internal indicators that it becomes plausible to think that the causal processes constitutive of behavior may actually be explained by facts about what these indicators indicate.... Only ... in this kind of learning do we find internal states assuming control functions *because* of what they indicate about the conditions in which behavior occurs. Only here do we find *information*, and not merely the structures that carry or embody information, being put to work in the production and the control of behavior. (EB, p. 96)

But the trouble is that it seems conceptually possible, according to our ordinary way of thinking about reasons and actions, for there to be a creature who instantiates genuine beliefs (and other propositional attitudes) – attitudes whose content is genuinely explanatorily relevant to its behavior even though the creature has not (not yet, anyway) learned anything at all. Imagine, for instance, a Frankenstein creature, created by Martians whose mastery of robotology and of human neurophysiology is vastly superior to ours. The Martians deliberately design the creature with neural circuitry very much like the circuitry that might have been instantiated by a sophisticated and well informed philosopher, in 1990 America, who has an enormous amount of knowledge about the world but has total amnesia about his own past. The creature, from its first moment of activation, has accurate beliefs (or seeming-beliefs) about a vast range of facts – including, let us suppose, facts about its own origin, about what Fred Dretske looks like, and about the content of Dretske's book *Explaining Behavior*. Imagine that the creature is activated in Dretske's presence, and immediately begins arguing vociferously with

him; it defends with great subtlety the contention that it already has
full-fledged propositional attitudes, whose content is genuinely explanatorily relevant to its own behavior. (Thereafter it continues behaving
intelligently and appropriately throughout its life, very much in the
manner of an intelligent, sophisticated academic.)

Or imagine a species of creatures very much like humans except that
their infants are born with both (i) an innate working knowlege (or
seeming-knowledge) of the language spoken by those creatures, and (ii)
physical capacities roughly comparable to those of human five-year-old
children. And suppose that these infant prodigies, promptly upon being
born, immediately engage in behavior (including verbal behavior) roughly
comparable to that of human five-year-olds. (Thereafter the children
grow up very much as do human children.)

Both kinds of creatures do seem conceptually possible. Moreover,
one's intuitive judgment about the mental lives of such creatures seems
strong and unequivocal: they are true believers, whose attitudes are fully
explanatorily relevant to their behavior, from the very first moment they
enter the world. Yet Dretske is committed to denying this, because these
creatures have not yet *learned* anything when they first enter the world.
Given his remarks in passage (9), he must say that prior to learning, these
creatures not only lack beliefs whose content is explanatorily relevant,
but that they lack beliefs altogether. A position this counterintuitive
begins to look seriously misguided.

One way to forestall this objection would be to withdraw the claim that
explanatory relevance (and also beliefhood itself) must derive from associative learning within the creature's individual history – and to allow
instead that actions can be explained by past-operative structuring causes
lying either in the evolutionary history of the creature's species (as in the
case of the infant prodigies), or in the creature's individual ontogenesis
(as in the Frankenstein case). This would require repudiating the reasoning in passages (8) and (9) above.[7] I leave open the question how
plausible it is, from the perspective of Dretske's own theoretical
framework, to deal with the objection this way. However that might be,
this way out would only exacerbate the third and most serious objection
to Dretske's account, to which I now turn.

Here-and-Now Explanatory Relevance

Consider performing some action oneself, such as walking to the refrigerator because one wants a beer and believes there's beer there. Our
common-sense belief about our own actions – a belief with enormous
force and vivacity, by virtue of the phenomenology of our own agency
(the "what it's like" of being an agent) – is that the content of the
operative belief and desire has an utterly *immediate* kind of causal/
explanatory relevance to the action. That is, we think of the reason, *qua*
reason, as relevant not merely (and not mainly) insofar as its content
might figure in some past-operative structuring cause of the present

acition, but rather as a full-fledged *triggering* cause of the action, and indeed as a *current* triggering cause. But Dretske is committed to denying that reasons, described as reasons, have this kind of here-and-now explanatory relevance.

Speaking for myself, I find that this belief in the here-and-now explanatory relevance of content is virtually unshakeable. I suspect it's the same for you. If so, then you will probably find yourself believing, as I do, that Dretske's treatment of reasons and actions is surely wrong, and that there must be some better approach. But in any case, here-and-now explanatory relevance is clearly central to our ordinary conception of how reasons explain behavior; Dretske's account thus falls quite far short of accommodating this conception. There is ample reason, therefore, to seek a different account – ideally, one that will end up closer to our ordinary ways of thinking about these matters, and that will do so at a manageable philosophical cost.

An Alternative Approach

In this final section I will briefly set forth and defend an alternative treatment of the soprano problem. This approach preserves the here-and-now explanatory relevance of content. It allows us to say that the Frankenstein creature and the infant prodigies have genuine propositional attitudes, with full-fledged here-and-now explanatory relevance, right from the moment they begin life. It allows us to say that reasons are causes of actions, rather than components of actions. And as a bonus, it handles the problem of explanatory exclusion too. The key to these benefits is a certain way of understanding explanatory relevance, together with some philosophical therapy to help expunge the idea that a property which does not supervene upon what's in the head cannot figure in genuine here-and-now causal explanation of action.

Explanatory Relevance

In causal explanation the effect phenomenon, described as instantiating a phenomenon-type E, is shown to depend in a certain way upon the cause phenomenon, described as instantiating a type C. This dependence largely involves the the way the properties C and E fit into a suitably rich pattern of counterfactual relations among properties. The following passage from James Woodward gives a sense of how certain patterns of counterfactual relations underpin causal explanation and explanatory relevance:

> A scientific explanation not only shows that the explanandum phenomenon was to be expected, but also enables us to answer questions of the form "What would have happened if...." A successful

scientific explanation accomplishes this by exhibiting the explanandum phenomenon as one of a range of states, any one which might have occurred had initial conditions, boundary conditions, and so forth been different in various ways from they actually were. We are shown why, conditions being what they were, the explanandum phenomenon rather that one of these alternative outcomes occurred. In effect we are not just shown why the explanandum phenomenon had to occur, but are given some sense of the range of conditions under which it would have occurred.... But why should this additional information have any explanatory signficance? One way to appreciate the significance ... is to note that if we simply require that an explanans provide a nomically sufficient condition for the explanandum we do not insure that the explanans is relevant to the explanandum. When we require, in addition, that the laws answer a set of what-if-things-had-been-different questions, we help to insure that the explanans will perspicuously identify those conditions which are relevant to the explanandum being what it is.[8]

To illustrate these remarks, Woodward cites an example from Wesley Salmon. Suppose that Mr Jones, a man who has been taking birth control pills regularly, fails to get pregnant. Even though the generalization "All men who take birth control pills regularly fail to get pregnant" satisfies standard criteria for being lawlike, this generalization will not sustain a genuine explanation of why Mr Jones failed to get pregnant. In his case the property *taking birth controls regularly* is explanatorily irrelevant. For, the pertinent what-if-things-had-been-different question – viz., "What would have happened had he not taken birth control pills regularly?" – receives the wrong answer.

On the other hand, suppose that Mrs Jones, a female who has been taking birth control pills regularly, fails to get pregnant. Now the very same property becomes explanatorily relevant; and a very similar lawlike generalization (pertaining to women) underpins a genuine explanation (albeit a crude one, too crude to count as scientific). For, now we have a pattern of counterfactual relations that makes for genuine explanatory relevance. Thus Woodward:

In an explanation involving [the lawlike generalization about pregnancy] there are in effect two possible initial conditions which may obtain – Mrs Jones either may or may not take birth control pills – and two possible explananda – Mrs Jones either may or may not get pregnant. In a successful scientific explanation we have a kind of generalized analog of this feature – the explanation identifies not two but a great range of possible explananda, and a range of possible initial conditions under which these different expananda will be realized. The explanation explains in part in virtue of showing us how it is that it was the explanandum rather than one of these many alternate possibilities that was realized and in doing so, perspicuously identifies those conditions which are relevant to the obtaining of the these various explananda.[9]

I will refer to this generic approach to explanatory relevance as the *counterfactual pattern* conception (for short, the CP conception). On this general view, the explanatory relevance of a pair of properties C and E, instantiated respectively by a pair of causally related events or states, consists largely in the fact that C and E fit into a pattern of counterfactual relations of the kind Woodward describes.[10] (I will refer such patterns as *CR patterns*.)

Under the CP conception, a single phenomenon can perfectly well be subject to a variety of different explanations, involving properties from a variety of different CR patterns. Often several distinct patterns, all explanatorily relevant to a single phenomenon, will involve different levels in the hierarchy of the sciences – e.g., microphysical, neurobiological, macrobiological, and psychological. Typically certain context-relative parameters of discourse will determine, in a given situation of inquiry, which sort of explanation is most appropriate for the purposes at hand. (These parameters operate in much the way that context-relative parameters typically determine, in a given discourse situation, what counts as the proper referent of a given definite description that is satisfied by several distinct objects in the contextually pertinent universe of discourse.)

In addition, in order for properties in a given CR pattern to have genuine explanatory relevance, no doubt this pattern must itself must figure in the right sort of inter-level fit with other properties, and other CR patterns, at lower levels (i.e., more fundamental ones) in the scientific hierarchy. What counts as an acceptable kind of inter-level fit is a large question, which I leave open here. In light of the potential multiple realizability of higher-level properties (e.g., psychological properties), evidently it would be excessive to demand the kind of intertheortic reduction traditionally discussed in philosophy of science, involving either type/type biconditional "bridge laws" or inter-level property identities. But one important constraint can be stated loosely and roughly: viz., the higher-level CR patterns should not turn out to be *merely coincidental*, and thereby explanatorily spurious, by virtue of the way they are connected to lower-level CR patterns.

Suppose, for instance, that a certain fatal disease always causes certain symptoms (say, a distinctive kind of skin rash) shortly before it causes death, and that these symptoms are never caused in any other way. Then there will be a higher-level CR pattern involving presence or absence of skin rash, and presence or absence of subsequent death. But this pattern will be explanatorily spurious: having the skin rash does not causally explain one's subsequent death; rather, the rash and the death are both the effects of a single common cause.

The Soprano Problem Reconsidered

Let us now return to the soprano problem, in light of the CP conception of explanatory relevance. As Dretske remarks in passage (1) above, "The soprano's upper-register supplications shatter glass, but their meaning is irrelevant to their having this effect." Under the CP conception, we would expect this explanatory irrelevance to stem from the fact that there does not exist a suitable CR pattern involving, respectively, the cause's property of meaning such-and-such and the effect's property of being a shattering. Pertinent what-if-things-had-been-different questions won't get the answers that are requisite for explanatory relevance.

And so it is, in this case. Passage (1) itself actually points us toward one pertinent kind of what-if question: What would have happened if the soprano had emitted sounds with the same pitch and amplitude, but with a different meaning, or with no meaning at all? The answer is that the glass would have shattered anyway, which reflects the absence of an explanatory CR pattern involving the meaning of the soprano's actual supplications. Other what-if questions are pertinent too. For instance, what would have happened if the soprano had emitted sounds with the same content as in her actual supplications, but with different pitch and amplititude? The answer – further reinforcing the absence of an explanatory CR pattern involving content – is that the glass would not have shattered.

In addition, there is another feature of Dretske's soprano example that also prevents the sounds' meaning from being explanatorily relevant to the glass's shattering: viz., it is *merely coincidental* that sounds with this meaning are followed by shattering of glass. This feature will remain, and will block the explanatory relevance of the sounds' content, even if we embellish Dretske's case in such a way as to build in a certain CR pattern. Even in such an embellished case, it will be true that the higher-level relations among properties are connected to lower-level CR patterns in such a way that the higher-level relations are merely coincidental.

Suppose, for instance, there is an all-female society of Amazons, each of whom can produce, and can perceptually distinguish, sounds with the properties that shatter glass. Suppose, also, that sounds instantiating these properties – regardless of any other acoustic features they do or do not possess – mean "shatter" in the Amazon language. When Amora, queen of the Amazons, first encounters something made of glass, she reacts by saying "shatter" (in Amazon), and it promptly shatters. Now, in this case there is indeed a certain CR pattern of the kind that sometimes underpins explanatory relevance: the glass's shattering or not shattering depends counterfactually upon Amora's uttering or not uttering a sound that means "shatter." (This pattern is quite crude and limited, but it does seem comparable, for instance, to the CR pattern in Woodard's example of Mrs Jones and the the birth control pills.) But the sound's meaning is explanatorily irrelevant anyway. For, the CR pattern in question is merely coincidental; it is not linked in an appropriate way to other, lower-level, CR patterns that do sustain genuine relevance.[11]

So it is not difficult, within the framework of the CP conception of explanatory relevance, to say why the meaning of the soprano's sounds is irrelevant to their effects of shattering glass. Furthermore, the account just offered makes no explicit appeal to the fact that the meaning of the sounds does not supervene upon their intrinsic properties. That fact *per se* is not necessarily problematic, under the CP conception of explanatory relevance.

Consider, on the other hand, explanations of actions on the basis of reasons. The intentional mental properties that constitute reasons (viz., belief-types, desire-types, and other attitude-types), in combination with act-types, clearly figure in rich and robust CR patterns. When someone performs an action A for a reason R, it is typically the case that if he had not possessed R, and also had not possessed some other sufficiently strong reason for performing A, then he would not have performed A. It is also typically he case that if he had possessed a sufficiently good reason for performing some other act A' rather than A, then he would have performed A' instead. Under the CR conception of explanatory relevance, intentional mental properties are excellent candidates for explanatory relevance, in combination with act-types. The fact that they don't supervene upon what's in the head is no mark against them at all.

There remains the question of inter-level fit, however. We still require some assurance that CR patterns involving propositional attitudes and actions are connected to lower-level CR patterns in such a way that the former can sustain genuine explanatory relevance, rather than being merely coincidental. Ironically, it is precisely in addressing this question where I think it becomes appropriate to invoke macrobiological ideas of the kind so central to Dretske's own position – ideas about Nature's solutions to design problems. What is crucial is the notion of "recruitment" of internal states to execute certain design functions, and the linkage between proper function and representational content. (The distinction between evolutionary recruitment and associative learning is no longer central.) Colin McGinn, who has recently proposed an account of the explanatory relevance of reasons that has a certain family resemblance to Dretske's account, puts quite crisply the ideas I want to stress. He writes:

> Let us start with the idea of *relational proper function*. The proper function of some organ or trait or process is what it is designed to do, what it is supposed to do, what it ought to do. Proper functions can come about either through the intentions of a designer or through a mindless process like natural selection.... An organism must be designed (by natural selection) according to the environmental constraints; indeed the given environment is the chief *architect* in constructing a species of organism, since it does the selecting of characteristics. And here is where relational proper

function comes in: proper functions are generally defined *relatively* to some environmental object or feature. Thus the function of the chameleon's pigmentation mechanism is to make it the same colour as its immediate environment.... In each case we specify the function of the characteristic in terms of a relation to some environmental item.... What natural selection must do is to install a causal mechanism of some kind which carries out the function selected for in a specific environment.... It is not difficult to see how this idea might be applied to traits of mind as well as to traits of body. The mind and its characteristic powers and properties are evolutionary products too, and as such may be expected to exhibit functional features: mental states will have their own distinctive relational proper functions. On general grounds, then, we may anticipate environment-directed functions on the part of such states as desire, belief and perception; they too will play their part in helping the organism adapt itself to the environmental contingencies.... *[T]he relational proper function of representational mental states coincides with their extrinsically individuated content.* That is to say, content is an upshot or concommitant of function; the relationality of the former reflects the relationality of the latter.... [T]his coincidence cannot be mere coincidence.... [F]unction fixes, and is fixed by, content.[12]

McGinn himself maintains, as does Dretske, that intentional mental properties do not have here-and-now causal/explanatory relevance with respect to behavior; in fact, McGinn holds that psychological explanation is not causal at all. There claims are quite radically at odds with our ordinary thinking about reasons and causes, and I think they are mistaken for largely the same reasons that Dretske's views are mistaken. But the point I want to emphasize here, so nicely brought to light in the quoted passage, is this: representational content and relational proper function are so intimately connected, in the case of propositional attitudes, that it is clearly no mere coincidence that attitude-types and act-types figure as they do in robust CR patterns. On the contrary, the requirement that propositional attitudes should figure in such patterns is crucial to their relational proper function; it is their *raison d'etre*, from the point of view of Nature-as-designer.

The upshot of this reconsideration of the soprano problem is as follows. Under a plausible looking, if admittedly sketchy and generic, approach to explanatory relevance, it turns out that although the content of the soprano's sounds is clearly explanatorily irrelevant with respect to the effect of the glass's shattering, the situation is just the opposite for typical cases of reasons causing actions. The content of reasons has full-fledged here-and-now cuasal/exlanatory relevance to the actions they cause, just as common sense supposes it does. Moreover, there is no need to claim that reasons are constituents of actions, rather than causing them. And there is no need to claim, either about Frankenstein creatures or about infant prodigies, that when they first enter the world they do not yet have genuine propositional attitudes with genuine explanatory relevance.

Scorekeeping in the Explanation Game

Dretske believes that since content does not supervene upon what's in the head, intentional mental properties cannot have here-and-how relevance in causal explanations of actions. He is not alone; many other philosophers believe this or something similar. Indeed, some philosophers believe that intentional properties cannot have any kind of relevance at all in causal explanations. Passages (2) and (3) formulate the reasoning for this stronger negative conclusion. In effect, Dretske accepts this reasoning in modified form. What he thinks it really shows, I take it, is that content cannot be relevant to *here-and-now* causal explanation.

If the position sketched earlier in this section is correct, however, then the reasoning in passages (2) and (3) should be repudiated entirely. Intentional mental properties are relevant to *bona fide* here-and-now causal explanation; for, they figure in the requisite way in suitable CR patterns, and their doing so is no mere coincidence.

It cannot be denied, however, that there is substantial intuitive plausibility in the claim that properties not supervenient upon what's in the head cannot be causal properties, i.e., cannot figure in here-and-now causal explanation. So I want now to propose an explanation of this claim's seductive appeal.

As I remarked above, often a given phenomenon is susceptible to several kinds of explanation; and when this is so, typically certain implicit context-relative parameters will determine which kind is appropriate for the purposes at hand. In the case of human behavior, any of several types of explanation might be the most appropriate – psychological, for instance; or neurobiological; or in principle, even microphysical.

Let me stress three important points about implicit context-relative parameters of discourse. First, as competent speakers we deal with them so naturally that we often don't even notice them. Take definite descriptions, for instance. As David Lewis points out,[13] frequently more than one object, within some contextually determined domain of discourse, will be a potentially eligible referent of "the F." When this happens, the proper referent will be the most salient F in the domain, according to some contextually determined salience ranking. We take this implicit context relativity so much in stride that we often are not even aware of it. Lewis gives this example:

> Imagine yourself with me as I write these words. In the room is a cat, Bruce, who has been making himself very salient by dashing madly about. He is the only cat in the room, or in sight, or in earshot. I start to speak to you:

> The cat is in the carton. The cat will never meet our other cat, because our other
> cat lives in New Zealand. Our New Zealand cat lives with the Cresswells. And
> there he'll stay, because Miriam would be sad if the cat went away.

At first, "the cat" denotes Bruce, he being the most salient cat for
reasons having nothing to do with the conversation. If I want to talk
about Albert, our New Zealand cat, I have to say "our other cat" or
"our New Zealand cat." But as I talk more and more about Albert,
and not any more about Bruce, I raise Albert's salience by conversational means. Finally, in the last sentence of my monologue, I am
in a position to say "the cat" and thereby denote not Bruce but
rather the newly-more-salient Albert. (SLG, p. 241)

Second, implicit context-relative parameters frequently get altered
through a process Lewis calls *accommodation*: something is said that
requires some parameter to have a new value, in order for what is said to
be true (or otherwise acceptable); so that parameter thereby takes on the
new value. Concerning salience and definite descriptions, he says:

> One rule, among others, that governs the kinematics of salience is a
> rule of accommodation. Suppose my monologue has left Albert
> more salient than Bruce; but the next thing I say is "The cat is going
> to pounce on you!".... What I have said requires for its acceptabil-
> ity that "the cat" denote Bruce, and hence that Bruce be once again
> more salient than Albert. If what I say requires that, then straight-
> away it is so. (SLG, p. 242)

Third, often if a context-relative parameter is one we would naturally
think of as involving standards that can be either raised or lowered, then
accommodating upward will seem more natural than accommodating
downward. Concerning context-relative standards of precision for terms
like "hexagonal" and "flat," for example, Lewis remarks:

> I take it that the rule of accommodation can go both ways. But for
> some reason raising the standards goes more smoothly than lower-
> ing. If the standards have been high, and something is said that is
> ... [acceptable] ... only under lowered standards, then indeed the
> standards are shifted down. But what is said ... may still seem only
> imperfectly acceptable. Raising of standards, on the other hand,
> manages to seem commendable even when we know that it inter-
> feres with our conversational purposes. (SLG, p. 245)

If we keep in mind the three points just mentioned, then we begin to
see why it should be so intuitively tempting – even though it is a mistake –
to think that intentional mental properties are barred from here-and-now
explanatory relevance by virtue of not supervening upon what's in the
head. One could arrive at this mistaken belief by undergoing a series of

cognitive steps something like the following. (Note that some of these steps are cognitive "acts of omission.")

1 Focusing on the causal explanation of behavior at some theoretical level more fundamental than the psychological level – e.g., neuro-chemical explanation of specific muscle movements.
2 Accommodating, automatically and subliminally, to the parameters of explanatory relevance appropriate for this kind of explanation.
3 Failing to notice that such accommodation has occurred, or that context relative parameters of explanatory relevance are operative.
4 Noticing that for the kind of explanation under consideration, pro-perties relevant to here-and-now causal explanation must supervene upon what's in the head. (The pertinent muscle movements are gener-ated by causes internal to the body; hence, at this explanatory level one seeks causal properties intrinsic to the creature's current internal neurochemical states and structures.)
5 Shifting focus to the role of mental properties in the causal explana-tion of action.
6 Failing to accommodate to the parameters of explanatory relevance appropriate for mentalistic explanation.
7 Finding it "intuitively obvious" that for any kind of causal explanation of behavior, here-and-now explanatory relevance requires superven-ing upon what's in the head.

The crucial component of such a process is step 6, which paves the way for the mistaken belief that arises at step 7.

Several factors are likely to contribute to step 6. First is the overarching failure to notice, at the level of reflective consiousness, that context relative parameters of explanatory relevance are operative at all, or that accommodation is going on. Second is a subliminal cognitive resistance to the kind of accommodation that actually would be appropriate at step 5. To accommodate properly would be to acquiesce in standards of explana-tory relevance that are lower, on a scale we might call "comparative degree of explanatory fundamentality," than the standards already opera-tive; and downward accommodation involving lowering of standards often does not go smoothly (as Lewis points out). Third is the extent of the qualitative gap between properties that supervene upon what's in the head and those that do not. When the gap is this glaring, the subliminal resistance to downward accommodation is likely to be much stronger than it otherwise might be. (The resistance would be substantially weaker, I think, if propositional-attitude types could be properly individuated in terms of "narrow functional role," involving merely their typical-cause connections to one another, to sensory stimuli, and to narrowly charac-terized behavior.[14])

A fourth contributory factor involves certain kinds of counterfactuals. Describing it requires a bit of preliminary stage setting. Suppose that in a given context of inquiry, actions are being explained in terms of reasons.

Suppose that Smith has performed an action A; and that he had two distinct reasons R-1 and R-2 (two distinct desire – belief combinations) each of which rationalized A. And suppose that the following two counterfactuals obtain:

(C1) If he had possessed R-1 without R-2, then he would have A-ed anyway.

(C2) If he had possessed R-2 without R-1, then he would not have A-ed.

These counterfactuals have a direct bearing upon questions of explanatory relevance, within the sphere of psychological explanation. Their joint truth indicates that R-2 probably was not explanatorily relevant to Smith's act of A-ing at all. Although R-2 was indeed a reason he had for A-ing, his act probably was performed only because of R-1 – rather than because of R-2, or because of both R-1 and R-2 together. [15]

Now, the factor I want to mention, pertinent to both steps 6 and 7 in the above sequence, is a tendency to regard certain pairs of inter-level counterfactuals as suitably analogous to intra-level counterfactuals like (C1) and (C2). Suppose, for instance, the Jones performed act A for reason R, and that N is the neuro-chemical state-type which physically realized R in Jones. (Assume that A is a narrowly individuated act-type; cf. note 14. N is presumably a conjunctive state-type, with separate components realizing each of the the distinct propositional attitude types which jointly constituted R.) Consider these two counterfactuals:

(C3) If he had been in neural state N without possessing reasons R, then he would have A-ed anyway.

(C4) If he had possessed reasons R without being in neural state N, and without being in some other R-realizing neural state N' that itself would have causally sufficed (under the circumstances) for A-ing, then he would not have A-ed.

In typical situations where an agent performs a (narrowly individuated) action A for a reason R, counterfactuals of the form (C3) and (C4) will have natural readings under which they are non-vacuously true.[16] (The conditional of form (C4) will be true because the person could have possessed R without being sufficiently motivated to engage in A-ing; and the conditional of form (C3) will be true by virtue of some appropriate "Twin Earth" scenario.) In addition, their antecedents actually straddle two explanatory levels as once. Consequently, when one contemplates such counterfactuals with the question of explanatory relevance in mind, one naturally accommodates to the standards of relevance that are appropriate for the more fundamental, non-psychological, level of explanation. And since the accommodation process is normally subliminal, one also tends to construe the truth of (C3) and (C4) as showing that the reason-type R is irrelevant *tout court* in explaining the action – even though the most their truth actually shows is is that R is explanatorily irrelevant *sub specie neurologis*.[17]

Admittedly, the past several paragraphs constitute a somewhat speculative account of the origins of the intuition that properties not superventient upon what's in the head cannot have here-and-now explanatory relevance to behavior. But if one keeps the account in mind as one reads Dretske's remarks in passages like (2), (3), (5), and (6) above, then it begins to look fairly plausible that his worries about the explanatory role of content stem from surreptitiously importing into psychology a constraint on here-and-now explanatory relevance that really is only appropriate at more fundamental levels of explanation.[18]

Notes

1 Fred Dretske, *Explaining Behavior: Reasons in a World of Causes* (Cambridge, Mass.: MIT Press/Bradford Books, 1988), henceforth EB; "Reasons and Causes," *Philosophical Perspectives*, vol. 3, ed. James Tomberlin (Mascadero, Cal.: Ridgeview Publishing, 1989), pp. 1–15, henceforth RC; and "Why Thinking Helps," unpublished, henceforth WTH.

2 On explanatory exclusion, see Jaegwon Kim, "Explanatory Realism, Causal Realism, and Explanatory Exclusion," *Midwest Studies in Philosophy*, 12 (1987), pp. 225–39; "Mechanism, Purpose, and Explanatory Exclusion," *Philosophical Perspectives*, vol. 3, ed. Tomberlin, pp. 77–108; and "Explanatory Exclusion and the Problem of Mental Causation," unpublished. On anomalous monism, see Donald Davidson, "Mental Events," in *Experience and Theory* ed. L. Foster and J. Swanson (London: Duckworth, 1970), pp. 79–101, reprinted with an appendix in *Essays on Actions and Events* (Oxford: Oxford University Press 1982), pp. 207–27.

3 Philosophical doubts sometimes are raised about the supervenience of phenomenal properties upon what's in the head – not because these properties are nonintrinsic, but rather because of the seeming imaginability of "inverted qualia" scenarios in which, for instance, color experiences are differently linked to brain states than they are in our actual world. For an attempt to defuse such doubts, see my "Supervenient Qualia," *Philosophical Review*, 96 (1987), pp. 491–520.

4 Kim, "Explanatory Exclusion and the Problem of Mental Causation," pp. 25–7. In this quotation the letters "C" and "M" have been inserted in place of Kim's symbols, in order to conform with Dretske's own notation – which I am following in this paper.

5 Determinism is not being assumed here. Rather, let the LaPlacean demon know the entire physical history of the universe, whether or not this history is itself deterministic.

6 In a recent conversation with Dretske, I asked him whether his concern was the soprano problem (as I call it), or the EEP problem, or both. He replied that although he had not explicitly distinguished these two problems in his own thinking, his real worry had been the soprano problem rather than the EEP problem. He does believe, he said, that a single phenomenon can be susceptible to several distinct kinds of explanation.

7 Even if one did repudiate this reasoning, however, one still might deny that

the content of a moth's representations is explanatorily relevant to the moth's behavior. Maybe explanatory relevance requires a richer and less tropistic behavioral repertoire than the moth's, and/or the capacity for learning and memory.

8 James Woodward, "Scientific Explanation," *British Journal for the Philosophy of Science*, 30 (1970), pp. 41–67, 54–5.

9 Ibid., p. 57.

10 For one proposed elaboration of the generic CP conception of explanatory relevance, with specific attention to the explanatory role of intentional mental propoperties, see my "Mental Quausation," *Philosophical Perspectives*, vol. 3, ed. Tomberlin, pp. 47–76.

11 I broach the case of Amora and the Amazons in "Mental Quausation," note 37.

12 Colin McGinn, *Mental Content* (Oxford: Basil Blackwell, 1989), pp. 145–7.

13 David Lewis, "Scorekeeping in a Language Game," *Journal of Philosophical Logic*, 8 (1979), pp. 339–59, henceforth SLG; reprinted in his *Philosophical Papers*, vol. 1 (Oxford: Oxford University Press, 1983), pp. 233–49. Subsequent page references are to the reprinted version.

14 By "narrowly characterized behavior" I mean behavior characterized in a way that would still be applicable in Twin Earth scenarios. An act description like "drinking a glass of water" is not narrow, because on Twin Earth the stuff they call water is not water at all.

15 I say "probably" because it seems possible for R-2 to be a genuinely contributory causal factor – a partially overdetermining factor, one might say – even though R-1 alone would have caused an act of A-ing, whereas R-2 alone would not have caused one. (I make a snide remark both because I think my colleague's statement requires a sharp refutation and because I dislike him; I would have made the remark anyway even if I'd had the former motive without the latter, but not if I'd had the latter without the former.)

16 Counterfactuals are subject to various readings because they too are governed by certain context-relative parameters of discourse. Under the standard possible-worlds semantics, a counterfactual "If it were that A, then it would be that C" is non-vacuously true iff some accessible possible world where both A and C are true is more similar to our actual world, overall, than is any world where A is true but C is false; cf. David Lewis, *Counterfactuals* (Cambridge, Mass.: Harvard University Press, 1973). Both the comparative similarity relation and the accessibility relation can vary from one context to another. In the case of comparative similarity, context relativity is exhibited by non-standard "backtracking" readings of counterfactuals; cf. David Lewis, "Counterfactual Dependence and Time's Arrow," *Nous*, 13, pp. 455–76, esp. 455–9. As for accessibility, there is convincing evidence that this relation is context relative *vis-à-vis modal* discourse; cf. Lewis, SLG, esp. pp. 246–7; and Angelika Kratzer, "What Must and Can Must and Can Mean," *Linguistics and Philosophy*, 3 (1977), pp. 337–55. So one would expect accessibility to be comparably context relative for counterfactuals too.

17 I do not mean to suggest that counterfactuals of the form C3 and C4 can never bear upon the question whether mental properties are explanatorily relevant under the appropriate higher-level standards of relevance (the standards appropriate to psychology itself). In fact, I think that sometimes such counterfactuals do bear upon this question, because sometimes they are pertinent to whether mental properties have the requisite kind of inter-level

fit with lower-level properties. (I have in mind certain inter-level counterfactuals involving so-called "phenomenal," or "qualitative," mental properties; cf. Horgan, "Supervenient Qualia.") However, I also would maintain that there are important connections between (i) the context-relative parameters determining the operative explanatory level (and the operative standards of explanatory relevance), and (ii) the context-relative parameters that govern counterfactuals themselves. In particular, under the accessibility relation that is appropriate in contexts of psychological explanation, the social and environmental factors that contribute to mental content remain fixed. (Jones *could not* have been in neural state N without possessing reasons R, given these factors.) Thus, possible worlds involving Twin Earth scenarios count as *inaccessible*, under the contextually appropriate accessibility relation; hence counterfactuals of the form C3 turn out vacuous rather than being non-vacuously true. (Of course, as soon as one begins contemplating such a counterfactual, one tends to accommodate by broadening the accessibility relation; but the resultant non-vacuous truth of the counterfactual does not undermine the explanatory relevance of intentional mental properties at all.) For further related discussion see Horgan, "Mental Quausation."

18 I thank Fred Dretske, John Tienson, and Jim Woodward for helpful discussion. Some of what I say in this paper grows out of philosophical interaction at the 1988 Conference on Mental Representation at the University of Missouri at Columbia, where Jerry Fodor and I both commented on Dretske's "Why Thinking Helps."

6

The Role of Mental Meaning in Psychological Explanation

Robert Cummins

Introduction

In his recent book *Explaining Behavior*,[1] Fred Dretske sets out an extended an admirably clear account of the role of mental meaning in the explanation of behavior. The account is unique in being the only well-informed, current attempt I know of to take seriously and attempt to explicate the idea that the semantic content of a mental state is *causally* relevant to the explanation of behavior. Dretske's effort can (and should), therefore, be read as, among other things, a response to what I call Stich's Challenge.[2] Given that, by definition, the semantic properties of a representation in a computational system are not relevant to its causal role, how can a computationalist take semantic content to be relevant to psychological explanation?[3]

Dretske's account is explicitly directed at ordinary common-sense explanation by reasons – i.e., at "folk-psychological" explanation, as it has come to be called. Dretske obviously takes this sort of explanation very seriously. He is not the kind of philosopher who would write a book about a kind of explanation if he did not think that kind of explanation is on the right track. Dretske, along with Fodor and many others,[4] assumes that common-sense explanation by reasons is, if not yet science, at least near to it, and bound to be (perhaps in regimented form) at the core of any serious psychology of cognition. Dretske is thus (again, along with Fodor and many others) making an assumption I call the Intentionalist Assumption (1A):

> 1A: the role of semantic content in folk-psychological explanation just is (or is our best line on) the explanatory role of semantic content in scientific cognitive psychology.

Dretske is also making what I will call the Causal Assumption (CA):

> CA: semantic content cannot have a serious explanatory role to play in psychology unless it has a *causal* role to play.

He writes:

> Something possessing content, or having meaning, can *be* a cause
> without its possessing that content or having that meaning being at
> all relevant to its causal powers.... If meaning, or something's
> *having* meaning, is to do the kind of work expected of it – if it is to
> help explain *why* we do what we do – it must, it seems, influence the
> operation of those electrical and chemical mechanisms that control
> muscles and glands. Just how is this supposed to work? This
> obviously, is as much a mystery as the interaction between mind
> stuff and matter.[5]

These assumptions – the ones I've labeled IA and CA – are background
assumptions for Dretske. They don't either into the analysis itself; their
function is rather to motivate the analysis. Without IA and CA in the
wings, the project to give an account of the causal role of content in
folk-psychological explanation degenerates into mere ordinary language
philosophy or folk-wisdom journalism.

I think Dretske's motivating assumptions are on the wrong track, or at
least seriously misleading. The explanatory role of semantic content in
most contemporary cognitive science is not causal and has little to do with
the explanatory role of reasons in folk-psychology. In order to substanti-
ate this charge – or at least make it intelligible and plausible – I will need
to contrast my view of things with Dretske's. This means that I will have
to begin with some critical exposition of Dretske's theory.

Contents as Causes

Exposition

Behavior   Dretske distinguishes the outputs (e.g., movements) of a system from its behavior. Behavior is the production of output by a cause
internal to the system. Behavior is thus a process – the causing of M by C
– rather than an event. It follows from this conception that to explain
behavior is to explain something of the form $C \to M$ (C's causing M). On
Dretske's picture, then, semantic content enters into a causal explanation
of behavior when we can explain why C causes M by appeal to the
semantic content of C.

Structuring Causes   To understand why Cs cause Ms in S, we need to
know something about the way S is structured. To understand, for example, why the bending of a bimetallic element in a thermostat causes the
furnace to go on or off, we need to know that the bimetallic element is a
switch that closes (opens) a circuit by bending into (away from) a contact
point. By a structuring cause of $C \to M$, Dretske means a cause of S's
having whatever structure underwrites the C to M connection in S. A

change in the room temperature can explain why the bimetallic element bent, hence why the furnace went on, but it cannot explain the system's *behavior*, for that requires explaining why a bending of the bimetallic element in the thermostat causes the furnace to go on.[6]

Putting these last two points together we arrive at the following result: the semantic content of C enters into a causal explanation of the behavior C → M of S when C's having a certain semantic content is a structuring cause of C → M. The semantic content of C has to be what allows us to understand the C to M connection in S.

Indication and representation   How could the semantic content of C help us to understand the C to M connection in S? Dretske's answer is that in some systems there is a C to M connection because of what C *indicates*: if Cs cause Ms in S because the occurrence of Cs in S covaries with the occurrence of Fs (in the environment or elsewhere in S), then, according to Dretske, (1) in S, Cs have the function of indicating Fs, hence (2) Cs are *representations* in S of Fs, and so we can say (3) that we have a C to M connection in S because C has the semantic content it does.

Learning   So the question of the explanatory role of content boils down to this: under what conditions, if any, do we have a C to M connection in S because of C's indicative powers? This happens, according to Dretske, when and only when M is learned as a response to F.

Let's begin with the "when" part. Suppose S responds to Fs with Ms. Then S must have some way of detecting the occurrence of Fs. That is, there must be some internal state C of S the occurrence of which covaries with the occurrence of Fs. Cs can then be *recruited* (Dretske's term) as specific causes of Ms. Since learning establishes a C to M connection – i.e., establishes a structure that underwrites a C to M connection in S – and since this happens *because Cs covary with Fs*, learning gives us just what the doctor ordered, viz., a case in which it is C's meaning that accounts for (is a structuring cause of) the C to M connection in S, i.e., of S's behavior.

Now for the "only when" part. Consider a bit of unlearned behavior, i.e., a case in which the C to M connection is S is innate. How could C's content enter into the explanation of the C to M connection in S? There seems only one possibility: Organisms with a C to M connection were selected for because Cs indicate (or indicated at one time) Fs and the capacity to respond to Fs with Ms conferred a selective advantage on S's ancestors. In an earlier work,[7] Dretske thought that this kind of selectional explanation should be regarded as a case of casual explanation of behavior by content. In *Explaining Behavior,* however, he rejects this view.

A selectional explanation of behavior is no more an explanation of an individual organism's behavior – why *this* (or indeed *any*) moth takes a nosedive when a bat is closing in – then is a selectional account of the antisocial behavior of prison inmates an explanation of why Lefty forges checks, Harry robs banks, and Moe steals cars. The fact that we imprison people who forge checks, steal cars, and rob banks does not explain why the people in prison do these things.[8]

The point of the passage is to argue that selectional explanations don't explain why Cs cause Ms, they only explain why individuals with the C to M connection occur (and, perhaps, predominate) in the current population.[9]

Summary statement   Putting all this together, we have the following.

1   S's behaviors are processes consisting of the production of an output M by a cause C internal to S.
2   The semantic content of C's explains why Cs cause Ms in S when C's having the content it does is a structuring cause of the C to M connection in S – i.e., when C's having the content it does explains why S has the structure that underwrites the C to M connection.
3   C's having the content F (C's expressing the property F) is a structuring cause of the C to M connection in S when C's cause Ms because it is a function of Cs to indicate Fs. When Cs cause Ms in S because it is a function of Cs to indicate Fs, Cs are said to represent Fs.
4   There is a C to M connection in S because Cs indicate Fs when and only when M is learned as a response to F, the underlying mechanism being the recruitment of Cs as causes of Ms.

Consequences

Several consequences of Dretske's view are worth emphasizing. They are these:

1   Only learned behaviors have explanations in terms of semantic content;
2   not even learned behaviors can be said to be explained by representations;
3   it isn't current meaning that explains current behavior;
4   whether current behavior is properly explained by the semantic content of an internal state depends essentially on the system's history.

   1   *Only learned behaviors have explanations in terms of semantic content.* It is worth pointing out that this runs directly counter to a central empirical claim of most cognitive science of the past twenty years, namely the claim that a great deal of learning is based on innate knowledge:

learning itself (some of it) is unlearned behavior explained in terms of unlearned knowledge. Dretske's rather surprising denial of this central claim is a direct consequence of his assumption that the explanatory role of content is its role in the causation of behavior (identified earlier as motivating assumption CA), together with the idea that behavior is a process consisting of the production of output by an internal cause. There is really only one way in which something x can be said to cause Cs to cause Ms in S: x restructures (or constrains) the system S in such a way that the occurrence of a C leads to the occurrence of an M. (If something jams the door, then the occurrence of smoke inside is going to make you come out a window.) But if x restructures S so that Cs cause Ms, then the C to M connection in S is *acquired*. Unacquired C to M connections cannot be caused to occur because you cannot cause the occurrence of what is already there. Dretske cannot allow for the explanation of unlearned behavior (e.g. learning itself) in terms of innate knowledge.

2 *Not even learned behaviors can be said to be explained by representations.* On Dretske's account, Cs acquire the function of indicating F precisely by being recruited to cause Ms because of the value of outputting M when F.

> Once C is recruited as a cause of M – and recruited as a cause of M *because of what it indicates about F* – C acquires, thereby, the function of indicating F. C acquires its semantics, a genuine meaning, at the very moment when a component of its natural meaning (the fact that it indicates F) acquires an explanatory relevance.[10]

It is thus trivial to say that C causes M because of what C represents, for C's status as a representation is constituted by the fact that its (past) indicative power is relevant to explaining the C to M connection. What makes it C's function to indicate F (what makes C a representation of F) is just that C causes M because of what C indicated during learning. "A belief is merely an indicator whose natural meaning has been converted into a form of non-natural meaning by being given a job to do in the explanation of behavior."[11] It is thus *natural meaning* that does the explaining, that has been given a job to do in the explanation of behavior. Non-natural meaning can't explain behavior because what makes it non-natural is, by definition, just the fact that the correlative *natural meaning* explains behavior.

3 *It isn't current meaning that explains current behavior.* Once the system is structured in a way that guarantees a C to M connection, Cs will continue to cause Ms regardless of what Cs indicate. (As Dretske is at pains to point out, it can be a function of Cs to indicate Fs even if Cs do not indicate Fs.) The structuring cause of the C to M connection is the fact that Cs indicated Fs *during learning*. The fact that it is *now* a function of Cs to indicate Fs – the fact that Cs now represent Fs is *not* a structuring cause of the C to M connection, hence does not enter into the explanation of the behaviors that are constituted by the production of Ms by Cs.

4   *Whether current behavior is properly explained by the semantic content of an internal state depends essentially on the system's history.* Dretske's account shares a disturbing feature with that of Millikan,[12] viz., that a just created molecule by molecule duplicate of me cannot behave for reasons. This is because, in the duplicate, the behaviors aren't learned but, as it were, preprogrammed.[13] On this conception of things, most of artificial intelligence is based on a conceptual error, for AI assumes that one can simply give an artificial system what natural systems have to learn, and one can do this without copying the physical structure of any natural system.

Two Pictures

Attractive as Dretske's picture is in many ways, it has, as we've just seen, some unattractive consequences. Three seem especially worth reiterating.

1   The account is incompatible with the plausible claim that much learning is dependent on innate knowledge.
2   The account is incompatible with the plausible claim that cognitive states can be synchronically specified.[14]
3   The account is incompatible with the widespread claim that it is current representations and their current semantic contents that (in part) explain current behavior.[15]

These consequences are disturbing enough, I think, to lead us to ask whether and how they might be avoided.

There are two strategies a revisionist might employ, depending on how the trouble is diagnosed. The conservative diagnosis assumes that the trouble is basically vibration that can be cured by careful tuning and tinkering. The radical diagnosis assumes that the trouble doesn't derive from the details, but from the assumptions that motivate the project – the assumptions IA and CA identified earlier. In the remainder of this paper, I want to explore a radical alternative to the picture that emerges if one begins with IA and CA.

The Causal Assumption

CA: Semantic content cannot have a serious explanatory role to play in psychology unless it has a *causal* role to play.

Remember functionalism? Functionalism was the idea that mental states could be individuated *via* their roles in the causation of behavior or rather, as Dretske has taught us to say, of output. What happens when a functionalist applies this treatment to belief and desire, i.e., to intentional states? Well, intentional states are mental states that are individuated by their semantic properties, i.e., by their contents. Two things seem to follow. First, semantic properties of mental states must somehow be a matter of causal roles: same causal role, same state (functionalism); different semantic properties, different state (individuation of belief); hence, distinct beliefs must differ in their causal roles. Second, functionalism is plausible to the extent that we think that what matters about mental states – what makes them important – is their role in the causation of output. From this point of view, talk of mental states gets into psychology – gets past the behaviorist gate-keepers – because mental states are deemed important to the explanation of output. It is still the behaviorist game – explain output – but mentalists win because it turns out that one can't explain output without mental states.

Putting these two points together what we have is this: the game is to construct causal explanations of output by reference to mental states.[16] Since what is distinctive about some mental states, namely the intentional states, is their contents, the game in the case of intentional states is to discover the causal role of content: if intentionality is to have a serious explanatory role to play, it must be the case that some states cause output in virtue of their semantic properties. We thus arrive at the causal assumption, viz., that the explanatory role of content is its causal role in the production of output.

This may not be the way Dretske got to the causal assumption, but it is a pretty common and natural way to go for a philosopher influenced by functionalism or a psychologist influenced by the behaviorist definition of psychology as a science in the business of explaining/predicting behavior. Natural as the causal assumption is, however, there are other ways to go, as we'll see shortly.

The Intentionalist Assumption

> IA: the role of semantic content in folk-psychological explanation just is, or is our best line on, the explanatory role of semantic content in scientific cognitive psychology.

Two facts should make this assumption look dubious to us.

First, the idea that belief and desire involve representation is a daring and controversial empirical hypothesis, an hypothesis I call the representational theory of intentionality. According to this hypothesis, championed by Fodor, to harbor a belief that Brutus had flat feet is a two part affair. It is (1) to harbor a representation that means that Brutus had flat feet, and (2) for that representation to be (computationally) available to the system as a premise in reasoning, and to be subject to evidential assessment. Representations, in this picture, are conceived as data structures, or something very like them, things that can be "read" and "written" in the computational senses of those terms. There is thus a large gap between the role of intentional states (belief, desire) and the role of representation, and a correspondingly large assumption is being made when it is assumed that the explanatory role of role of intentional state contents is a good guide to the explanatory role of the semantic contents of mental representations.

Second, talk of mental representation, and hence of the relevance of semantic content to psychology, got a serious scientific start in psycholinguistics, and in the computational modeling of reasoning. In both cases, the contents of the representations invoked were not plausible candidates for the contents of intentional states (by which I mean ordinary propositional attitudes such as belief and desire), a point misguided critics were at pains to make at the time. Representational psychology (as opposed to intentionalist psychology) didn't start out with belief and desire and branch out into phrase structure and goal hierarchies; it went the other way around.

Given these facts, we should, as I said, be suspicious of the intentionalist assumption. I think suspicion is rare in this context because the rules set by the intentionalist assumption seem (to philosophers) to define the only game in town. But there is another game in town.

The Interpretationist Picture

The computational theory of cognition (CTC) seeks to explain cognition by appeal to two correlative explanatory primitives, representation and computation. It is central to this approach that these are assumed to be well understood in virtue of uncontroversial applications in the explanation of non-cognitive capacities such as calculation and elementary character manipulation. Essential to the appeal of the CTC is the idea that the very same elementry processes that account for the arithmetic capacities of a calculator and the character manipulating capacities of a word-processor can be made to account for sophisticated cognitive capacities as well. For the CTC, it is elementary data structures – e.g., the stored value of a variable – rather than beliefs, that are the paradigm cases of representation. Advocates of the CTC reject what I have called the intentionalist assumption and are thus free to remain agnostic about the representational theory of intentionality.[17]

The CTC takes as its paradigm of the explanatory role of representation not the explanation of behavior by reasons (which may not involve representation at all!), but the computational explanation of calcuation and symbol manipulation. To understand the picture from the perspective of a theoretical framework that rejects both the intentionalist assumption and (as we'll see shortly) the causal assumption, we do well to begin by examining the explanatory role of representation in elementary calculators and other symbols manipulators.

Adding machines To add is to compute the plus function. But + is a function on numbers, and numbers are not physical states of calculators. How, then, can calculators traffic in numbers? The answer is simple and familiar: adding machines *instantiate* + by computing representations of its values from representations of its arguments. A typical adding

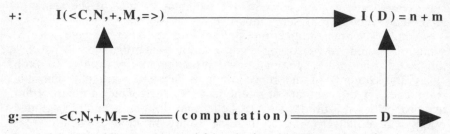

Figure 6.1 An adding machine satisfying the function g instantiates the function +.

machine computes a numeral for the number seven from a pair of numerals for the numbers five and two. The numerals in question are physical states of the machine – relative cog wheel positions, say, or relative dc levels. In figure 6.1, the points along the double line represent physical states of the machine, points on the single line above represent the numbers which are the interpretations of the corresponding physical states. What makes a physical state a numeral is just that it is properly interpreted as a number. A physical state is properly interpreted as a number just in case the diagram commutes, i.e., just in case the conjunction of A_1 and A_2 causes S iff + $(I(A_1, A_2) = I(S)$.

Typically, of course, the mapping from numeral to number is made obvious by the labels on the keys, and by the use of a display featuring numerals in some standard notation. This makes it easy to miss the distinction between what the states of the machine represent *in the machine* (if anything) and what the states of the machine mean *to us*. But there is a difference: whether or not the states of the system are really numerals in the system, and which numbers they represent, depends on whether we have properly designed the system so that its states really do represent what we intend them to (our intentions being recorded as our choice of labels).

That there is a fact of the matter concerning what is represented that is independent of standard conventions or the intentions of designers or users is made clearer by a different sort of example, viz., Galileo's discovery that the elements of geometrical figures represent mechanical magnitudes. Consider a body uniformly accelerated from rest that travels a fixed time t. When time runs out, it will have achieved a velocity v. Now consider a body that travels at a uniform velocity v/2 for the same time t. It turns out that both bodies will cover the same distance. Galileo's proof of this result involves a revolutionary use of geometry. In figure 6.2, the height of the triangle/rectangle represents the time t. The base of the triangle represents the terminal velocity v of the uniformly accelerated object, and hence the base of the rectangle represents the constant velocity v/2 of the unaccelerated object. The area of the rectangle represents the distance traveled by the unaccelerated object (vt), and

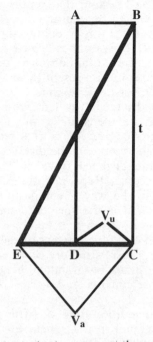

Figure 6.2   Galileo's use of geometry to represent the relationship between mechanical variables.

the area of the triangle represents the distance traveled by the accelerated body.[18] Proof of the result reduces to the trivial demonstration that the triangle and the rectangle have the same area.

The crucial point is that, given Galileo's interpretation of the lines and volumes, the laws of Euclidean geometry discipline those representations in a way that mirrors the way the laws of mechanics discipline the represented magnitudes: the geometrical discipline mirrors the natural discipline of the domain. That is, geometrical relationships among the symbols have counterparts in the natural relations among mechanical variables[19] in such a way that computational transformations on the symbols track natural transformations of the system.[20] This is what makes it correct to say that the symbols – lines and volumes – *represent* times, velocities and distances.

Of course, this is what Galileo *intended* them to represent: that is the interpretation he stipulated. But it's one thing to intend to represent something, another to succeed. Galileo's figures *actually do* represent mechanical variables because the computational discipline *actually does* track the natural one – the natural discipline we have in mind when we say the system behaves according to natural law. Galileo's interpretation is a *proper interpretation* because, under that interpretation, the natural system and the geometrical system that represents it march in step: the geometrical system *simulates* the natural one. Representation, in this context, is simply a convenient way of talking about an aspect of more-or-less successful simulation. The volumes behave in the geometrical system in a way analogous to the way certain distances behave in the natural one. Hence, the volumes are said to represent those distances; those distances are proper interpretations of those volumes. For instance, the volume of the triangle tracks the distance traveled by the uniformly accelerated body; the volume of the triangle is the *geometrical analog* of the distance traveled by the accelerated body. This is what makes it correct to say that the volume of the triangle *represents* the distance traveled by the acceler-ated body, i.e., that the distance traveled by that body is a proper interpretation of that volume. Representation enters into this story in a way exactly analogous to the way it enters into the story about adding machines. In both cases, it is the fact that one function simulates the other under a fixed interpretation that makes it possible to think of the arguments and values of one function as representing the arguments and values of the other. The causal structure of an adding machine – the fact that it executes an appropriate program and hence satisfies the function g – guarantees that the arguments and values of g track the numbers; guarantees, for example, that "3" is the computational analogue (in the machine) of three in the addition function. This is what makes it possible to think of "3" as a symbol *in the system* for three. Analogously, the formal structure of Euclidian geometry guarantees that the volume of the rectangle will track the distance traveled by the unaccelerated body, and this is what makes it possible to think of that volume as representing that distance.[21]

The important point about this example is that it brings out the fact that the notion of representation we are investigating is no more arbitrary or "imposed" than the use of mathematics in science generally.[22] Galileo's discovery counts as a *discovery*, not an invention, because his interpretation is a proper interpretation: nature disciplines the rela-tionships between the mechanical magnitudes in question in a way that is mirrored by the way the laws of geometry discipline the corresponding elements of the figure. Galileo makes an historic contribution by dis-covering that the formal structure of geometry (properly interpreted) represents the structure of nature. Science has never been the same since. His task, far from being one of arbitrary imposition of interpretations, was to discover whether and how geometrical relations represent mecha-nical relations.

Every programmer will recognize Galileo's problem. When program-ming, it isn't enough to baptize one's data structures (or use a natural language); you have to write a program that imposes a discipline on the symbols that mirrors the discipline nature imposes on the things one hopes to symbolize. When you get the algorithm wrong, the representa-tions fail to represent what you intend them to represent.[23] Galileo had this problem himself: Euclidian geometry doesn't quite do the job for mechanics, so the representation is imperfect.

The Explanatory Role of S-Representation

I propose to call the sort of representation I've been discussing "s-representation" to distinguish it from other sorts of representation, and to emphasize that its essential feature is that there be a kind of simulation relation between the formal structure of the representational and the natural structure of the domain represented.[24] It should be obvious by now that the explanatory role of s-representation isn't anything like the explanatory role Dretske assigns to mental meaning. The idea behind s-representation is rather that, *under proper intepretation* what was seen as mere computation (or any other discipline embedding the symbols) is revealed as something else: adding, chess playing, reasoning.

What makes this idea appealing in its application to cognition is just the old idea that cognitive behavior – rational behavior in some sense – is epistemically assessable behavior. The difference between cognizing an environment and simply responding to it is that cognitive behavior is behavior that satisfies epistemic constraints.[25] But epistemic constraints are defined over propositional contents. Thus, to be capable of epistemic constraint satisfaction, and hence of cognition, a system must be capable of states that have propositional contents. Cognizers are thus systems that have propositional contents. Cognizers are thus systems whose states have proper propositional interpretations. The CTC's central idea is that it is computational structure (dispositions to compute) that provides the relevant discipline on the states. The hypothesis is that there is an interpretation that will reveal the right cognitive structure. It is an hypothesis analogous to Galileo's hypothesis that there is an interpretation that will reveal geometry as mechanics. The jury is still out on the CTC's hypothesis.

So s-representation is just a name for what you've got when there is a proper interpretation linking two structures/disciplines. Interpretation (and hence representation) contributes to understanding by effecting what Haugeland calls a dimension shift: the hope behind the CTC is that mere computation (of just the right kind) will be revealed by proper interpretation as thinking.

Semantic interpretation is just a special case of the sort of redescriptive conceptual filtering that good scientific taxonomy accomplishes generally. Good scientific taxonomy allows one to describe a situation or domain in a way that filters out everything except the information relevant to the explanatory problem at hand. Equipped with the glasses of Newtonian mechanics, what one sees when one looks at an otherwise colorful and complex scene from *The Hustler* is a plane normal to g (the surface of the pool table), populated by various vectors (momenta originating at the centers of gravity of the balls). Similarly, equipped with the glasses of proper interpretation, what one sees when one looks at the otherwise complex transactions in an adding machine is calculation. The latter is no more in the eye of the beholder than the former.

Conclusion

Dretske's target is the role of content in the common-sense explanation of behavior by reasons. It might, therefore, seem unfair to tax him with failure to be compatible with the special empirical assumptions of theories in artificial intelligence and cognitive psychology. But Dretske's project degenerates into mere ordinary language philosophy or folk-wisdom journalism unless he accepts what I have called the intentionalist assumption, the assumption that the ultimate scientific relevance of semantic content to our understanding of the mental is best seen in common-sense explanation of behavior by reasons. I have tried to argue that the intentionalist assumption is by no means inevitable (or even plausible), and that there are other routes into the problem of mental semantics, viz., the use made of it by actual science. Pursuing this route leads me to reject Dretske's other motivating assumption, the causal assumption, according to which the explanatory role of mental content is to be found in its contribution to the causation of behavior. Instead, I find that semantics enters into current scientific attempts to understand the mind as bridge over the gap produced by what Haugeland has called a dimension shift.

I have, of course, ignored a major aspect of Dretske's motivation, which is to give a naturalistic account of "original intentionality" i.e., of the ordinary propositional attitudes – belief, desire and so on. But representations and their semantic properties were not introduced into the science of the mind to account for belief and desire, they were introduced to account for the capacity to solve problems, and to parse speech; to account for psychological phenomena such as the Sternberg effect,[27] the "chunking" effect,[28] the verbal transformation effect,[29] or the scanning effect.[30] Indeed, there is no *common-sense* reason to suppose that belief and desire involve representation at all, and some common-sense reasons to deny this.[31] Perhaps propositionally interpretable states computationally available as representations of premises for a reasoning algorithm aren't "real" beliefs, and perhaps propositionally interpretable GOAL states aren't "real" desires. But they seem to be just what the doctor ordered. I don't know what "real" belief and desires are, but I have yet to see any compelling reason why a serious science of the mind should care.

Notes

1 Fred Dretske, *Explaining Behavior* (Cambridge, Mass.: MIT Press /Bradford Books, 1988).

2   Stephen Stich, *From Folk Psychology to Cognitive Science: The Case Against Belief* (Cambridge, Mass.: MIT Press/Bradford Books, 1983).

3   Stich's Challenge can be generalized to constitute a challenge to any framework that takes representations to be realized in a medium whose relevant causal properties are presumed independent of the semantic properties of the representations realized.

4   Jerry Fodor, *Psychosemantics* (Cambridge, Mass.: MIT Press/Bradford Books, 1987).

5   Dretske, *Explaining Behavior*, pp. 79–80.

6   C → M is a process. If we think of a process as a causal chain, then one way causally to explain a process is to cite a cause of its initial event. This is what Dretske calls a triggering cause of C → M. If Bs cause Cs in S, and a B occurred in S at t, then the process C → M will be initiated at t. Triggering causes explain why the C → M process occurred when it did, but do not explain the C to M connection in S. That requires a handle on the structure of S.

7   Fred Dretske, "The Explanatory Role of Content," *Contents of Thought: Proceedings of The 1985 Oberlin Colloquium in Philosophy* (Tucson: University of Arizona Press, 1987), pp. 17–36.

8   Dretske, *Explaining Behavior*, p. 95.

9   Dretske (following Sober, following Lewontin) distinguishes selectional from developmental explanations. See Elliot Sober, *The Nature of Selection* (Cambridge, Mass.: MIT Press/Bradford Books, 1984), and R. Lewontin, "Darwin's Revolution," *New York Review of Books*, 30 (1983), pp. 21–7.

10 Dretske, *Explaining Behavior*, p. 84.

11 Ibid.

12 Ruth Millikan, *Language, Thought and Other Biological Categories* (Cambridge, Mass.: MIT Press/Bradford Books, 1984).

13 For the careful: On Dretske's account, as on Millikan's only an accidental duplicate fails to represent. A *copy* – a duplicate made by copying the original – does have its structure because of the learning history of the original, though it has no learning history of its own.

Taken together, points 2 to 4 have the consequences that minds, conceived as systems whose states are, in part, semantically individuated, are very peculiar systems in that their theoretically relevant states do not supervene on even the entire current physical state of the universe. This follows from the fact that physical states are ahistorically conceived, while representational states are, according to Dretske, essentially individuated by actual learning histories.

14 Cognitive state should be distinguished from epistemic or justificatory state: whether I am currently justified in representing the world the way I do doubtless depends on my history. But whether I currently represent the world as, say, containing black swans does not seem to depend on my history. Russell's suggestion that we might, for all we know, have been created five minutes ago, having just the *beliefs* we now have, doesn't appear to be trivially dismissable on the grounds that beliefs and so on are historically individuated.

15 For an argument that indicator semantics of the sort that Dretske favors is also incompatible with some fundamental empirical claims of cognitive science, see Robert Cummins, *Meaning and Mental Representation* (Cambridge, Mass.: MIT Press/Bradford Books, 1988), chapter 6.

16 This looks fishy already because functionalists define mental states in terms of their role in the causation of output, so it seems circular to causally explain output by reference to mental states as causes. What happened to Hume's sound insistence on independent access to cause and effect?

17 If, as some suppose, intentionality presupposes rationality, those who accept the intentionalist assumption are bound to wind up thinking mental representation requires rationality too. The CTC is not burdened with this implausible result.

18 The area of the triangle, of course, is half the base times the height: $vt/4$. To see that this is the distance traveled by the accelerated object requires some mathematical reasoning that was not formulated explicitly until the invention of the integral calculus.

19 By mechanical variables, here, I mean real mechanical properties that vary in magnitude. I do *not* mean symbols.

20 The tracking referred to here is not causal, of course. A computational system can simulate a natural one without there being any significant causal relations between a symbol and the property it tracks in the simulated system. This is important because it allows for the fact that a computational system can simulate hypothetical systems and counter-factual systems, as well as abstract systems and systems that are actual and concrete but not in any significant causal interaction with the simulator.

21 Notice that we are not talking about a particular distance here – three meters, say – but *whatever* distance an unaccelerated body travels for an arbitrarily specified velocity and time. Plug a velocity and time into the geometry as the base and height of the rectangle respectively, and the volume is the distance traveled.

22 Dretske thinks that cases of this sort are cases of derived intentionality, i.e., cases in which what meaning there is is meaning only *for us*, the effect of convention and or arbitrary imposition.

> Let this dime on the table be Oscar Robertson, let this nickel (heads uppermost) be Kareem Abdul-Jabbar, and let this nickel (tails uppermost) be the opposing center. These pieces of popcorn are the other players, and this glass is the basket. With this bit of stage setting I can now, by moving coins and popcorn around on the table, represent the positions and movement of these players. I can use these objects to describe a basketball play I once witnessed (Dretske, *Explaining Behavior*, pp. 52–3)

If only Galieo had known it was this easy!

23 They always manage to represent something, of course: take them as numerals and there is some arithmetic function the program computes (though probably not a familiar or useful one). This bothers those who accept the intentionalist assumption because their paradigm is belief, and beliefs aren't always about numbers as well as people places and things.

24 Notice that s-representations cannot come one at a time.

25 John Haugeland, "The nature and plausibility of cognitivism," *Behavioral and Brain Sciences*, 2 (1978), pp. 215–60.

26 John Haugeland, *Artificial Intelligence: The Very Idea* (Cambridge, Mass.: MIT Press/Bradford Books, 1985).

27 S. Sternberg, "Mental Processes Revealed in Reaction Time Experiments," *American Scientist*, 57 (1969), pp. 421–57.

28 George Miller, "The Magic Number Seven, Plus or Minus Two: Some Limits on our Capacity for Processing Information," *Psychological Review*, 63 (1956), pp. 81–97.
29 R. Warren and R. Gregory, "An Auditory Analogue of the Visual Reversible Figure," *American Journal of Psychology*, 71 (1958), pp. 612–13.
30 S. Koslyn, T. Ball an B. Reiser, "Visual images Preserve Metric Spatial Information: Evidence from Studies of Image Scanning", *Journal of Experimental Psychology: Human Perception and Performance*, 4 (1978), pp. 46–60.
31 Daniel Dennett, *Brainstorms* (Cambridge, Mass.: MIT Press/Bradford Books, 1978), and, more recently, Dennett, *The Intentional Stance*, (Cambridge, Mass.: MIT Press/Bradford Books, 1988).

7

Ways of Establishing Harmony

Daniel C. Dennett

Folklore has many tales in which the hero goes in search of some precious thing – a holy grail, a magic talisman – and eventually, thanks to his many virtues, acquires the sought-for treasure *but only after rejecting it, unrecogized, several times*. In the final dénouement, he is shown that what he wanted so badly he had already had within reach.

One can see in Fred Dretske's career just such a quest – with just such a happy result. I am pleased to be the bearer of glad tidings, especially since, in Dretske's particular saga, he has often mistaken me for one of the villains (or better: worthy opponents), rather than the protector, all along, of the magic key. What Dretske has sought, with increasing clarity of purpose over the years, is the key to *how meaning makes a difference to us*, and now that he has described his quest so vividly, the rest of us can see better what we were trying to say and do as well.

In a recent paper (1985, p. 31), Dretske gives a particularly clear and telling example of the difference that he is trying to capture: the marijuana-detecting dog whose tail wags because an event occurs in its brain "meaning" (carrying the information) that marijuana is present, but which doesn't wag *because* the event means what it means. Unlike the dog's tell-tale tail-wag, Dretske insists, *our* bodily actions often happen *because of* what the states that cause them mean: "it is the structure's having this meaning (its semantics), not just the structure that has this meaning (the syntax), which is relevant to explaining behavior" (personal correspondence, quoted in Dennett, 1987, p. 307).

In a more recent paper (Dretske, SOFIA conference, 1988), on which this will focus,[1] he puts it even better: he has been "increasingly preoccupied with the question, not of what meaning (or content) *is*, but what meaning (or content) *does*." He wants to give meaning "some explanatory bite," (p. 5 of Dretske's conference paper, hereafter MS) and ideally, this would involve showing "the way meaning ... *can* figure in the explanation of why" an event causes what it does.

What difficulty lies in the way of this goal? The arguments, from myself and others, to the effect that the meaning of a particular event always must be, in Dretske's terms, *epiphenomenal* with regard to that event's actual causal powers. In *Content and Consciousness* (1969) I argued that the intentional interpretation of neural events is always at best a "heuristic overlay", and in "Intentional Systems" (1971) I tried to show how physical-stance predictions of the effects of structures always had hegemony over predictions based on the powers attributable to those structures (in idealization) in virtue of their meaning – as discerned from the intentional stance. More recently (1981, 1983, 1987), I have spoken, as Dretske notes, of the *impotence* of meaning; the brain is first and foremost a syntactic engine, which can be fruitfully viewed as reliably mimicking a semantic engine, but in which meanings themselves never overrule, overpower, or so much as influence the brute mechanistic or syntactic flow of local causation in the nervous system. (A semantic engine, I claim, is a mechanistic impossibility – like a perpetual motion machine, but a useful idealization in *setting the specs* for actual mechanisms.) Others have made similar claims: Fodor has long insisted on the inescapability of what he calls the Formality Constraint, and Dretske attributes to Schiffer (1987) the view that meaning is an "excrescence" which can do nothing and explain nothing.

Dretske's response to these claims is ambivalent. On the one hand he makes it entirely clear that he would truly love to defend a doctrine of brains as real semantic engines, with real meanings locally throwing their weight around and making the most direct imaginable difference – but he knows better. He is convinced by the arguments that show, in LePore and Loewer's terms, that the historical facts on which the meaning of a structure supervenes are *screened off* from the explanation of the structure's causal powers and behavior. (In a similar vein, I have spoken of "inert historical facts.") In fact, his own presentation of the argument, drawing the analogy to the difference between value and perceived value, is the clearest yet. He has reached the First Camp, and he finds it a hateful place but one he must endure now that he has cleaned it up.

What he will not endure, however, is any of the paths to the Second Camp. The well-known responses to the Lesson of the First Camp all involve finding some more indirect way in which there can be a regular, reliable correspondence between the meaning of a (neural) structure and its effects on behavior. For instance, Fodor's *language of thought* hypothesis is essentially an attempt to describe a system that satisfies what Haugeland has called the Formalists' Motto:

> If you take care of the syntax, the semantics will take care of itself. (1985, p. 106.)

This motto lies at the heart of what Haugeland calls GOFAI (Good Old Fashioned AI) and I call "High Church Computationalism" (Dennett, 1986). There are other, more noncommittal, ways in which materialists who have reached the First Camp can postulate a reliable correspondence between semantics and mechanism, but Dretske finds them all intolerable. I think it is wonderful that he chose to illuminate this "corner materialists have painted themselves into" by some old-fashioned labels: "epiphenomenalism" and "pre-established harmony." These dreaded relics of prescientific philosophy of mind, these desperate and doomed escape routes from Cartesian dualism, are sure to strike terror in the heart of complacent materialists, and Fred tells us exactly why he cannot abide them: any view of meaning according to which there is merely a pre-established harmony between the causal facts and the facts of meaning may permit us to *predict* an agent's behavior, and *control* an agent's behavior, but will not permit us to *explain* an agent's behavior – "and that," he says quite reasonably, "is what it takes to vindicate belief-desire psychology or our ordinary view about the causal efficacy of thought – that we stopped, for example, *because* we thought the light was red."[2]

But since Dretske has reluctantly accepted the conclusion of the First Camp, he realizes that a straightforward vindication of this intuition is not in the cards. What he offers us instead is an attempt to salvage, if not *locally potent meanings*, then the next best thing: "the fact that *A* means *M*, though it fails to explain why *B* occurred, may help explain a closely related fact, the fact that events of type *A*, when they occur, cause events of type *B* . . . And this fact, especially when we are trying to explain the behavior of a system, is a fact eminently worth explaining" (p. 11 of Dretske's conference paper).

What we need, in short, is not just a brute pre-established harmony, but an *explanation* of why and how the harmony is pre-established. Moreover (if Dretske has his druthers) this explanation will make an ineliminable appeal to the meanings of the elements thus linked. Now apparently he thinks that we pre-established harmony guys have failed to offer such an explanation, for he is forthright in his opposition: "I don't think this works. Or, if it does work, it does so at a cost that I'm not prepared (unless forced) to pay" (p. 9 of Dretske's conference paper). But this is where he makes his mistake, for in the end, he does not offer us an alternative to pre-established harmony, but a version of it, a truncated version, in fact, of the very version I have offered. (We have reached the turning point in the saga. Reach out, Fred, and *take the key!*)

There are exactly five ways in which such a correspondence – a "pre-established harmony" between the meanings of structures and their causal powers – could (in principle) come into existence. Fred encounters them all, but fails to recognize them for what they are.

First, there are the Three Cousins:

1. the correspondence is designed by natural selection;
2. the correspondence is designed by a learning process of some sort in the individual brain;
3. the correspondence is designed by an engineer creating an artifact, such as a robot or computer.

Then there is the Philosopher's Fantasy:

4. the correspondence is the result of a Cosmic Coincidence.

Finally, there is the Theologian's Hope:

5. the correspondence is created and maintained by God.

Desperate though he is to wed meaning and causation together, Fred rightly dismisses this fifth possibility with only a passing allusion, for the obvious reason that it would be, quite literally, a *deus ex machina*. It is interesting to me that philosophers who would be embarrassed to spend more than a passing moment dismissing this fifth alternative are nevertheless irresistibly drawn to extended discussions of the implications of the fourth, Cosmic Coincidence, which is actually a more fantastic and negligible "possibility in principle."

Notice that there really cannot be a sixth route to pre-established harmony. If such a harmony is not just a single, large ("Cosmic") coincidence (4), or a miracle (5), it must be the product, *somehow*, of lots of tiny, well-exploited coincidences, for the moral of the First Camp is that meanings cannot *directly* cause things to happen – and hence they cannot *directly* cause themselves to correspond to any causal regularities in the world. So it will have to be via an indirect process of fortuitous coincidences that are duly "appreciated" or "recognized" or "valued" or "selected" by something – either something blind and mechanical, such as natural selection or operant conditioning or "neural Darwinism" (Edelman, 1988) (1 and 2), or something foresightful and intelligent, such as an engineer (3). Any such process is a design process, and must consist, at bottom, of such generate-and-test cycles, where the generation of diversity to be tested is somewhat random or coincidental (see "Why the Law of Effect Will Not Go Away", Dennett, 1974, 1978).

Let me preview Dretske's encounters with the Ways, before setting out the details: he *endorses* the first two Cousins, natural selection and conditioning, while *rejecting* the third Cousin, engineering, never recognizing that *by his own principles* they are inseparable kin who stand or fall together. He then uses his allies, the first two Cousins, to defeat the fourth Way, Cosmic Coincidence, which really doesn't pose a threat in the first place. What clouds our hero's vision? As we shall see, it is his overzealous vow of allegiance to the intuitions of folk-psychology.

Now the details. Dretske begins his attempt to give meaning explanatory bite by nicely distinguishing between explaining B's happening (A caused it) and explaining A's causing B. He then tells a story about how a neural assembly can come to have a meaning, either via species evolution or via phenotypic learning – a kind of intra-cerebral evolutionary process of conditioning. The upshot is that such a story can explain why it is that As, meaning what they do, cause Bs. So far as I can see, this account follows precisely the path I laid out in *Content and Consciousness*, in my discussion of "the evolution of appropriate structures" (pp. 47–63).

Dretske describes an organism with a need to develop an avoidance mechanism against the highly toxic condition F, while I described different strains of organism which were different wired up to avoid, approach, or ignore a particular stimulus condition that happens to be "more often than not" – an important proviso – injurious (p. 49). The result of both thought experiments is the same: the lucky ones who happen to be wired up to avoid the toxic, *ceteris paribus*, are the ones who survive to reproduce, their coincidentally happy correspondence being selected for by natural selection. Dretske goes on to suggest that the same result could also be achieved by redesign during an individual organism's lifetime via a conditioning process, or as I put it, via a process of "intra-cerebral evolution" which can, in principle, yield all and only the new designs which the much slower process of species evolution could produce (pp. 56–63).

Note, however, that while Dretske now agrees with me about this, his doing so requires that he abandon, or at least soften, the hard line he has previously taken on these issues, in *Knowledge and the Flow of Information* (1981), and more recently in "Machines and the Mental" (1985) and "Misrepresentation" (1986). In his book, he attempted to erect meaning on a foundation of information. That is, he developed an account of semantic information (the sort of meaning needed for psychology – a *functional* notion that applies only to *designed* channels) from a base of nonfunctional, nonsemantic information channels, through which traveled items with "natural meaning" – items that informed (by definition) with *perfect reliability*; where natural meanings are concerned, no misrepresntation is possible. The task then was to turn the corner, somehow, from natural meaning to semantic or "natural functional meaning" (in which misrepresentation *is* possible), without, as he has more recently put it, "artificially *inflating*" the attributions of meaning to a structure one is so interpreting. Dretske has tried to hold the line against inflation by insisting on what he now calls the "indicator relation." But, although the current paper is not forthright about it, the indicator relations he now endorses (thanks to his endorsement of natural selection as a Way) can only approximately carry information about the distal conditions one is tempted to say they are designed to inform the organism about.

The indicator relation, which he heralds as "a plausible, at least a *possible*, partial basis for meaning" need only be a rough-and-ready guide to the meaning of the chosen structure. At least Dretske *ought* to recognize this, for that is how evolution, at the species or neural level, works. Mother Nature is a stingy, opportunistic engineer who takes advantage of rough correspondences whenever they are good enough for the organism's purposes, given its budget. Fred correctly wants to boast that his account *does* find an explanatory role for meanings: it is *because of what a structure happens to indicate* that it is "selected for" or "reinforced in" a further causal role in the economy of control of the organism, but it will be selected for, or reinforced in, this role *whenever* it is "close enough for government work" as the engineers say.

The most Dretske can get out of Cousins (1) and (2), then, is an explanatory account that makes ineliminable appeal to *quasi-indicator relations* or *approximate meanings*. Mother Nature never holds out for high-priced indicator relations.

As my frequent allusions to engineering suggest, and as I have argued in *The Intentional Stance* (chapter 8), the design processes one encounters in (1) and (2) are not only fundamentally the same, but fundamentally the same as the *artificial* design process encountered in (3). It is striking that Dretske resists this conclusion, most emphatically in "Machines and the Mental" but still strongly in evidence, with somewhat difference emphasis, in the current paper. If it is an engineer or computer scientist – rather than natural selection or a learning history – who does the selecting (who esteems a structure for its quasi-indicator relations and harnesses it in a particular functional role in a robot's control structure), this somehow gives the structure an illegitimate ancestry, in Dretske's eyes. But why?

Why should selection by an engineer disqualify a structure for one of Dretske's why-explanations, while "natural" selection does not? One might even suppose that engineer-selection had an advantage over its "blind," inefficient competition. One might say: whereas one must use scare-quotes when talking of natural selection's "appreciation" of the potential meaning of a structure, engineers sometimes really and truly respond to these potential meanings in the course of their conscious, deliberate, designing. But Dretske does not find this line of thought palatable, in spite of the fact that in the present paper his illustration of the wiring of the light switch explicitly appeals to just such different appreciations or intentions on the part of circuit designers. Is it just because he has a bad case of *orqanophilia* (otherwise known as *silicophobia*)? I think not. I suspect that he is distracted by an illusion: the illusion that somehow in ways (1) – and (2) – but in (3) not – the organism itself (or even: its mind or soul) does the understanding – responds directly to the meaning. After all, one might naturally but confusedly say, if some engineer is responsible for appreciating the meaning of a neural or computer structure, and is responsible for designing its further role in the light of that meaning, there is nothing left for the organism or robot to do – no *task of understanding* left over. But of course if *that* were so, the very same consideration would disqualify natural selection, for if it is the process of natural selection that has set up an innate correspondence between meaning and causation, there would likewise be no supervisory role for the organism (or its central, understanding homunculus) to play. (For more on this see my commentary on Ewert's "Prey-Catching in Toads," in *Behavioral and Brain Sciences*, (1988) "Eliminate the Middletoad!")

Now the reason I suspect that Dretske is beguiled by this line of thought is that in earlier work, he endorsed only (2), a learning history, and resisted endorsing (1), natural selection, as a legitimate Way to Harmony.[3] Both in his book, and more recently in his articles (and in personal correspondence, quoted in *The Intentional Stance*, p. 306), he held the line against innate, unlearned meanings. "Beliefs and desires, *reasons* in general (the sort of thing covered by the intentional stance), are (or so I would like to argue) invoked to explain patterns of behavior that are acquired during the life history of the organism exhibiting the behavior (i.e., learned)."

Why then has Dretske been tempted to favor individual learning histories exclusively? Because, apparently, they seemed to give the organism itself a proper role in the acquisition and appreciation of the meanings in question. But once again, of course, if "mere conditioning" is responsible for the redesign of the individual organism's brain, this too looks like taking responsibility away from the inner understander that Dretske is so loath to lose.

"But where does the *understanding* happen?" One might ask this, having been treated to an account of the way in which an organism was caused, thanks to its design, to respond appropriately (first internally, and eventually externally) to events impinging on it. It is as if one held out the hope of *locating* a moment of understanding by using a more powerful microscope, but in fact the understanding is, must be, located more diffusely, in the happy interactions of all those well-designed mechanisms.

This is, I think, the primary source of Dretske's earlier (and continuing!) opposition to natural selection and his continuing opposition to engineering design as sources of Harmony. In fact, in recent correspondence with me, he made it quite clear that he put so much stock in learning history, that he was prepared to grant real meaning even to the structures in an artifact, *so long as they were produced, in part, by individual learning* by the artifact: "I think we could (logically) create an artifact that *acquired* original intentionality, but not one that (at the moment of creation as it were) *had* it " (personal correspondence, quoted in *The Intentional Stance*, p. 305).

Now here we must distinguish two claims, one plausible and important, and the other – Dretske's – obscurely motivated and, I think, strictly negligible. The plausible and important claim is that it is astronomically unfeasible to create, by the usual engineer's methods, the sorts of structures that are naturally and efficiently created by learning histories of the sort he champions. This suspicion strikes at the heart of a particular fantastic hope of some in AI, who would *hand-craft* the myriads of beliefs that would constitute the "world knowledge" of an adroit robot. Not only have some thought this was possible in principle; there is a multi-million dollar project in AI with that as its explicit goal: Douglas Lenat's CYC project, an effort which Lenat himself supposes will take *person-centuries* of programming to accomplish. (See my discussion in *Daedalus* (1988a).) The majority opinion in AI, however, is that this is a hopeless approach, for reasons well-canvassed by David Waltz (1988).

Dretske's point, in contrast, is philosophical, not practical. It is that even if the engineers could hand-craft all those structures, they wouldn't have any meaning until they had been somehow annealed in the fire of experience. He puts the astronomically unfeasible product of engineering design in the same category with the even more astronomically unlikely case of Cosmic Coincidence, in spite of the fact that in the former case, there would be explanations of the provenance of structures that made appeal to meanings. He imagines that a physical duplicate of himself might "materialize – miraculously or randomly – out of some stray collection of molecules" (ms p. 19), and goes to some length to insist that this biological twin's motions would not be *actions*, with *meanings* behind them.

> I move my arm in this way *in order* to frighten away a pesky fly. With such a purpose I am, let us say, *shooing away a fly*. That is my *action*. My biological twin, though he moves his arm in the same way (with the same result) does not shoo away a fly, He doesn't have wants or beliefs, the kind of purposes I have in moving my arm. He isn't therefore, performing the same action. (ms, p. 19)

Your intuitions may agree with his, or recoil, but in either case, they concern something negligible, for as he goes on to acknowledge, there is a loophole: this metaphysically shocking state of affairs is apt to be short-lived, since it will persist only "until the twin accumulates enough experience – until, that is, his internal processes acquire the requisite extrinsic relations – to give his control processes, the processes governing the movement of his hand, the same kind of explanation as mine" (ms, p. 20).

How long, one wonders, should "acquiring the requisite extrinsic relations" take? I should think it would be instantaneous.[4] Signals from the bio-double's peripheral vision (or perhaps a faint blip from cutaneous sensors on the shoulder) happen to put the bio-double into what would be a bogus fly-out-there-sensing state – except that this time it is caused by a real fly. Moreover, the real fly's trajectory intimately determines the hand – eye coordination series that promptly leads to the (bogus or real?) "shooing" motions. How many flies must buzz around the head of a bio-double before he can start shooing them? If that isn't an angels-dancing-on-the-head-of-a-pin question, what would be?

This curious question, of how much traffic with the world is enough, somehow, to ensure that genuine meaning has been established, is simply the enlargement (via a *Cosmic* Coincidence) of the curious question that has bedeviled some evolutionary theorists: how much selection is required to endorse a tiny coincidence (a random mutation) as a genuine *adaptation*? (See my discussion in *The Intentional Stance*, pp. 320–1 and footnotes on those pages, and in my response to commentary in *BBS*). But if nothing but arbitrary answers (e.g., 42 generations of selection) could "settle" the question for natural selection, only arbitrary answers (e.g., 42 flies must buzz) could settle the question for a learning history, for the processes have the same structure – they must begin with a fortuitous or coincidental coupling, thereupon favored – and they have the same power to design structures in indirect response to meaning.

One might hold out some hope of a less arbitrary answer in the special case of design by conscious, deliberater engineers, for one could require that a structure could acquire only those meanings that were "explicitly recognized" by the designers, but such a reliance on the Word would be of dubious value since, as I argued in *The Intentional Stance* (pp. 284–6), and as Dretske has also shown in his current arguments in support of *screened off history*, the results of the three different processes can be indistinguishable: there is no surefire way of telling, for instance, that some correspondence in your own brain is *not* the result of ancient tampering by visiting extraterrestrial bio-engineers.

There remains a marginal sense in which (1) and (2) are more "natural" ways of establishing meanings, but this is a sense of no theoretical importance. In just the same sense, a weasel's short legs are natural, while a dachshund's, as a product of *artificial* selection, are not. It is an interesting historical fact, but it makes no difference to the integrity of any explanation that appeals to the function, or meaning, or implications, of those features.

This should leave us, and Dretske, with three equally legitimate Ways to Harmony, and indeed he comes within a hair's breadth of granting this. Consider the fundamental claim that underlies his paper: his analysis of why the meaning of a structure cannot figure in causal explanations of its effects:

> If meaning supervenes, at least in part, on the *extrinsic* properties of an event – historical and relational facts that *need not* be mirrored in the event's current (= the time at which it has its effects) physical constitution or structure – then if *A* causes *B*, then the fact, if it is a fact, that *A* means *M* will not – indeed, cannot – figure in a causal explanation of *B*. It cannot because, in *similar circumstances* [my italics] an event lacking this meaning, but otherwise the same, will have exactly the same effects. So it isn't *A*'s having meaning *M* that explains why *B* occurred. (Ms p. 10)

This would be a significant worry if "similar circumstances" were apt to be forthcoming with non-zero probability in cases where *A* did not mean *M*, but we can rest assured that we will never encounter such an anomaly. That is to say, it is no accident that events with the meanings they have get to play the causal roles they play (and Fred gives a good account of this), but the other side of that coin is that the odds are astronomical against the occurrence of an event or structure that *lacked* the relevant meaning somehow arising to cause a bogus *B*-type event. We don't need any special history of experience to ensure that any harmonies we encounter are robust, and Dretske's own arguments show that a learning history, "acquisition of *extrinsic* relations," *could not* impart any *intrinsic* power to those harmonies.

Let me review Dretske's view, and compare it with the view he *says* he will not accept, unless forced to. On Dretske's view, an account of the historical process of "acquiring the requisite extrinsic relations" explains *why* structure types (As) cause their associated Bs. This is fine, even if he slights some perfectly good varieties of historical process. But, to quote Dretske's earlier remark: "Meaning, on this view of things, has to do with the etiology of a structure type, with how (and perhaps why) it was developed to service an organism's needs." (ms, p. 7). Dretske ends up showing how, even if meaning cannot be locally potent, it can be put into reliable pre-established harmony with locally potent structures.

So I think Dretske and I end up, if not yet in perfect harmony, at least in possession of all the same themes with which to explain how – and to what extent – meanings can be cited in the explanation of events.

Postscript

So matters seemed to me until Dretske's Postscript arrived, recanting his endorsement of natural selection (or more fairly, denying that he had ever meant to endorse natural selection as a Way to Harmony). He gives this account of the difference between a learning history and a selection history:

> Natural selection gives us something quite different: reflex, instinct, tropisms, fixed-action-patterns, and other forms of involuntary behavior – behavior that is (typically) *not* explained in terms of the actor's beliefs and desires (if any). These genetically determined patterns of behavior often involve (as triggers for response) internal indicators (information-carrying elements), but, unlike, belief, it isn't *their* content that explains the way they affect output. That is determined by the genes.

What exactly is the contrast?

> In order to get meaning itself (and not just the structures that have meaning) to play an important role in the explanation of an *individual's* behavior (as beliefs and desires do) one has to look at the meaning that was instrumental in shaping the behavior that is being explained. This occurs only during individual learning. Only then is the meaning of the structure type (the fact that it indicates so-and-so about the animal's surroundings) responsible for its recruitment as a control element in the production of appropriate action.

The only difference I can discern, however, is that the "structure type" in the case of natural selection is a type that is identified in the genotype, while the structure type in the case of intra-cerebral evolution is a type that is identified only in the phenotype. In both cases "meaning was instrumental in shaping the behavior" – that is, in shaping the behavior-*type*, and in neither case was meaning instrumental in shaping any particular, individual token of a behavioral type.

Let us compare the particular case Dretske describes – his shooing of the fly – with a near neighbor produced, presumably, by an evolutionary history rather than a learning history – the shooing of a fly by a horse swishing its tail. Whatever the actual facts about such cases, let us stipulate that Dretske's arm-swing is a genuine *action*, for the reasons he gives, and that the horse's superficially similar tail-swing is a mere reflex, genetically programmed.

The horse's tail-swing belongs to a type which is designed to be provoked or caused by various other internal types, normally produced by flies buzzing around its rump; if these mediating types hadn't meant what they have meant over evolutionary history, the horse wouldn't be wired up to caused by them now to issue one of the tail-swing type behaviors. But of course, right now, given the way nature has set up the horse's wiring, a particular event of one of these mediating types *however it in particular is caused, and regardless of what, if anything, it in particular means*, will cause a tail-swing. That's the way it is with reflexes: no locally potent meaning.

Is there a contrast, however, in the case of Dretske's shooing action? In virtue of his individual learning history, he has come to acquire various beliefs and desires, among them the belief that when he sees or feels something roughly *like that*, it is apt to be a fly or bug or something in need of shooing, and a desire to shoo whatever needs shooing. Such belief–desire pairs, when provoked by particular circumstances, are designed to cause the formation of shooing intentions which forthwith get executed. (The particulars of this rough-and-ready account of beliefs, desires and intentions is not meant to bear any weight; I assume that Dretske has some such scheme in mind, and I mean to address what must be true of any such scheme.)

Now let us look at a particular case: at time t the fly buzzes and at $t + \delta$ Dretske shoos. What has happened during δ? The fly causes a mediating perceptual event p, which causes the mediating belief-state b, which, along with desire-state d, causes the intention i, which causes Dretske's arm to move – something like that. In short, a lot of internal events happen, and all together they amount to his coming to think a fly is buzzing and then deciding to take some action, viz., shooing. And in fact, given his learning history, all these mediating events and states mean what they ought to mean and cause what they ought to cause, but *had any particular component been "wild"* the sequence would have occurred just the same; that's the way it is with actions: no locally potent meanings. Now Dretske says, in the postscript quoted above, that "one has to look at the meaning that was instrumental in shaping the behavior that is being explained," but no meaning was "instrumental" in shaping *this particular action*; it would have happened just as it happened, no matter what each element occurring during δ meant or failed to mean. We do have room to advert to meanings if what we want to explain is how it comes to be that events of these (structural) types cause a behavior of this (structural) type at time $t + \delta$. But that is also what we do when we account for the etiological ancestry of reflexes. It is not that there is no difference at all between a reflex and an action. Of course there is. But it does not lie in the domain that Drestske explores.

Notes

1 This paper is an elaboration of my reply to Dretske at the SOFIA conference on information-based semantics at Tepoztlan, Mexico, August, 1988. The proceedings of that conference are published by Basil Blackwell in *Information, Semantics and Epistemology* (1990) edited by Eurique Villanueva. Dretske composed a postscript to his paper, published in that volume, responding to the objections I had raised in Tepoztlan, and the present paper responds in turn to that postscript.

2 It is interesting that here Dretske announces his allegiance to the same goal that motivates Fodor – the vindication of folk psychology taken neat – while dismissing Fodor's own solution as insufficiently responding to the folk-psychological intuition that (the Formality Condition be damned) *meanings make it happen.*

3 As Dretske's postscript makes clear, he did not intend to endorse natural selection in the paper under discussion. See the discussion of this postscript below.

4 See, for instance, my discussion (in "Mechanism and Responsibility," in *Essays on Freedom of Action* (London: Routledge and Kegan Paul, 1973), ed. T. Honderich, of the parallel case of the bogus belief (that he has an older brother living in Cleveland) surgically inserted into Tom (in *Brainstorms*, pp. 251–3); the discussion of the Panamanian debut of the two-bitser (how long does it take for the new functions to be "real"?); and my reply to Goldman, forthcoming in *Behavioral and Brain Sciences*.

References

Dennett, D. 1969: *Content and Consciousness*. London: Routledge and Kegan Paul.

—— 1971: Intentional Systems. *Journal of philosophy*, 8 (1971), pp. 8–106.

—— 1975: Why the Law of Effect Will Not Go Away. *Journal of the Theory of Social Behavior*, 5, pp. 169–87.

—— 1978: *Brainstorms*. Cambridge, Mass: MIT Press/Bradford Books.

—— 1981: The Kinds of Intentional Psychology. In *Reduction, Time and Reality*, ed. R. Healey, Cambridge, Cambridge University Press.

—— 1983: Intentional System in Cognitive Ethology: the Panglossian Paradigm Defended. *Behavioral and Brain Sciences*, 6, pp. 34–90.

—— 1986. The Logical Geography of Computational Approaches: A View from the East Pole. In *Representation of Knowledge and Belief*, ed. M. Harnish M. Brand, University of Arizona Press.

—— 1987: *The Intentional Stance*. Cambridge: MIT Press/ Bradford Book.

—— 1988a: When Philosophers Encounter Artificial Intelligence. *Daedalus*, winter (issue on Artificial Intelligence), pp. 283–95.

—— 1988b: Précis of *The Intentional Stance*. *Behavioral and Brain Sciences*, 11, pp. 493–544.

Dretske, F. 1981: *Knowledge and the Flow of Information*. Cambridge, Mass.: MIT Press/Bradford Book

—— 1985: Machines and the Mental. *Proceedings and Addreses of the American Philosophical Association*, 59 (1985), pp. 23–33.

—— 1986: Misrepresentation. In *Belief*, ed. R. Bogdan Oxford, Oxford, University Press.

Edelman, G. 1988 *Neural Darwinism*. New York: Basic Books.

Haugeland, J. 1985 *Artificial Intelligence: The Very Idea*. Cambridge, Mass.: MIT Press/Bradford Books.

Schiffer, S. 1987: *Remnants of Meaning*. Cambridge, Mass MIT Press/ Bradford Books.

Waltz, D. 1988: The Prospects for Building Truly Intelligent Machines *Deadalus* winter (issue on artificial intelligence), pp. 191–212.

8
Causal Contents

Frederick Adams

Cognitive Content: What Good Is It?

If purposive systems (creatures) possess mental states with cognitive content (concepts, beliefs, desires), but its possession is causally impotent, then content is a quite useless extravagance of a type that nature ought not to tolerate, much less proliferate. Clearly, if *we* succeed in building artificially intelligent systems, causationless content is something that we should *leave out!*[1] Even if *nature* does not abhor extravagances of this type, it is a mystery *why* she would cough up something so decadent as causationless content (systems that possess it).

I suspect that, in part, this is why Dennett delights in suggesting that there really is *none* – at least not outside the intentional stance. Dennett, like Spinoza, thinks there is no objective teleology – nothing happens literally *for a reason*, it only appears that way "from the intentional stance."[2] But, if one pursues this line, the smoke does not clear. Why would nature allow the *appearance* of content *within* the intentional stance? Either there really *is* content *in the stance itself* – the original mystery – or there really is *no* content, not even *in* the intentional stance – which is completely hopeless. What is one doing in taking a *contentless* stance and why would nature allow it? Choose your mystery. If there *is* content what good is it? If there is *no content*, of what does the intentional stance consist?

Surely, there could be *information* (natural content or meaning) in intelligent systems, even if *it* caused nothing. Information comes into existence solely as a result of causal and/or objective probability relations between events. Metal expansion carries information about increased temperature. Barometer-needle movements (when working properly) carry information about atmospheric pressure changes; and so on. But it need not be *the information* (an event's carrying it) that causes anything in such cases.[3] The information carried by events may well *supervene* on *physical properties* of the events that do *all of the causal work*. The *expansion* of the metal may cause things, not the information it carries about temperature change. The pointer *movement* on the barometer may cause things, independently of the fact that its movement carries information about a fall in atmospheric pressure. The same may hold for mental events of intelligent systems.

But cognitive content (the possession of it) is *more than* mere information.[4] It is information that has been encoded and readied for important cognitive roles: such as believing that the enemy is attacking, or believing that this (plant) is edible. The cognitive content of states like these *seems* to have a job to do in the behavioral *guidance* and *success* of purposive systems. If, as some believe, the possession of content by such states has *no* causal role to play, then it is an utter *mystery* why nature tolerates and promotes such extravagance. Why endow any organism with the capacity to acquire information and *process it* to a degree of detail sufficient to generate *propositional attitudes*, if there is no work to be done *by the content* (possession) once an attitude is formed? It is *that* kind of extravagance that we try to weed out of our bureaucracies. Why should nature be any different? My bet is that she is not different – and I think that is Dretske's bet too. There must be a job for content to do or it is too unlikely that there would be cognitive content at all. Nature is just *not that extravagant*.

What job is there for content? Dretske's answer[5] is simple, traditional, and quite conservative (by historical standards) – although his view has come to be considered "radical" in some circles. The job of cognitive content in nature is *to cause purposive behavior* – behavior that literally is goal-directed.

Perhaps I should say the job is to cause behavior purposively. For one and the same type of behavior may be tokened purposively in one system and nonpurposively in another (or in the same system at a different time). My dropping of the kerchief may be accidental on one occasion, and the signal to start the festivities on another. But when it is not accidental, it is the job of content to appropriately cause it. *That* is what content is *for* – to make it *possible* for behavior to be purposively caused and, thereby, *successful*.

The job of content in a *science* of purposive behavior is to *causally explain* that behavior – when nondeviantly caused. If there were no purposive behavior to explain, it is unlikely that there would be a job for a science like *cognitive* psychology. In principle, any bodily movement or effect E that is caused by an internal cause C (or set of causes D) devoid of cognitive content, should be able to be explained entirely by physics, chemistry, neurophysiology, or some combination of these – *minus cognitive* psychology. Furthermore, in principle, there should be no need to describe E in the language of the intentional idiom. God could explain E, in all its glory, without appeal to content.

Intelligent, purposive behavior, on the other hand, is *etiologically dependent upon intelligent, purposive causes*. Within an individual system S, no behavior E can be done *on purpose* and emanate from a meaningless cause C (or set of causes D) – causes without content or of content that is causally inert. Furthermore, intelligent, purposive behavior can only be described (nonmetaphorically,) in a way that captures its distinctness form nongoal-directed behavior, by using intentional terms. And, importantly, behavior purposely caused can only be truly (nonmetaphorically) *explained* by appeal to its contentful causes. In S, if E is an effect of an internal state C (or set of states D) that has cognitive content, and if E is such that it is sensitive to the content of C (or D), then E will not be causally explainable *without* appeal to the content of C (D). Even God could not adequately explain E without appeal to the content of C (D).

Caterpillars do not purposively crawl towards the light unless something inside means or indicates *light*. Cats do not stalk mice unless something in the cat means (refers to, is about) *mice*. People do not vote for presidents unless something inside means president *and* they have the goal of voting for one. Contentful states are necessary, even if not sufficient, to cause purposive behavior.

Of course, purposive behavior can be *simulated* by things that cause bodily limbs to move in ways that are, perhaps, physiologically and geometrically indistinguishable from purposive activities. But that does not mean that a robot caterpillar *crawls in order to get to the light*, nor that a robot cat is *stalking mice*, nor that a remote controlled robot "voter" *votes* for president. Merely going through motions physically indistinguishable from those of a system exhibiting genuinely purposive behavior is not sufficient for purposively behaving. There must be purpose in the cause of behavior for there to be purpose in its expression – in the behaving. The only way to get purpose in the behaving is to put purpose in the causing. And *that* takes cognitive content – reasons, beliefs, and desires, or internal states that are to some degree *contentful*.[6] Furthermore, the only way to *explain* the purpose expressed in the behavior of a goal-directed system is by reference to the purpose (contentful states) in its causes. This, then, is the job of cognitive content – to cause (and causally explain) genuinely goal-directed behavior.

Dretske's Theory of Content (Naturalized)

Dretske's program for explaining content comprises an interlocking puzzle with three key pieces.[7] They include: (1) tracing cognitive content to its etiological origins in *information content* (in the environment and perceptual systems of the organism); (2) the transformation of information content, perceptually acquired, into *cognitive* (semantic) *content* – encoded in a form that is capable of being harnessed to beliefs and desires; and (3) the *causation* of behavior *by* the cognitive *content* of mental states (their possession of it).

Pieces (1) and (2) have been well-worked in the literature.[8] I plan to say little about them. *Information* is the crucial element of piece (1). Dretske develops a technical sense of information content, based on the mathematical theory of communication. This provides an objective sense in which information exists independently of the mind of an interpreter or stance. The project for naturalizing content requires a naturalistic base. If minds acquire content as a result of being placed in certain environmental contexts, then there must *be something* to be acquired, some content to be picked up. Natural causal relations between events (probability relations between them, on communication theory) generate information that is available to a system with the tools to extract it. Dretske designates "information" as the *thing* that systems pick up, *the basic ingredient* that goes into the making of a contentful mind.[9]

The "flow" of information is along the following path, according to Dretske: Information $\longrightarrow$ Perception $\longrightarrow$ Cognition (or Concept Formation). Information exists objectively in each stage (not stance-dependent) and its existence in the former stages does not depend on the existence of the latter stages.[10] Very crudely, the story is as follows. A subject S may acquire a *primitive empirical concept* of an F (being F) – where primitive means that S's concept of an F does not have further concepts as parts. S will acquire this concept of an F only by coming into perceptual contact with Fs. (Let a = a ball, F = being red – under white light, and S = a child learning the concept of red).

Now, suppose object a acquires the property of being F. This generates information (a could have been G or W, etc.) that is now available in the local environment. Suppose further, that the wavelength of light reflected from a is such that it is nomically dependent, under the locally stable conditions, upon a's being F. The light contains (carries) the information that a is F and S's visual system receives the light. Since S's perceptual episodes are nomically dependent, under the locally stable conditions of the environment, upon a's being F, S's perceptual episodes contain (carry) the information that a is F. If this happens long enough or if S encounters enough F-things (under these conditions), and S has the requisite cognitive capacities, S will be able to form a concept of F-things. The point is that, if S is to form the concept of an F (something's being F), its content must come *from somewhere*. Dretske wants to trace the content to the environment and the information about Fs that exists there independently of minds or stances. (That is the rough idea. From this point forward the *fine details* of building up empirical knowledge from primitive concepts go in familiar ways.)

Many people, wrongly in my view, have taken Dretske to task for allowing his *epistemology* to influence his views of content. But, without a firm understanding of his theory of knowledge, one will find it difficult to appreciate fully Dretske's theory of content. I have come not only to appreciate his epistemology, but to think that, basically, it is *right*.[11] The epistemic influence is revealed by an example. Dretske holds that one cannot know that p unless one's belief that p is caused (or sustained) by the information that p.[12] Colleen cannot know that Chimega is a Doberman unless Colleen receives the information that Chimega is a Doberman. But, for Colleen to receive this information, some event (signal, percept) must carry the information that Chimega is a Doberman. For Dretske, this means some event(s) e must be such that the objective probability that Chimega is a Doberman, given e (+ a stable communication channel), is one (unity).

Some critics think that, in principle, there could be no event(s), like e. The world is simply not that stable – not even locally. Dretske's reply *is* and *should be* that *if* the critics are right, then Colleen does not, and could not, know that Chimega is a Doberman (even though she has lived with the family pet for the past six years). His theory says that *in order to know that p*, one must have the "right stuff" (= *information that p*). It does not say that anyone *has* the "right stuff." If the world is not stable enough to give us knowlege that p, because no events carry the information that p, Dretske's epistemology need not be at fault.

This is thought to *infect* Dretske's theory of content because, if no event carries the information that Chimega (or any other dog) is a Doberman, then no one can form the *concept* of a Doberman. For example, if no environment is such that only Dobermans would cause Doberman-percepts in it, then no Doberman-percept is uniquely a *Doberman-percept*. It is a *Doberman-or-whatever-else-percept* (whatever else would cause the percept). The best information that anyone's perceptual experience could convey is *disjunctive* information. *All* empirical concepts, depending as they do upon perceptual episodes, would be disjunctive.

Hence, we face the familiar "disjunction problem."[13] Most see it as a problem for Dretske's second piece of the puzzle of content and some (Fodor) for the third. But, if it is a problem, it must start at the *first* piece of the puzzle. However, we should not be anxious to see it begin here, for it may fuel skepticism. At any rate, although Dretske offers a solution,[14] I shall not consider it fully now (I return to it below). Presently, we are interested in how content can have causal powers and even if all concepts were, by nature, disjunctive, that would not mean that they could not cause things in virtue of their possessing (disjunctive) content. Furthermore, it is an empirical question whether an environment is locally stable enough to yield nondisjunctive information. It is also an empirical question whether purposive systems can transform disjunctive information into nondisjunctive concepts (but this takes us beyond puzzle piece (1)).

Piece (2) of Dretske's theory is an attempt to explain how information content must be changed or modified to be transformed into cognitive (conceptual or semantic) content. Two tasks characterize this piece:[15] (a) explain how cognitive structures can acquire a more or less *unique* or *exclusive* content, and (b) explain how cognitive structures, given a unique content, can *misrepresent*. These are actually two sides of a single coin. An event that carries the information that p cannot possess *false* information that p – or it would *not carry* the information *that p*. And an event that carries the information *that p* may also carry the information *that q*, for the reason that p nomically, logically, or analytically entails q. However, cognitive systems, like Pam, can believe that a is F without believing that a is G even if there is a physical law that correlates being F with being G. Pam can also *falsely* believe that p. These are features that systems comprised solely of noncognitive events (states) do not have. If beliefs that p are built from the information that p they must undergo an important cognitive transformation from the *information that p* (transparent context/no misrepresentation possible) to the *belief that p* (opaque context/misrepresentation possible). Thus, piece (2) is an attempt, to describes the transition from the information content of an event, signal, or structure, to the cognitive (semantic) content of an event, state or structure (like belief or desire).[16]

Dretske's official solution to the second piece of the puzzle has taken several turns. The most recent explanation, as previously, turns on the notion of *learning*. It is essential that there be a learning history that determines why an organism's concept has the specific content that it has. The disjunction problem is to be solved by showing that although an organism's internal structure C (its concept of an F) may be triggered by Fs that are also Gs and Hs, it may be only *because* C carries information about Fs (not because it carries it about Gs and Hs) that C causes successful behavior and that, through this specific learning history, the organism, survives. So, although C carries information about Fs, Gs, and Hs, it is only the carrying of information about Fs that explains the role that is *causally sustained* by C in the organism's behavioral profile. Thus, it is the intensionality of the causally explanatory context concerning C's cognitive role that accounts for the specificity of semantic content of C and yields the solution to the disjunction problem. This draws us directly into the third piece of the puzzle.

At piece (3), content has a job to do in the *causal production* and *explanation* of purposive behavior. If a system S does B in order to achieve goal G, then B is goal-directed behavior. Dretske puts this in terms of S's *reasons*. When S's reason for doing B is R (= to achieve G), and S's doing B *causally* depends upon R, a causal *explanation* of S' doing B must include R.

Of course, even this is not sufficient to insure that the *content* of R is doing *work* in the causation or explanation of B by S. A causal explanation of B may include the reason R without regard to the fact that R *is a reason* that *has a content* (is *about G*). For it need not be R's content (R's having content) that enables R to cause B in S. R may cause B solely in virtue of its noncontentful properties (purely neurophysiological properties, say). R's content may be causally *inert*.

In order to show that content (the having of it) is not inert in purposive systems, it is necessary to find a job in S that R's having content does (causes and explains) *in virtue of R's having content*. Then, assuming that the job is causally relevant to the purposiveness of the behavior and is not contrived,[17] the causal potency of R's content in S's doing B will be *secured*. In the explanatory context "S did B because of reason R," the content of R will not be idle.

The job Dretske picks for content is that of *structuring cause* (versus triggering cause). He says that reasons are structuring causes of purposive behavior *in virtue of their content*.[18] (Let C = an internal state, or set of states, that causes bodily movement of type M in system S.) Dretske says that a *triggering* cause is the thing that caused C which caused M *now* (rather than at another time). Whereas, a *structuring cause* is the thing (process) that caused C to cause M (rather than another movement N).[19] However, Dretske also characterizes structuring cause this way: the process that explains why C (rather than some other state or set of them D) causes M.[20]

By my lights, the introduction of structuring causes is Dretske's way of making the point that I made above. There must be purpose (or at least content) in the causes of behavior (behaving), if there is to be purpose (goal-directedness) in the behavior (behaving). A nonpurposive system *S1* may be identical in bodily movement to a purposive system *S2*, but the explanations of *S1*'s and *S2*'s *behaviors* need not be the same. There may be no teleological *why* to be explained with respect to *S1*'s behavior (nor its bodily movements), but there may well be a teleological *why* to be explained concerning *S2*'s behavior. Let *S1* = a nonintelligent robot cat. Let *S2* = a real cat with mental states controlling its behavior. Both may seem to be stalking a mouse. That does not mean that their behavior has the same explanation, not even if the robot cat has a "brain" that has structures that resemble the real cat's brain in physically relevant ways. For there may be nothing in the robot cat that is in any way *about* a mouse (or the catching of one). There will be something in the real cat that *is about this* and that, given its learning history and a desire for a mouse, explains its stalking. Though their bodily movements are identical, their behavioral need not be. It would be stretching things to say that *S1* was "stalking" and it would be nonsense, teleologically, to try to explain why. It would be quite sensible to say *S2* was *stalking*, and would make perfect teleological sense to explain why – in order to attempt to catch a mouse.

How does this translate into talk of structuring versus triggering causes? We need a test for purposiveness in behavior and for content in its causes. Hence, the structuring-cause test. A structuring cause, like a teleological function, causes what it is causing *now*, due to what it caused in the *past*. If I find that my old railroad spike holds papers nicely, I may leave it on my desk to continue to hold papers there because it is efficient at this. Then, its continuing to hold them in the future becomes its acquired function. However, if you simply drop a rock on my desk (equal in size and mass to the spike) and, fortuitously, it holds papers fast on my desk too, it is not necessarily the rock's acquired function to do so (not unless someone continues to use it for this purpose). One of them (spike) continues to hold papers fast because it has acquired the function to do so (a structuring or sustaining cause of the papers staying put). I cause it to cause them to stay put via an artifact-selection process. The other (rock) is a cause of the papers staying put, but not a sustaining or structuring cause of this. A triggering cause, like a fortuitous but nonteleologically functioning item, causes something now, independently of what it caused in the past. Not so for a structuring cause.

Let S be an organism in a locally stable environment (no tricks). Let S's goals (or survival needs) include the need to avoid Fs (predators). If S flees ($M1$) in the presence of Fs, S is likely to survive. If S frolics ($M2$) in the presence of Fs, S is likely to be eaten. Under these conditions, S's fleeing (rather than frolicking) in the presence of Fs is *the thing to do*, and if S does this nonaccidentally, it will constitute goal-directed behavior. But, if fleeing is purposive behavior, there must be purpose in the cause (structuring cause).[21] Now, for S's fleeing in the presence of Fs to be goal-directed (not accidentally fortuitous), something in S must indicate to S that Fs are present. Call that thing C. And let C be what is causally responsible for S's fleeing. Why C? States other than C could, let us suppose, trigger fleeing movements. But the reason why C sustainingly causes fleeing is that C contains information about Fs. That gets S to flee *at the right times* (when Fs are near). And the past successes of C at doing this explain why C (rather than some noncontentful cause D) continues, in S, to cause fleeing in the presence of Fs. It is because C (not D) has *reliably* got S to flee in the presence of Fs in the past. So here we have C's being a structuring cause of $M1$ – both in the sense that C causes $M1$ (not $M2$, etc.) and in the sense that it is C (not some D) that causes $M1$. A *structuring cause*, therefore, is a sustaining cause whose sustained causal role is explained by the fact that its job (teleological function) is fixed by *past success*. In C's case, its successful functioning as an F-detector teleologically explains, given its prior history, its sustainingly causing $M1$ – in contrast to some other structure D's causing $M1$, where D does not indicate anything about Fs. D might cause $M1$, not as a sustaining (structuring) cause, but only as a triggering cause. However, since D contains no information about Fs, S is not likely to *survive* and D is not likely to have the *sustained* role of causing $M1$. Unlike D, C's sustained causing of $M1$ is *explained by* C's being an F-indicator.

The basic idea is that an R-state may cause M (bodily movement). And if all one is interested in is the trigger for M (how R caused M), citing the purely neurophysiological properties of R may do the trick. Yet, if one is interested, not in how M was produced, but in why M rather than some M' was produced (by R), then the purely intrinsic properties of R will *not* do the trick. For, the purely intrinsic properties of R could cause any of an indefinite variety of Ms. That is proved by the fact of neural plasticity. To explain why R caused an instance of this particular type of movement M, we must appeal to R's history (specific learning history). Specifically, in system S in environment E, the fact that R has the content that it does explains why it causes what it does. It is because R indicates F (not F') that it causes M (not M').

As may be clear, Dretske takes a stand on what I shall call the "component" view of behavior. A mental state C is a *component of behavior*, as is the bodily movement it causes. Behavior becomes the *causing* of the bodily movement M by the internal state C, with the result that mental states do not cause behavior. Behavior *is* their causing bodily movement ($B = C$'s *causing* M).

Piece (3) may not depend on the component view. Even on a "product" view of behavior ($B = M$), Dretske's claims about the causal role of content can be made. On the component view, if I shout obscenities for the reason that I do not like Quayle's remark, my behavior (heckling Quayle) *is* my reason's causing my making these sounds. The real job is to explain how a state's having a content can cause anything, especially a bodily movement of the relevant sort (one made purposively). Also, the job of content may be to explain why I did *that* (shout obscenities) rather than something else (applaud). But that would still be the job of content even on the *product* view. Whether we *locate* the behavior *in the causing* of one bodily product or another, or identify the behavior with *the product itself*, the job of content is to explain why we get *one product rather than another*. The answer is that the reason had one content rather than another. So, even if Dretske were wrong about the "component" view of behavior, that alone would not show that there is no causal work for content in the explanation of behavior. I think, in fact, that Dretske may place too much emphasis on the "component" view and not enough on the *contrastive role* that content plays in the explanation of relevant bodily movements. For even on the component view, it is *contrastive explanatory force* that explanation by content requires.

Next, Dretske's model needs to be instantiated. The "design problem" asks how must nature engineer a system such that the content of its R-state becomes a structuring cause of R's causing M? (Reasons are two-factor items, beliefs + desires. To avoid complication, assume that S desires to avoid things that are F.) We shall look at how S's acquiring a belief that something is F will causally explain S's behavior (contrastive bodily movements). Why does S's belief cause one movement rather than another (as structuring cause)?

The solution to the design problem consists of four steps (let $M =$ fleeing, $F =$ predators and $C = S$'s concept of a predator): (1) find (evolve) a system S that is capable of learning and has need and desire to avoid Fs (it now needs only beliefs that Fs are near to have the *goal or reason* to avoid Fs), (2) equip S with an *F-detector* (that can informationally mean that something is F), (3) equip S with the learning capacities to form a concept (cognitive structure) that semantically can come to mean that something is F, and (4) equip the system S with the capacity for its cognitive structure C to cause M in virtue of the fact that C semantically means that something is F. Then C can cause something M because (structuring cause) it means that something is F – because of an internal structure's semantic content.

Step 1 is to find a system *capable of learning*. S's internal states must be capable of being modified by interaction with its environment, and in turn, be capable of modifying S's bodily movement *depending upon* whether the bodily movement succeeds in contributing towards the satisfaction of S's goals.

Step 2 is to get S to do M (have C cause M) reliably in the presence of Fs. To preserve S in a hostile environment filled with Fs, S must be equipped with an F-indicator (*F-detector*). Therefore, some perceptual state of S, C, must be selectively sensitive to the presence or absence of

Fs. But, so far, we have reached only perception, not conception. S's internal state C may carry information about Fs, but it cannot misrepresent. C has information content, not semantic content. C must become S's concept of an F to complete the picture. C must come to mean (semantically, not just informationally) that something is F and, in virtue of meaning that, be able to cause M.

Step 3 is the equivalent of concept formation and alternately is labeled "meaning$_f$" and sometimes "recruitment" for causal role due to (information) indicator capacities. But, whatever it is called, this is the transitional stage from information content to semantic content. Structure C must receive information about Fs. Then, C's causing M will contribute to S's goal of avoiding Fs. That is, C's *continuing to cause* M, when the information that something is F is delivered to C, secures C's *cognitive function*. This means: (a) C is activated by the information that something is F, (b) C, when activated, causes M (not M'), (c) C's causing M (not M') is rewarding for S (contributes to goal-satisfaction) in the sense that C's continuing to cause M in the presence of Fs in the future is causally sustained by the outcome of its causing M in the presence of Fs in the past.[22] Hence, C comes to *mean$_f$* that something is F due to its teleological causal role in S – its feedback sustained causing in the presence of Fs, if you will.[23]

C semantically means (or means$_f$) something is an F, not just informationally means this, since: (1) C can be falsely tokened, and (2) although the information that something is F upon which C was formed may contain, nested within it, information that something is G or H, this need not be what C means.[24] C can be activated by something other than the information that something is an F – C can be wildly (falsely) tokened. So, when wildly tokened, C does not carry the information that something is and F. Still, the wild tokening does not *rob* C of its ability to (nondisjunctively) mean semantically that something is an F, because C's teleological function historically depends upon its ability to cause M when in the presence of Fs (not Gs, Hs, etc.). Basically, if it were not for C's ability to be activated by information about Fs, and, when doing so, cause M, S would not still be around and C would not still be causing M (as opposed to M'). Failure to avoid Fs would have led to S's demise.

Step 4 is that even though C can be wildly tokened and even though when nonwildly tokened by the information that F there may be more information nested within, it is C's sensitivity to Fs *alone that explains C's sustained causal role* of causing M (not M') in S (due to S's learning history). Thus, C's cognitive (semantic) content is causally responsible for its causing M.

What's Not To Like?

Intrinsic intentionality: Dennett thinks that Dretske, Searle, and Fodor, have gone off the deep end in claiming that the content (intentionality) of mental states must be "intrinsic" or "original" and not derived or extrinsic. He thinks that they *need* to say this to be realists about content, but that the very idea is wrongheaded. I shall not enter into the fray between content realists and instrumentalists, but I think that Dennett misrepresents the upshot of Dretske's support of intrinsic intentionality.

By "intrinsic intentionality" Drestske means simply intentionality (or meaning) that is not derived or stance-dependent. If something gets a meaning or content from the stance or interpretation we take toward it, then its content depends on us (on *our content*). But upon what does our content depend? The buck stops with us.

One might think that saying there is intrinsic intentionality is like saying that the brain *secretes* meanings. However brains acquire their intrinsic intentional contents, computers or robots never could acquire them, no matter how complex *they* become. Searle holds the latter view (and is sometimes, perhaps falsely, thought to hold the former). Dretske clearly holds neither. He is on record[25] as holding that it is possible, as far as we know, to create thinking machines. If we did create them, they *would* possess intrinsic intentionality. For if they did not, they would not really be *thinking* machines. At best they would simulate thinking – simulate having internal states which cause things in virtue of their (underived) semantic contents.[26]

One might also think that to say there is intrinsic intentionality means that nothing extrinsic (outside the skin of the system), can causally explain the origin of that intentionality. This too is clearly *not* Dretske's view. An organism must causally interact with its environment and be capable of modifying its behavior, based on *learning*, for it to acquire intrinsic intentionality (genuine meaning). *S* only acquires an internal state that *means F*, if that internal state is capable of indicating *F*s in its natural environment, and if that internal state was recruited (through *S*'s learning history) to have the *function* of being an *F*-detector by being a structuring cause of behavior appropriate for *S* in the presence of *F*s. Intrinsic intentionality is clearly *causally* derived from outside causes (*F*, the environment, learning mechanisms). It is just not *semantically* derived from outside meanings. The internal state means *F* due to its causal origins, not due to someone (or something) else *intending* for it to mean *F*.

Dennett seems to blur the causal/semantic derivation distinction. For he seems to say that, if a system derives its intentionality through a causal process like natural selection, then its intentionality is derived and unmasked as a sham – not really intrinsic intentionality at all. Of course, it is hard to tell if Dennett really means this. In his scheme of things, to talk about "selection" is already "intentionally loaded."[27] But surely, if selection-talk were *true*, that would not show that a state of *S* selected for its ability to indicate *F* has semantically derived intentionality.

Dennett's only hope of showing that there is semantically derived intentionality, by this line of attack, would be to show that the forces of selection are *themselves* semantically intentional. He would have to show that natural selection was itself a process that had a mind (purposes) – the "real intrinsic intentionality." Our intentionality would be unmasked as a mere artifact of Mother Nature's. But even Dennett does not think that Mother Nature has a mind. How could the semantic content of our minds (our intentionality) derive from the semantic content of hers? Clearly, it could not. Therefore, natural selection (or processes like it) could not rob us of intrinsic intentionality.[28]

Of course, Dennett does point out that forces in selection can be described in ways that generate "intensional" contexts. Selection for an X which is F is not necessarily selection for an X which is G even if X is both F and G (nomically). But since intensionality-with-an-s is not sufficient for intentionality-with-a-t, this does not show that anything that counts as aboutness, meaning, or content is going on in natural selection. Thus, he has not unmasked our intentionality as a "fake" or "imposter" merely because something like the forces of selection (viz., learning) may be involved in its causal origins.

Lastly, perhaps Dennett is saying that no statements about selection-like forces are true. That is, Dretske's theory of content involves, essentially, appeals to teleological functions of certain content-bearing states (states with the cognitive function of being F-indicators, etc.). Dretske maintains that an organism's learning history can, at least sometimes, determine that being an F-indicator is a state's acquired cognitive function. But Dennett points out that this can be true only if there can be such a thing as a structure's natural cognitive function. Dennett thinks (or seems to) that there cannot be teleological cognitive functions.[29] For "teleological function" talk is a part of the intentional stance. Statements about functions, or the selection which determines them, are metaphorical, and instrumental, according to Dennett. So, if anyone's account of intrinsic intentionality rests upon their being true, it is doomed to failure from the start.

If he means this, and it surely seems that he does, then if teleological accounts of intrinsic intentionality are the "only games in town" and they all fail, the clear result is that there is no content. But then there is no content even in the intentional stance. "No intrinsic intentionality" means none at all. If we are products of nature and nature cannot cough up systems that have content (intrinsic content), then nothing we can do, including taking the intentional stance, can yield content. Surely Dennett does not mean this. Right? And if he does, what should one say next?

Even if Dennett believes that the analysis of teleological functions (cognitive or otherwise) is hopelessly indeterminate, are his reasons good ones? I think not. He quotes Sober,[30] with approval, on whether to call the first dorsal fins to appear on Stegosaurus an adaptation for cooling. Sober says:

> Suppose the animal had the trait because of a mutation, rather than
> by selection. Can we say that the trait was an adaptation in the case

of that single organism? Here are some options: (1) apply the concept of adaptation to historically persisting populations, not single organisms; (2) allow that dorsal fins were an adaptation for the original organism because of what happened later; (3) deny that dorsal fins are adaptations for the initial organism but are adaptations when they occur in subsequent organisms. My inclination is to prefer choice 3. (*The Nature of Selection*, p. 197)

Dennett seems to conflate something's *having* a natural teleological function with our *saying* or *learning* what that function is. First, the fact that there is controversy over how to analyze natural functions, in general (or the function of the first dorsal fins, specifically), does not show that there is no fact of the matter. Nor would any case(s) like it show this. Second, Sober chooses (3) for a good reason. It seems the most likely to be *true*. There are quite good theories analyzing natural functions that explain why it is most likely to be true.[31] Third, Dretske discusses exactly this type of controversy surrounding intrinsic intentionality and with the same type of preference as Sober. That is, the very first instance in which an *F*-indicator causes a bodily movement that leads to satisfaction of an organism's need, does not count as a case in which the *F*-indicator state *means* (has the semantic content) that something is *F*. It has not yet acquired this cognitive function via learning. To acquire the function via learning is to have a causal dependency set up such that it is because the state is of the type that is an *F*-indicator that the state *continues* to cause bodily movements of the appropriate sort.[32] The point is that there are quite good accounts of learning, and natural functions, that make perfectly good sense of Dretske's use of the teleology involved in learning. They make attributions of function neither purely instrumental nor hopelessly indeterminate, despite Dennett's pessimism. Dennett clearly has not given us good reason to believe none of these theories could be correct, nor reason to believe that Dretske's project to naturalize content is incorrect.

Epiphobia: Some may object to Dretske's theory on the ground that the content of mental states is epiphenomenal. Although mental states may have it, having it does not really cause anything.

Dennett does not think there really is content – so, he is not exactly epiphobic. But he does think that talk of content is ultimately eliminable. He thinks that all intentional-stance talk is eliminable in favor of descriptions which are not "intensional." If we knew enough, we could describe the events we are interested in explaining in terms that are not intentionally loaded with content-talk, function-talk, selection-talk, or any other sort of teleology-infested language. The things to be explained would not, newly described, create "intensional" contexts, and we would not need explanations of them that made use of "intentional" terms. This is all vintage Dennett.[33]

However, Dretske's theory holds that the job of content (in causing and explaining behavior) is one that *nothing else could do* no matter how much more we knew. Even God would need to refer to *it* to explain our behavior's purposiveness – *when it is purposive*. So Dennett's claim that we only appeal to content in the face of human ignorance or out of convenience (even if partially true now), cannot show that, when science is done, we won't need it to explain the things we now use it to explain. Knowing all the neurophysiology in the world will not explain (teleologically) *why S* did *B* (not *B'*). Only a *reason R* can do that.

Causal powers: Fodor claims not to be epiphobic about content, but constructs the causal powers[34] argument that is designed to show that wide-content will drop out of a scientific psychology. Fodor's complaint is that the property of *having content* (at least, wide-content) is not the kind of property that can do causal work – a relational, non-natural kind property that is scientifically ill-behaved. If a content psychology is to be salvaged, Fodor is in favor of saving it via narrow content (not wide). I think that this cannot work. If content refers outside the head *at all* (as narrow content must, in order to be more than mere causal role), then any differences in the difficulties facing wide versus narrow content are a matter of degree, not of kind. At any rate, the differences between Dretske and Fodor can be couched in terms of wide-content alone.

Fodor utilizes an instructive and simple example in his causal powers argument. For simplicity, I shall borrow it. Suppose Jerry says "Bring water" on Earth and Twin-Jerry says "Bring water" on Twin-Earth. Fodor and Dretske agree that the contents of the utterances are *different*. They also agree that the contents of the utterances (what they mean) do not *supervene* on the physical properties of the sounds (as, say, registered in formant structure of acoustic wave forms from their lips). However, Dretske and Fodor disagree about whether differences in *wide-content* can make a causal difference. Fodor says it cannot, for the reason that the *causal powers* of Jerry's utterance are exactly the same as the causal powers of Twin-Jerry's utterance. And the only way the difference in content could be reflected in the instantiations, is if there were some difference in formant structure – which there is not (by hypothesis). How else *could* content of an utterance cause something, but by virtue of its physical instantiation's causing something? There is no other way. So, with no difference in physical instantiations, there cannot be a difference in causal powers of Jerry's and Twin-Jerry's utterances, even if there is a difference in the wide-contents of their utterances.

Furthermore, Fodor thinks that identity of causal powers must be assessed *across* contexts, not *within* contexts. So, it will not help to point out that, on Earth, Jerry's utterance causes H_2O to appear, while Twin-Jerry's utterance causes XYZ to appear. For, on Earth, Twin-Jerry's utterance would cause H_2O to appear and, on Twin-Earth, Jerry's utterance would cause XYZ to appear. How could they cause anything else? How can the difference in content show up? It can't. Since these utterances have different wide-content, but they have the same causal powers in all contexts, their differences in wide-content must drop out. Or, so Fodor has said. Thus, how could wide-content be causally relevant for psychology?

If we look closely, I think Dretske has an answer. (Let $\longleftarrow$ = a wide-content meaning relation, and let $\longrightarrow$ = a causal relation.)

	Earth	Twin-Earth
Step 1	"BW" $\longrightarrow$ H_2O appears	"BW" $\longrightarrow$ XYZ appears
Step 2	H_2O $\longleftarrow$ "BW" $\longrightarrow$ H_2O appears	XYZ $\longleftarrow$ "BW" $\longrightarrow$ XYZ appears
Step 3	XYZ $\longleftarrow$ "BW" $\longrightarrow$ H_2O appears	H_2O $\longleftarrow$ "BW" $\longrightarrow$ XYZ appears

Step 1: Surely Fodor is right that "Bring water" ("BW") has the same causal powers across contexts. If Jerry were to utter "BW" on Twin-Earth (step 3), it would have the same causal result (XYZ would appear) as if Twin-Jerry uttered "BW" on Twin-Earth. And if Twin-Jerry (step 3) were to produce "BW" on Earth, it would have the same causal result (H_2O would appear) as if Jerry (step 2) had produced "BW" on Earth. (By hypothesis, people will hear the utterance, want and be able to comply with the request, etc.)

Step 2: Surely Dretske is right that *something* must *explain* the fact that Jerry's utterance of "BW" on Earth results in H_2O's appearance (not a martini's) and the fact that Twin-Jerry's utterance of "BW" on Twin-Earth results in XYZ's appearance (not a Twin-martini's). Dretske's explanation is that Jerry's utterance of "BW" *means* bring H_2O and that Twin-Jerry's utterance of "BW" *means* bring XYZ.

Step 3: Fodor will not be impressed. For, at step 1 we agreed that we could bring Twin-Jerry to Earth have him utter "BW." If we do, H_2O will appear (not XYZ). So, Fodor would maintain that the causal powers of the respective utterances are still the same – despite differences in wide-content. He takes this to show that, if the wide-contents of two states differ, though their causal powers are the same across contexts, then their difference in wide-content does not make a causal (or explanatory) difference. It is a difference that can do no work. But this is *false* for two reasons: (1) differences in wide-content might causally *explain why* the causal powers of different instantiations of contents are the *same* across contexts, and (2) we can only expect differences in contents to result in differences in causal powers when the two states are themselves relativized to the *same context* (not when we switch contexts).

First, when we bring Twin-Jerry to Earth and have him utter "BW," what explains or accounts for the fact that his tokening of "BW" has the causal power to make H_2O appear? Surely something must explain this? The explanation cannot fall straight out of the formant structure (solely physical properties) of the utterance. For it is a historical accident that this physical type of token came to mean H_2O. Given a different history, it could have meant something different.

Second, that Twin-Jerry's tokening "BW" *means* bring *XYZ* cannot itself explain the appearance of H_2O. Fodor is right about that. "BW" from Twin-Jerry's lips means something than "BW" from Jerry's lips. Still, they *both* have the same causal powers on *Earth* – both cause H_2O to appear there.

Third, it does *not* follow that wide content is not causally explanatory of H_2O's appearance (on Earth). For now Twin-Jerry is in a context where utterances of "BW" typically mean bring H_2O. It is *this fact* about the wide-content (meaning) of typical tokenings of "BW" on Earth that, in part, causally explains H_2O's appearance (plus things in the background that we are holding fixed – e.g., people hear Twin-Jerry clearly, want to be helpful, and so on.) It is because (on Earth) "BW" typically means being H_2O that H_2O shows up when Twin-Jerry utters "BW." If one looks at the XYZ ⟵ "BW" relation to explain why H_2O appears, *of course* it will seem that wide-content is causally impotent. But that is because one would be looking in the *wrong* place.[35] One must look at the H20 ⟵ "BW" meaning relation to see that wide-content does causally explain why Twin-Jerry's tokening of "BW" causes H_2O to appear. (A corresponding story exists, *mutatis mutandis*, for the cases where Jerry goes to Twin-Earth and tokens "BW" which is followed by the appearance of XYZ.)

Dretske's theory of content is built on the premise that one will *not* find the causal efficacy of content if one looks only *inside* the head of an organism. The theory is non-individualistic to the core. Dretske's theory helps us see that it is *only* in a world where tokens of "BW" typically mean to bring H_2O that it would be likely for Twin-Jerry's tokening of "BW" to cause H_2O to show up. (I trust there is no overwhelming difference between a mental tokening of the thought to bring water and a public tokening of "BW." We could easily imagine a drink-fetching machine wired to Twin-Jerry's brain that reads the thought token "BW" and causes H_2O's appearance). So, contrary to Fodor's supposition, wide-content *does* contribute causally to the explanation of this effect of TwinJerry's utterance.

The general lesson is this: If we relativize content to a context, as we must to fix wide-content, then it *may* be *true* that mental states with different contents will be mirrored by differences in the brain. Colleen's belief that Chimega is a dog is different in content than her belief that Chimega is a cat. And, for Colleen change her mind, go from believing that Chimega is a dog to believing that Chimega is a cat, *would* result in a change in Colleen's brain. This is true within a fixed environmental context. And Dretske tells us why it is true. For Colleen to acquire a mental concept that has *dog* as its semantic content requires that it be formed on information about dogs. The state acquires its cognitive function by causing (with some plasticity) bodily movements of a type appropriate to the presence of dogs. That is, there was a "design problem" such that there was some purpose in being able to recognize and respond to dogs (even if only to learn to recognize them). For

Colleen's mental states to have solved that problem required an information story and a causal story with respect to appropriate behavior (maybe she utters "dog" when shown dogs). The point is that there will be a different design problem for dogs (acquiring the concept of them) than for cats (acquiring the concept of them). Causes and effects will be different and be reflected in the internal workings of Colleen's brain. A change will occur with each concept acquired *within* a single context.

When we look *across* contexts, not within, all bets are off on what we will find. There may be differences in neural states and structure that correspond to differences of (wide-) content. But there may not be differences. Twin-Colleen's brain, when she believes Twin-Chimega is a cat, may be qualitatively identical to Colleen's brain when she believes Chimega is a dog. However, the fact that differences in content may not be reflected by differences in brains, does not show that differences in content are not causally relevant or that content plays no causal role in the explanation of behavior. It shows only that one should *not* look *solely* to *differences in brains* to discover content's causal powers. Colleen's standing in a cognitive relation to Chimega and Twin-Colleen's standing in a cognitive relation to Twin-Chimega may be responsible for Colleen's and Twin-Colleen's brains being causally equipotent.

Of course, our example may not impress individualists. For they may say that "BW" means bring clear, colorless, odorless, liquid (CCOL).[36] Meaning this (narrow content) plus environmental context determines reference. So, "BW" plus the fact that, on Earth, the only CCOL-stuff is H_2O causally explains why H_2O shows up – when it does.

However, this fails to show that content does not figure in the causal explanation of H_2O's appearance. For now the content of "BW" is just *less wide* than if it means bring H_2O (on Earth) and bring XYZ (on Twin Earth). Since "BW" now (narrowly) means bring CCOL, the meaning of the utterance extends *widely enough* to be about stuff that has properties of being cool, clear, odorless, and liquid. Wide versus narrow, here, is a difference of degree, not of kind. Having the content "bring CCOL" is not an intrinsic property of the utterance, but as much a relational property as meaning "bring H_2O." Now when Jerry's (or Twin-Jerry's) utterance of "BW" results in H_2O's appearance, it is still the fact that on Earth (or Twin-Earth) "BW" means *bring CCOL* that *causes* CCOL to show up. The remainder of the story may be that the property of being CCOL is co-extensive with H_2O on Earth. If we are forced to move the content back, from H_2O to surface properties like *CCOL*, there will still be a causal story to tell that involves content – a story not eliminable from the explanation of the *utterance's causal powers*.

Dretske, himself, may respond to Fodor differently. He realizes that Fodor will say: (let "same" = qualitatively identical) same brains, same causal powers. Same causal powers, same bodily movements. Same bodily movements, same behaviors. So, same brains, same behaviors. If there are two mental states that have different (wide-) contents, not reflected by differences in their brains, the difference in content must be causally impotent. That kind of difference is not a causal difference and it will not appear in a cognitive *science*.

Dretske may break the chain here: same bodily movements, same behaviors. If S and twin-S have the same brains and their brains cause them to produce the same bodily movements, it does not follow that S and twin-S have produced the same behaviors. This is because he identifies behavior as internal state C's causing bodily movement M. The causing relation may extend well into the environment and beyond S's (or twin-S's) bodily movements. Two qualitatively identical bodily movements may have different environmental effects, thereby constituting *different behaviors*.

This blocks the causal-powers argument because mental states with different contents may cause different *behaviors* even if they cause the same *bodily movements* – in virtue of having been caused by qualitatively identical brains. So, Jerry's brain (when on Earth) causes him to drink H_2O, while Twin-Jerry's brain (when on Twin-Earth) causes him to drink XYZ. Different contents, same brains, same bodily movements (geometrical trajectories, muscles contracted, etc.), but different behaviors. One is H_2O-drinking. The other is XYZ-drinking. Furthermore, these different behaviors are constituted by causes, beliefs and desires, with different (wide-) contents.

Fodor anticipates this reply with the objection that it proves too much.[37] If true, it proves that qualitatively identical *brains* can cause different behaviors. If Jerry's brain causes H_2O-drinking, while Twin-Jerry's brain causes XYZ-drinking, and these are genuinely different types of behavior, then the brains of Jerry and Twin-Jerry have different causal powers. But, by hypothesis, their brains are exactly the same. So, their brains cannot have different causal powers. Therefore, the behaviors that their brains cause cannot be different. The conclusion Fodor needs is that H_2O-drinking and XYZ-drinking are the same *behaviors* and that their causal explanation is exactly similar due to the exact, qualitative similarity in the *brains* of Jerry and Twin-Jerry.[38]

However, Dretske would *deny* that H_2O-drinking and XYZ-drinking are the same behaviors and *deny* that brains do cause behavior. The work of the brain is a constituent of behavior not a cause.[39] Brains cause *bodily movements*. The brain's causing bodily movement *is* behavior – not a cause of behavior. Even though the bodily movements of Jerry and Twin-Jerry are the same (when they are on their home planets), it does not follow that their behaviors are the same. The equality of their brains explains the equality of their bodily movements, but says nothing about whether their behaviors are the same or different.

Behaviors have effects relative to an environment. Jerry's raising his arm may causally contribute to his H_2O-drinking. If it does, then his brain's causing the bodily movements involved in his H_2O-drinking becomes an environmental extension of his behavior. But still his brain events are constituents, not causes, of these environmental extensions.

And, to explain his H_2O-drinking behavior, we need to look beyond his brain events. What causes behavior (why Jerry is H_2O-drinking rather than martini-drinking) is the *content* of his beliefs and desires (his reasons). It is because he wants water (not a martini) and believes it is water (not a martini) in the cup, that he is H_2O-drinking: (A similar story would explain Twin-Jerry's XYZ-drinking behavior, *mutatis mutandis*.) Thus, content is a causally relevant factor in explaining the relevant differences in Jerry's and Twin-Jerry's *behaviors* – even if not required to explain bodily movements, since there are no relevant differences there.

Fodor's second line of reply is that if H_2O-drinking and XYZ-drinking were different behaviors, there would have to be a difference in causal mechanism to explain the differences in behaviors. But, since Jerry's and Twin-Jerry's brains are identical, there will be no differences in causal mechanism. Thus, there will be no real differences in behaviors.

The problem, of course, is that Fodor is still looking in the wrong place for the mechanism. Its *not in the head*. Its in the head + environment + learning history. If Jerry's and Twin-Jerry's behaviors are different, the differential explanation of their respective behaviors will require reference to *all three* of these factors, not just *one* (what's in the head). It is not that there is *no* mechanism, but that the mechanism is not where Fodor is looking.

Bring Twin-Jerry to Earth, and he will exhibit the same behavior as Jerry. They both will exhibit H_2O-drinking behavior. But they will do this because of different learning histories and different belief-contents. There are different links in the causal mechanisms behind the explanation of their similar bodily movements. Jerry's includes a learning history with H_2O. Twin-Jerry's includes a learning history with XYZ. If Twin-Jerry had not had a learning history with XYZ on Twin-Earth, then Twin-Jerry would not be brain-identical with Jerry and Twin-Jerry would likely not be behaving the same as Jerry here on Earth.

The last objection to Dretske's theory that I will consider is a boundary dispute argument over the proper objects of explanation for a cognitive science. First, consider the fan-diagram below. (S_1 to S_N = cognitive systems, "F_1" to "F_N" = syntactic structures to represent Fs, P_1 to P_N = physical instantiations of the systems' F-representations, F = a predator, and M = fleeing.)

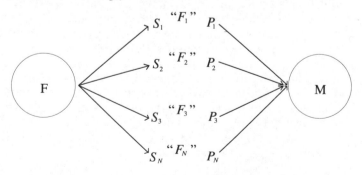

Dretske's theory allows that the only relevant thing that different physical systems S_1-S_N have in common may be that their internal structures all carry information about Fs. In virtue of this they may each cause M-type behavior. If the internal structures of S_1-S_N are all different, there may be different physical instantiations that cause (triggering cause) M. The only relevant thing that all systems have in common may be that their syntactic F-representations all carry information about Fs in environment E.

The first obvious reply is that it may be in virtue of a *syntactic* (non-semantic) feature of the instantiations that they all cause M. But that will not work. For the syntactic instantiations are *not* identical. So, in virtue of what do we explain the commonality of behavior? It may well be only in virtue of the relational fact that the syntactic items were caused by Fs in environment E and acquired the cognitive function of being F-representations. But that relational fact is *content*. The structures will carry information about Fs and, in virtue of sustained causal role, come to mean semantically that Fs are present (consistent with Dretske's overall theory).

The second obvious reply is that we should be able to produce the physical instantiations and syntax in each individual S_1-S_N, without the structures meaning anything about Fs. Brain-in-vat S could be wired up so that S thought it was seeing Fs and, because of that, S produced efferent signals that would (outside the vat) lead to M-ing. Suppose that we caused in S F-images, and these caused syntactic "F"-symbols which in turn caused the efferent correlate of M-ing. Now we get the M-ing without the "F" tokens actually meaning Fs are present. Then we put S's brain back in S's skull where it belongs, plop S in the home environment of systems like S, and presto – S Ms in presence of Fs. So, there is no need for "F"s to mean F, to get S to M in the presence of Fs.

But this will not work. For now "F" *means* (something like) F-image in S's brain. These syntactic items have been recruited for a cognitive role. If the experimenter is clever enough to figure out how to cause in S F-like images, she must also be clever enough to cause experiences of the type that correspond to M-ing (fleeing), and being safe, and so on. The envatted brain goes through a *learning simulation* of real life (as would a pilot training in a flight simulator). Thus, a "design problem" for the envatted brain must be solved for the "F" tokens to acquire content. Then, only because "F" means F-image (or whatever) does the "F" cause S to M in the presence of Fs, when put back in the body and returned to its home environment. And it causes this reliably only because F-images are reliably correlated with the presence of Fs in S's home environment. (After enough experience back in its body, S's content may become wide, but not at first.) "F" need not mean F to cause M, but it will need to *mean something*, even if it is supposed to have only narrow content. It will need to mean something or S's bodily M-ing will not be purposive behavior. It will not be caused by states with cognitive content and, thus, will not be something that falls under the jurisdiction of cognitive psychology. If S's M-ing *is* purposive, then the "F" token will have a meaning (narrow content). Furthermore, the content of S's mental tokens will be causally explanatory of S's behavior. Thus, explanation via content survives both Twin-Earth examples and envatted brain examples. (Notice that Dretske's theory permits narrow content. Wide or narrow content, there will be a learning history that is essential to content acquisition and to the explanation of its causal efficacy.)

But we are not home yet, for there is the *replacement-move*.[40] Find someone, S_2, just like S_1, but with *no learning history*. There are variations of this in the literature. Sometimes the replacement is constructed molecule for molecule out of physically identical stuff. Sometimes the replacement is a biological offspring with "innate structures" physically identical to the learned structures in S_1. In fact, these structures may have the same causal role (computational role). S_2's "F"s will not mean F. They will *not mean anything*. But if S_2's brain is identical with S_1's, they will both M in the presence of Fs, whether S_2's internal states mean anything or not. So, it looks like meaning is irrelevant to explaining even S_1's M-ing. But this is to say that movements caused by internal states without cognitive content of any kind are within the province of psychology (cognitive science).

Here is where teleology helps (at least, it helps me). The replacement argument asks us to accept that if the function of x in S is to do y, then the function of x' (where x and x' are identical in all relevant physical respects) in a replacement organism S' is to do y. But in these simple terms it is clear that the argument has to *fail*. Into physically type-identical systems we can build physically type-identical structures x and x'. Although they both do y (at some level of description), they may have quite different functions. The exact same calculation on my computer may have the function of balancing my checkbook or the function of calculating a student's grades. I may build a door stop that looks for all the world like your bowling ball with a flat holder under it. That does not make your bowling ball a doorstop (because physically type-identical to mine), while the one I made is *just that*. Examples are easy to come by. Causal history, particularly sustaining causal history, is crucial for whether an artifact has a function. When you set your bowling ball by my door, it holds it open. But that is not why its there (not its function). However, that is why mine is by my door. It has acquired that function. Thus, replacement of one structure by another that is molecule for molecule physically identical is never sufficient for having the same function.

For natural functions as well, it is widely accepted that no structure has a teleological function in its first occurrence. It is only when its causal role accounts for *success* in the *next* occurrence (generation) that we ascribe a genuine function (as opposed to a merely "fortuitous effect"). A biological structure in daddy frog may conceivably have a different causal role and function in grandson frog, and so on. And, the more adaptive the structures in question – such as structures in the brain – the more likely it is that changes of function will occur. So, the fact that a structure in daddy frog is a bug-detector does not settle the matter of what the structure is in grandson frog. For grandson frog may grow up in the Purina Frog Chow laboratory where the structure is tokened only by moving particles of Frog Chow. The fact that, in daddy, the activation of his structure meant "bug" does not settle the issue of what it means in grandson. It may mean "chow." Learning history alone will tell – because it alone can tell us the causal sustaining story. This is what the design problem tells us.

Of course, someone may still protest that cognitive psychology *is* in the business of explaining only bodily movement (or brain movement, nervous system events, etc.). But it is surely not in the business of explaining what Dreske says that content can cause. It is not in the business of explaining structuring causation, or purposive behavior.[41]

However, this reply is not plausible.[42] Psychology *is* in the business of explaining purposive, intelligent behavior. Not just any bodily movement that is caused by an internal state is a kind of thing that it is psychology's job to explain. The brain controls heart pace, blood sugar, body temperature, breathing, and on and on. All of these require significant information to be processed in the brain – but *not cognitively*. No one thinks that we need a cognitive science or psychology of digestion, temperature control, perspiration or heart rate. Neuroscience is satisfactory. Only events or bodily movements that are goal-directed, caused by contentful mental states are in the true domain of *cognitive* psychology. Of course, there are psychological subsystems that subserve causal roles within cognitive systems, and that do not process information at the level of cognition. But surely an entire system of such, without cognitive content anywhere in the picture, is not a system ripe for psychological explanation. An arm's movement is not necessarily a waving hello, unless it is caused by the intention with the right content. An utterance of "Bring water" is not a request for water unless it has the right beliefs and desires producing it. And so on. Some think cognitive science and psychology are not about purposive, intelligent, goal-directed behavior. They are only about physical movements describable purely in terms of muscle contractions and geometrical space-time worms of those movements. Neurophysiology, biology, physics, and chemistry may explain these without aid or need of a content psychology. But if that was all that minds or cognitive psychology was for, we would *not need* minds or *cognitive psychology* – which takes us back to our opening query. Why would nature cough up impotent minds filled with causationless content? The answer that thought-mates of Dretske prefer is that she would not. The reason we need content (and cognitive psychology) is to explain teleological behavior of the variety caused by mental states, viz. waving good-bye, exchanging marriage vows, signing a contract, drinking a martini, and so on.

Notes

Thanks to the CMU philosophy of mind group for friendly resistance and to Fred Dretske, John Barker, and Kevin Possin for helpful discussion.

1　Unless, of course, it is *we* who will exploit the content. But if we are building intelligent systems that are not to exist solely for our exploitation, causation-less content would be of no use *to them* – so why put it in?

2　Dennett, as Davidson, would subscribe to the view reasons may cause things, but not in virtue of their content.

3　As we shall see, Dretske's view *demands* that information can and does *cause* things (or an event's carrying it does). If an indefinite number of physically dissimilar events e_1 to e_n all cause the same type of thing R, and if they share no single causally relevant physically properties in common in virtue of which they could all have caused R, then it may *only* be in virtue of their sharing the same information content that e_1 to e_n all cause R. I shall return to this point.

4　Actually, cognitive content is *less than* information content for the reason that the information that this body of water is freezing contains nested within it the information that this body of water is expanding. But the belief with the content that this body of water is freezing need not be a belief that this body of water is expanding. So cognitive systems are in the business of *selectively ignoring* excess information content that is not essential to the cognitive businesss at hand. What I mean by "more" is that it takes more biological (and, perhaps, mental) machinery to get to the stage where a system is capable of this selectivity.

5　Fred Dretske, *Explaining Behavior: Reasons in a World of Causes*, (Cambridge, Mass.: MIT Press/Bradford Books, 1988).

6　Of course, this is all contentious and the opposition has been famously recorded by Jerry Fodor, *Psychosemantics: The Problem of Meanings in the Philosophy of Mind*, (Cambridge, Mass.: MIT Press/Bradford Books, 1987); Stephen Stich, *From Folk Psychology to Cognitive Science. The Case Against Belief*, (Cambridge, Mass.: MIT Press/Bradford, Books, 1983) and a cavalcade of sympathizers.

7　All three pieces can be found, to some degree, in Fred Dretske, *Knowledge and the Flow of Information*, (Cambridge, Mass.: MIT Press/Bradford Books, 1981). Piece two is further developed in "Misrepresentation," in *Belief: Form, Content and Function*, ed. Radu Bogdan (Oxford: Clarendon Press, 1986), pp. 17–36, and piece three is in *Explaining Behavior*, chapter 4. I think that the pieces can stand independently of one another. I am not sure that Dretske would agree, however.

8　I will not try to list all of the references. The main ones can be found in Fodor, *Psychosemantics*; the "Open Peer Commentary" on Dretske's *Knowledge and the Flow of Information*, in *Behavioral and Brain Sciences*, 6 (1983), pp. 63–90; and the special issue of *Synthese*, 70 (1986), ed. Barry Loewer and devoted to Dretske's work.

9　Several commentators have posed objections to Dretske's attempt to borrow the technical concept of "information" for this purpose. Yet, the more insightful among them see that the important concept being explicated is that of natural meaning or natural representation – however that is to be satisfactorily analyzed.

10 As is widely known, Dretske maintains that there can be *nonepistemic seeing* (perceptions of *F*s which contain the information that something is *F* prior to formation of a concept of *F*s – prior to believing or knowing that the things perceived *are F*s). Whether one is sympathetic or not, it is clear that this supports his attempt to naturalize the theory of *cognitive* content. See Dretske, *Seeing and Knowing* (Chicago: Chicago University Press, 1969) and *Knowledge and the Flow of Information*, chapter 6. For opposition, see D. M. Armstrong, *Belief, Truth and Knowledge* (Cambridge: Cambridge University Press, 1973) and John Heil Heil, *Perception and Cognition* Berkeley, Cal.: University of California Press, 1983).

11 For extension of Dretske's views on epistemology, see Frederick Adams, "The Function of Epistemic Justification," *Canadian Journal of Philosophy*, 16 (1986), pp. 465–492; and Adams and Kline, "Nomic Reliabilism: Weak Reliability is not Enough," *Southern Journal of Philosophy*, 25 (1987), pp. 433–43.

12 Dretske, *Knowledge and the Flow of Information* p. 86. For the critical responses to this condition on knowing, see "Open Peer Commentary," pp. 63–82.

13 See Fodor, *Psychosemantics*, chapter 4.

14 There is a complex reply to the disjunction problem in Dretske, "Misrepresentation." However, the reply simplifies in Dretske, *Explaining Behavior*, p. 84, n. 4.

15 See Dretske, *Knowledge and the Flow of Information*, chapters 7 and 8; "Misrepresentation;" and *Explaining Behavior*, pp. 64–77.

16 To my mind, this transition represents the struggle with the "mark of the mental" – or what is left of it these days. However, Dretske cares little for boundary-drawing and, unless such cognitive structures were harnessed to behavior, he would deny that this piece of the puzzle alone would provide the "mark" anyway. But, pretty clearly, in Dretske, *Knowledge and the Flow of Information*, this step was the distinctive thing that beliefs had that other states lacked (opacity of the right order – "third-order intentionality"). I think that what convinced Dretske that this was not enough to distinguish genuine minds from non-minds was that even non-minds seem capable of the right order of opacity "third-order intentionality". See Berent Enc, "Intentional States of Mechanical Devices," *Mind* 91, pp. 161–82.

17 Cummins objects that Dretske has changed the subject on us by finding a causal job for content, but not one that is relevant to cognitive psychology. I disagree and explain why below, but see Robert Cummins, "Commentary" on Dretske's "The Explanatory Role of Content," *Contents of Thought: Arizona Colloquium in Cognition*, ed. Robert Grimm and Daniel Merrill (Tuscon: University of Arizona Press, 1988), pp. 44–55.

18 Dretske, *Explaining Behavior*, pp. 50 and 83.

19 Ibid., pp. 42–4.

20 Ibid., p. 91.

21 Since reasons are two-factor items, beliefs + desire, let the desire component be fixed for the sake of the example. That is, let *S*'s desire to avoid *F*s constantly be *on*.

22 This is basically Larry Wright's theory of teleological functions. Dretske adopts it as a model of cognitive functions and meaning$_f$. See Dretske, *Explaining Behavior*, p. 111, and "Misrepresentation," and Larry Wright, "Functions," *Philosophical Review*, 82 (1973), pp. 139–68.

23 Dretske seems to add to Wright's analysis the role that feedback plays in
    learning and the instantiation of the conditions for something's having a
    function. Compare Frederick Adams, "A Goal-State Theory of Function
    Attribution," *Canadian Journal of Philosophy*, 9 (1979), pp. 493–518, and
    Frederick Adams and Berent Enc, "Not Quite By Accident," *Dialogue*, 27
    (1988), pp. 287–297.
24 Dretske, *Explaining Behavior*, p. 84, n. 4.
25 Dennett seems to lump Dretske with Fodor and Searle on this. Daniel
    Dennett, *The Intentional Stance* (Cambridge, Mass.: MIT Press/Bradford
    Books, 1987), p. 297. But see Dretske, "Mentality and Machines," *Proceed-
    ings and Addresses of the American Philosophical Association*, 59 (1985),
    pp. 23–33.
26 Dennett criticizes Dretske for saying that currently existing computers have
    "no access" to the meaning of their symbols, as though Dretske might have
    meant by "access" "being in a position to know or recognize or intuit or
    introspect that fact [the meaning] from the inside." But, of course, this is not
    what Dretske meant. He meant that *no causal role* is played by the semantic
    content of symbols in currently existing machines. If symbols in computers
    caused things in virtue of their having semantic content, *that* would be the
    type of access of which he was speaking – causal access, not epistemic.
27 Dennett seems to think that if even the process of natural selection contri-
    butes to our ability to have states with content that this will rob us of intrinsic
    intentionality. See Dennett, *Intentional Stance*, p. 305.
28 Dretske explicitly denies that selection can create cognitive content; see
    Explaining Behavior, pp. 92f. But we can think of learning as selection within
    individuals (within an organism's lifetime) versus natural selection which
    is across individuals (lifetimes). He ties content to specific learning history.
    But Dennett is right that there will be some process with selectional or teleol-
    ogical elements.
29 Dennett, *Intentional Stance*, pp. 320–1.
30 Elliott Sober, *The Nature of Selection*, (Cambridge, Mass., MIT Press/
    Bradford Books, 1984)
31 Compare Adams, "A Goal-State Theory," and Adams and Enc, "Not Quite
    By Accident."
32 Dretske, *Explaining Behavior*, p. 98, n. 10.
33 Daniel Dennett, *Brainstorms: Philosophical Essays on Mind and Psychology*
    (Montgomery, VT: Bradford Books), and Dennett, *Intentional Stance*.
34 Fodor, *Psychosemantics*, chapter 2.
35 The surprise is that Fodor has made a similar move about false belief that
    could have led him to the right place. On Fodor's view of false tokening,
    "horse" can be caused by a cow and be a false tokening only because:
    (1) horses cause "horse" tokens (in a counterfactual-supporting way), and (2)
    cows would not cause "horse" tokens unless (1) were true. See Fodor,
    Psychosemantics, chapter 4.
36 Thanks to the CMU reading group for this point: David Drebushenko, Gary
    Fuller, Bob Stecker, and Paul Yu.
37 Fodor, *Psychosemantics*, pp. 37f.
38 Fodor could also say (and does consider) that these behaviors may indeed be
    different, but not the proper objects of psychological explanation. I consider
    this below.
39 Compare: our seeing the book is not caused by the book, but is a constituent

of our seeing it. The book causes our bookish percept which, when caused nondeviantly by the book, comprises one of the relata – the other being the book – of the perceiving relation. The book and the percept are constituents of perceiving the book.

40 See Stich, *From Folk Psychology*, pp. 165–70.
41 This is Cummins' complaint, "Commentary on Dretske."
42 For support of this (though put to slightly different purposes), see Jennifer Hornsby, "Physicalist Thinking and Conceptions of Behavior," in *Subject, Thought, and Context*, ed. Philip Pettit and John McDowell (Oxford: Clarendon Press, 1986), pp. 95–115.

9

Belief Individuation and Dretske on Naturalizing Content

Brian P. McLaughlin

When are two beliefs identical?[1] In a word, "never:" No *two* beliefs are ever identical. The answer to the question when is a belief identical with itself can also be given in a word: "always."[2] A more interesting question is how to fill in the following blank:

No two beliefs can be exactly alike in their____.

While this question is more interesting, it is fairly widely held that it too can be answered in word, namely "content."[3] That is, it is fairly widely held that the following is a correct *nonduplication principle* for beliefs:[4]

> *The Content Principle for Beliefs:* No two beliefs can be exactly alike in their *content*.

My aim in this paper is two-fold: (1) to challenge the content principle and, thereby, (2) to defend a recent proposal of Fred Dretske's against an objection that appeals to the principle. Dretske's proposal (1988) implies that a certain condition D (which I will state later) is a sufficient condition for a state token's having the content that p, rather than some other content. As we will see in due course, if the content principle is true, then Dretske's proposal faces a dilemma: Either the proposal is false *or* Dretske has failed to explain how D could be satisfied, and, moreover, it is hard to see how it could be. I will offer a partial defense of Dretske's proposal by making a case against the content principle.[5] Exploiting an insight of Jerry Fodor's (forthcoming a), I will make a case that from the fact that the belief that p ≠ (means "not identical") the belief that q, it does not follow that the content that p ≠ the content that q. Two beliefs, I will argue, can have the same content.

The paper has two parts that can, for the most part, stand independently of each other. In the first part, after a brief discussion of belief individuation, I argue that Dretske's proposal faces a dilemma if the content principle is correct. In the second part, I make a case against the content principle.

I
Belief Individuation

Before presenting Dretske's proposal, it is useful to note that, as Dretske himself has stressed, beliefs individuate very finely. One can believe that water is nearby, for instance, without believing that H_2O is nearby, even though it is metaphysically necessary that water is H_2O (Dretske 1981, pp. 217–18). One can believe that the solution to the problem is 23 without believing that the solution to the problem is the cube root of 12,167, even though it is logically necessary that 23 is the cube root of 12,167 (ibid., p. 173). Indeed, as Dretske (1981) has noted, "We distinguish the belief that s is F from the belief that s is G ... even (sometimes) when the expressions 'F' and 'G' are synonymous" (ibid., p. 215). (Cf. Mates 1952, Burge 1978, and Fodor forthcoming a.)

To illustrate this last sort of case: One can believe that Mary will return in a fortnight, for instance, yet not believe that Mary will return in fourteen days, even though "fortnight" and "fourteen days" are *synonyms* (Mates 1952).[6] For one might mistakenly think that a fortnight is ten days. We can all make conceptual mistakes. One can be under such a misconception about what a fortnight is. One can fail to *realize* that a fortnight is fourteen days while *knowing* well and good that fourteen days is fourteen days. (Likewise, one could, for example, *wonder* whether a fortnight is fourteen days or *doubt* that a fortnight is fourteen days without wondering whether or doubting that fourteen days is fourteen days.) As Tyler Burge (1978) has pointed out, nonphilosophers seem to have no trouble in taking the following sort of remark at face value: "For years I believed that a fortnight was ten days, not fourteen, though of course I never believed that fourteen days were ten days" (p. 126). If, as Burge has persuasively argued, this remark *should* be taken at face value, then synonyms fail to substitute *salva veritate* in that-clauses in belief sentences.[7]

From the failure of synonyms to so substitute, Burge (1978) concludes that the denotations of that-clauses in belief sentences are "more fine-grained than ordinary linguistic meanings" (p. 136). Presumably, he assumes the content principle when drawing this conclusion. Such failures of substitution indeed imply difference of belief: If one can believe that Mary will return in a fortnight, yet not believe that Mary will return in fourteen days, then, of course, the belief that Mary will return in a fortnight is distinct from the belief that Mary will return in fourteen days. One can have the one belief without having the other. Moreover, if the content principle is correct, then the beliefs have different contents. The that-clauses used to denote or express the contents of the beliefs in question are synonymous; they have the same "linguistic meaning." So, given the content principle, it would indeed follow that contents are "more fine-grained than ordinary linguistic meanings." But if the content principle is false, then it is an open question whether the beliefs differ in content. It is an open question whether from the fact that the belief that Mary will return in a fortnight ≠ the belief that Mary will return in fourteen days, it follows that the content that Mary will return in a fortnight ≠ the content that Mary will return in fourteen days. The contents may be the same despite the fact that the beliefs are different. Of course, if the contents are the same, then two distinct beliefs can have the same content, and so the content principle is false. But more about this in part II.

The point to note for now is just that if the beliefs in question are distinct and if the content principle is correct, then even synonymous that-clauses will express different contents. As I remarked above, beliefs individuate very finely indeed. If the content principle were correct, contents would individuate just as finely. This noted, turn to Dretske's account of content.

Dretske's All-Natural Recipe for Intentionality

Dretske (1981, 1988) has attempted, in his own words, to provide an all-natural recipe for baking an intentional cake.[8] The recipe is intended to be a solution to Brentano's Problem (cf. Field 1978).[9] This is, roughly, the problem of explaining how it is possible for a physical organism to have intentional states. Its solution requires that one state a (broadly) phisical condition satisfaction of which suffices to make it the case that a given state is an intentional state of some sort.[10] By stating such a condition, one would show how to break into the so-called intentional circle. If I understand him, Dretske intends to state a condition that is causally possible (i.e., that obtains in some causally possible world). For he hopes to explain how it is *causally* possible for a physical organism to have intentional states.

As we shall see, the central ingredients of Dretske's all-natural recipe are the notion of Gricean natural meaning and a notion of natural function. Dretske combines these ingredients to serve up a notion of natural indicator function, and this notion is the primary ingredient in his recipe for intentionality. The intentional cake he tries to bake is that of a state's being a belief that p, or at least a proto-belief that p. But more about all this shortly. Before discussing these matters I should note first that I won't attempt to determine whether Dretske solves Brentano's Problem. Any responsible attempt to do this would take me too far afield of my central concerns. Rather, I will focus on one consequence of his solution, namely a proposal of the following form:

(X)   A state token b has the content that (an) F is present, rather than some other content if D.

In what follows, I will first show that Dretske is committed to a proposal of form (X). Then, I will invoke the content principle to pose a dilemma for the proposal.

I will begin by rather baldly summarizing some of Dretske's views and giving them names to make for easy reference.

Dretske (1988) is *sympathetic* with the following proposal:

> *The Belief Proposal.* A state token b is a belief and has the content that (an) F is present, rather than some other content *if* D [(i) b is state of an organism O, (ii) b is a token of a state type B that has, in O, the natural function of indicating that (an) F is present, and (iii) B has this natural indicator function in O in virtue of the fact that B was naturally recruited for a control duty in O because tokens of B in O indicated that (an) F was present, and not because of the indication of any other condition by tokens of B in O].

Condition D is intended to be a causally possible, (at least broadly) physical condition. One of the central ideas in D is, of course, the idea of a *natural indicator function*.[11] This is, as I mentioned, the central ingredient in Dretske's all-natural recipe for intentionality, the naturalistic wedge he attempts to drive into the so-called intentional circle. Dretske (1988, chapter 3) contrasts *natural* indicator functions with *assigned* indicator functions. An alarm's ringing, for instance, might be assigned the function of indicating that it is quitting time. Assigned functions depend on intentions and purposes of cognizers: They are intended functions. Natural functions, in contrast, do not depend on intentions and purposes of cognizers. Where natural indicator functions are concerned, Mother Nature herself determines the indicator function by means of natural processes whereby a state type is recruited or selected for a control duty. Condition (ii) implies that B has a certain natural indicator function in O, and (iii) purports to cite a fact in virtue of which B has the natural indicator function in O.

Conditions (ii) and (iii) require much discussion. Before discussing them, however, I want to make two points that can be appreciated with an understanding of the consequent of the belief-proposal alone, and so without a detailed understanding of (ii) and (iii). First, while Dretske is sympathetic to the belief proposal, he does not actually commit himself to it. Rather, he revises the proposal by replacing "belief" in the consequent with "proto-belief," thereby making a "proto-belief proposal." I will say why shortly. Second, both the belief proposal and the proto-belief proposal imply a proposal of form (X), namely:

> *The Indicator Function Proposal.* A state token b has the content that (an) F is present, rather than some other content if D (as stated above).

I will, in due course, pose a dilemma for this proposal.

I propose to proceed as follows. I will first discuss conditions (ii) and (iii) of D in detail; then, I will briefly discuss why Dretske shifts from the belief proposal to the proto-belief proposal; and, finally, I will pose the dilemma.

To begin then, let us explore conditions (ii) and (iii) in turn and reserve critical evaluation for later.

Consider condition (ii): b is a state token of type B that has, in O, the natural function of indicating that (an) F is present. B is a type of *intrinsic* state of O; it might, for example, be a type of neural state. To say that B has, in O, the natural function of indicating that F is present is to say that when tokens of B are naturally functioning properly in O, they indicate that F is present. F is a kind (e.g., water) or a property (e.g., square-ness). The notion of *indication* is, essentially, the Gricean notion of natural meaning (Grice 1957): Tokens of B in O indicate that F is present *iff* the fact that a B occurs in O naturally means that F is present. Dretske suggests (roughly) that either side of this biconditional is true *iff* a B would not have occured in O unless F were present (1988, p. 57).[12] To say that B has, in O, the natural function of indicating that F (e.g., water) is present is, then, to say (roughly) that a properly functioning token of B would not occur in O unless F (water) were present. Now indication does not admit of misindication. If a token of B indicates (naturally means) that F is present, then F is present. In contrast, a token of B can have (*qua* token of B) the natural function of indicating that F is present, even when F is not present. Tokens of B can thus fail to function properly (*qua* tokens of B): They can fail to indicate that F is present. Natural indicator functions are *normative*: If B has, in O, the natural function of indicating that F is present, then tokens of B in O are *supposed* to indicate that F is present. But they can fail to do what they are supposed to do; they can fail to discharge their function. Thus, it is possible for B to have, in O, the natural function of indicating that (say) water is present yet be tokened in O on an occasion on which water is not present. When this happens, the state token *misrepresents* O's environment. Thus, tokens of B can be, so to speak, *mistokens*.

Condition (iii) is, you will recall, this: B has this natural indicator function in O in virtue of the fact that B was naturally recruited for a control duty in O because tokens of B in O indicated that (an) F was present, and not because of the indication of any other condition by tokens of B in O. This condition purports to cite a fact in virtue of which B has, in O, the natural function of indicating that F is present. According to Dretske, the fact that B has a natural indicator function in O thus consists of a forward-looking fact and a backward-looking fact. The forward-looking fact is that B has a control duty in O. This is a foward-looking fact concerning the role tokens of B would play in producing bodily movements of O in various circumstances. State type B's having a control duty in O consists in its tokens having a certain causal role in O *vis-à-vis* some bodily movements of O's. The backward-looking fact concerns how B was recruited for a control duty in O. The sort of backward-looking fact that is relevant to belief (or proto-belief) is this: B must have been naturally recruited for a control duty in O because tokens of B in O indicated that F was present, and not because of the indication of any-thing else by those tokens. As Dretske points out, if tokens of B indicate anything, they will indicate a great many things. But, he claims, it can happen that B is naturally recruited because its tokens indicate that F is present, and not because of the indication of anything else by its tokens. When this happens, B's indicating that F is present is elevated to the status of a *representation*; B acquires the natural function of indicating that F is present. Moreover, according to Dretske, B will continue to have this natural indicator function as long as (1) B continues in a control duty and (2) it does not so continue because of its tokens' indicating anything else (i.e., some condition other than F's being present). If it continues in a control duty because of its tokens indicating some condi-tion other than F's being present, then B will acquire a new natural indicator function.

By what natural means can B be recruited for a control duty in O because its tokens in O indicated that F is present, and not because of the indication of any other condition by tokens of B in O? According to Dretske, this can happen by means of O's undergoing a process of *operant learning*.[13] Dretske's appeal to operant learning is legitimate in the context of his attempt to solve Brentano's Problem. For operant learning does not require the possession of prior intentional states and is suitably naturalistic. Here is a very beief summary of Dretske's account of how a state can acquire a natural indicator function by means of operant learning. Suppose that tokens of B (say, a neural state type) in O indicate that (an) F is present. Suppose further that tokens of state type D (say, another type of neural state) in O render O receptive to a certain sort of reward R: D is, in O, a state of receptivity *for* R (Dretske 1988, p. 110). When O is in D, O's behavior can be reinforced by R. Now a token of B and a token of D might jointly contribute to causing a movement M in circumstances in which F is present, and this might result in O's a receiving reward of type R.[14] If, for whatever reason, this happens often enough, B might come, through a process of association, to have control duties in O: B might acquire, as a result of the learning process, the control duty of (contributing to) producing movements of type M. O becomes *disposed* to M when in B and D. Dretske claims that by means of O's undergoing such a process of operant learning, state type B acquires such a control duty in O *because* tokens of B in O indicate that F is present, *and not because they indicate anything else*. When B is so recruited for a control duty in O, it, thereby, according to Dretske, acquires the natural function of indicating that F is present; and that it, thereby, has the *content* that F is present, rather than some other content (or no content at all) (ibid., p. 84; pp. 95–107).[15] On Dretske's view, then, operant-learning history determines indicator function, and indica-tor function, in turn, determines a unique content. More about this shortly.

For B to have the natural function of indicating that F is present, tokens of B must indicate that F is present during the period of operant learning. They need not do so after the learning period, however, in order for B to retain its indicator function. That, in a nutshell, is why it is possible for tokens of B to misrepresent O's environment. Let us explore this in more detail. The learning period ends when B acquires a control duty as a result of the learning process. After the learning period, circumstances can change in such a way that tokens of B cease to indicate that F is present, despite the fact that B retains its indicator function. The fact that tokens of B in O indicate that F is present might well depend on nomologically contingent circumstances of O's environmental niche. Those circumstances might change, or O might move to a different environment, without any change in B's control duty. And as a result of such changes, tokens of B in O might cease to indicate that F is present. However, as we noted earlier, if B's control duty remains unchanged and does not do so because of its tokens indicating that some other condition is present, then, claims Dretske, B retains its natural indicator function. Thus, it can continue to be the case that tokens of B are *supposed* to indicate that F is present, even though they no longer *reliably* do so. If this happens, then B will admit of mistokens. Error will be possible. (This completes my explication of conditions (ii) and (iii).)

These bold and imaginative proposals raise a host of questions some of which I will address shortly.[16] First, however, a brief comment is in order about Dretske's shift from the belief proposal to the proto-belief proposal.

Here, in a nutshell, is the reason he makes the shift: He concedes, for the sake of argument, that it *may* be the case that D fails to suffice for b's being a belief since the fact that D holds *may* fail to suffice for B's having an elaborate enough functional role in O to count as a belief. Perhaps, he says, for tokens of B to count as beliefs, B must occupy a certain position in a network of state types that exhibits a rational structure, and D does not guarantee this. He thinks, however, that whether B must occupy such a position to be a belief is largely a verbal issue. He gives the following reason for not debating it: "I have, as I say, no great interest in what seems to me to be a terminological boundary dispute of negligible philosophical interest" (1988, p. 107). Rather than debate the issue, he revises the belief proposal as follows:

> *The Proto-Belief Proposal*: A state token b is a proto-belief and has the content that (an) F is present, rather than some other content if D.

A proto-belief, Dretske tells us, is a kind of intentional state that is very similiar to belief, but perhaps one with a less elaborate functional role than belief. This proto-belief proposal is Dretske's would-be solution to Brentano's Problem. As I mentioned earlier, I will not be concerned with whether his solution succeeds. A word about proto-beliefs is in order, however, before turning to the indicator function proposal.

The proto-belief that F is present has, Dretske holds, the same content as the belief that F is present. If the proto-belief in question is distinct from the belief, the difference, according to Dretske, is in their intentional modes, not in their contents. The hope that F is present and the belief that F is present, for example, have the same content but differ in their intentional modes; the same is true of the proto-belief that F is present and the belief that F is present. What makes proto-belief especially interesting in this context is of course that we have a (would-be) naturalistic sufficient condition for a state's being a proto-belief. Conditions in addition to (i)–(iii) might be needed to provide a sufficient condition for b's being a belief rather than a mere proto-belief; but those conditions will be extraneous to b's content. No condition beyond (i)–(iii) is required for b to have the content that (an) F is present, rather–than some other content (or no content at all). Or so Dretske claims.

A Dilemma

Turn to our central concern:

> *The Indicator Function Proposal.* A state token b has the content that (an) F is present, rather than some other content *if* D [(i) b is state of an organism O, (ii) b is a token of a state type B that has, in O, the natural function of indicating that (an) F is present, and (iii) B has this natural indicator function in O in virtue of the fact that B was naturally recruited for a control duty in O because tokens of B in O indicated that (an) F was present, and not because of the indication of any other condition by tokens of B in O].

One issue that arises is whether the natural indicator function of a state determines a unique content for the state; another issue is whether Dretske has succeeded is describing a natural process that can determine the natural indicator function of a state. I want now to appeal to the content principle to propose a dilemma: If the content principle is correct, then either the indicator function proposal is false since the natural indicator function of a state will fail to determine a unique content for the state *or* Dretske has failed to describe a natural process that can determine the natural indicator function of a state.

To begin, consider the following three statements:

1 B has, in O, the natural function of indicating that (an) F is present.
2 F = G (and "F = G" is metaphysically necessary).[17]
3 B does not have, in O, the natural function of indicating that (a) G is present.

Either (1)–(3) are consistent or they are inconsistent. Either way there is a problem. If they are inconsistent and if the content principle is correct, then the indicator function proposal is false. If they are consistent, then Dretske has failed to provide an explanation of how a natural process can determine the natural indicator function of a state; moreover, it is hard to see how there could be such an explanation. Let us consider each horn in turn.

If (1)–(3) are inconsistent and if the content principle is correct, then D will not suffice for b's having the content that F is present, rather than some other content, and so the indicator function proposal is false. To see why on these assumptions D will not suffice for b's having a unique content, suppose that (1)–(3) are indeed inconsistent. That is, suppose that when (2) holds, then B has, in O, the natural function of indicating that F is present *iff* B has, in O, the natural function of indicating that G is present. Then, if the content principle is correct, D will fail to suffice for b's having the content that (an) F is present, rather than some other content. For if the content principle is correct, then, even when (2) holds, the content that F is present *can be* distinct from the content that G is present. To see this, consider the following. The belief that water is present has the content that water is present. The belief that H_2O is present has the content that H_2O is present. The belief that water is present is distinct from the belief that H_2O is present: One could have one of the beliefs without having the other. So, given the content principle, the beliefs cannot have the same content. It follows that the content that water is present $\neq$ the content that H_2O is present. We see, then, that if (1)–(3) are inconsistent and if the content principle is correct, then D fails to state a sufficient condition for b's having the content that F is present, rather than some other content. Natural indicator function thus fails to determine a unique content. It follows that the indicator function proposal is false.

Here is the second horn: If (1)–(3) are consistent, then we lack an explanation of *how* a natural process could determine the natural indicator function of a state. For we lack an explanation of how, when (2) holds, a state can have the natural function of indicating that F is present yet not have the natural function of indicating that G is present. And, as we saw above, given the content principle, it must be possible for these to be distinct natural indicator functions if the natural indicator function of a state determines a unique content for the state. We thus lack an explanation of how condition (iii) of D could be satisfied, and so of how D could be satisfied. What is wanted is an explanation of how it is causally possible for it to be satisfied. Dretske maintains, you will recall, that operant learning is a natural process that can determine the natural indicator function of a state. For operant learning to determine that B has the natural function of indicating that F is present, however, it must be the case that by means of operant learning, B can be recruited for a control duty because its tokens indicated that F was present, and *not because of the indication of any other condition by its tokens*. And it is hard to see how that could happen if, for example, the condition of water's being present $\neq$ the condition of H_2O's being present. Operant-learning history underdetermines natural indicator function if (1)–(3) are consistent. If, for example, by means of operant learning, B was *naturally* selected for a control duty because it tokens indicated that water was present, then it is also true that it was so selected because its tokens indicated that H_2O was present. Operant-learning history won't distinguish B's having the natural function of indicating that water is present from B's having the natural function of indicating that H_2O is present. *If* there is a difference between the condition of water's being present and the condition of H_2O's being present, it is not a difference the mechanisms of operant learning are sensitive to: For there is no metaphysically possible way for Mother Nature to "split the stimulus." Likewise, the mechanisms will be insensitive to the difference, if there is one, between tokens of B indicating that water is present and tokens of B indicating that H_2O is present. I am *not* assuming here that, when (2) holds, B's indicating that F is present is *ipso facto* explanatorily equivalent to B's indicating that G is present. Rather, my point is just that I do not see how, when (2) holds, B could, by means of operant learning, acquire a control duty because its tokens indicated that F is present and not also acquire a control duty because its tokens indicated that G is present.[18]

Moreover, I fail to see what sort of natural process could determine that B has the natural function of indicating that F is present yet not the natural function of indicating that G is present, when (2) holds. The reason is that these seem to me to be the *same* natural indicator function. Natural indicator functions are relations that state types relative to an organism or system bear to a condition. And when (2) holds, then F's being present = G's being present, and "F's being present = G's being present" is metaphysically necessary. So, whatever bears the natural indicator relationship to F's being present bears it to G's being present. Indeed, the natural function of indicating that F is present = the natural function of indicating that G is present.[19] For example, water = H_2O and squareness = right−angled equilaterness; and, moreover, the statements "water = H_2O" and "squareness = right-angled equilateralness" are metaphysically necessary. So, I claim, water's being present = H_2O's being present; and a square's being present = a right-angled equilateral's being present. Moreover, the natural function of indicating that water (a square) is present = the natural function of indicating that H_2O (a right-angled equilateral) is present. Natural functions differ in this way from *assigned* functions. Something can have the assigned function of indicating that F is present yet not have the assigned function of indicating that G is present, even when (2) holds. But that is because assigned indicator functions are *intended* functions. And the relevant cognizer(s) might be ignorant of the fact that F = G.

Dretske might of course reject this and try to defend the claim that (1)−(3) are consistent. But he must, then, answer this skeptical challenge: to explain how, even when (2) holds, B could come to have the natural function of indicating that F is present yet not come to have the natural function of indicating that G is present.

I think Dretske should instead maintain that (1)−(3) are inconsistent.

As we saw in the first horn, he must, then, either reject the indicator function proposal or reject the content principle. I suggest that he reject the content principle. Before purusing this, however, I want to consider briefly the option of rejecting the indicator function proposal.

Dretske might concede that the indicator function proposal is false since natural indicator function does not itself determine a unique content, but claim that, nevertheless, natural indicator function can be a central ingredient in a recipe for content. Thus, he might, for example, propose a two-factor theory of content (cf. Field 1977; McGinn 1982, 1989; and Block, 1986). He might maintain, for example, that content can consist of natural indicator function *and* functional role. The idea would be that the indicator function relation pairs a state with one component of a belief content, and that having a certain functional role is the other component of content. Indeed Dretske (1988) says that his view on content is now "closer to" a two-factor view than was his earlier view in 1981. But despite his sympathies with some aspects of two-factor theories of content, he does not actually embrace a two-factor theory of content in 1988.[20] Moreover, he does not think that content *essentially* consist of two-factors (personal correspondence): He holds that if B has the natural function of indicating that F is present, then its tokens have the content that F is present, rather than some other content (or no content at all). It is, I think, all to the good that Dretske does not embrace a two-factor theory of content. Formidable problems have been raised for such theories (see LePore and Loewer 1986; and Fodor 1987). These problems concern how functional role figures as a component of content and how the two components relate to add up to content. But since Dretske does not actually propose a two-factor view of content, rather than pursue these difficulties in order to block the move in question, I will instead turn to my positive suggestion: Dretske should maintain that (1) (3) are inconsistent and deny that the content principle is a correct nonduplication principle for beliefs.

II
The Encoded Content Principles

What, then, *is* a correct nonduplication principles for beliefs? I propose the following:

> *The Encoded Content Principle for Beliefs*: No two beliefs can be exactly alike in their content and in the manner in which they encode their content.

This is implied by, but does not imply, the content principle for beliefs. Unlike the content principle, it leaves open whether two beliefs can have the same content.[21] In this second part of the paper, I will, among other things, try to make a case that two beliefs with the same content can differ because of the way they encode the content.

A belief's content is encoded in its conceptual constituents and constituent structure.[22] And the content of a belief is a function of the contents of its constituent concepts together with its constituent structure. As Dretske himself (1981) has pointed out, one can believe that water is nearby without believing that H_2O is nearby, for example, because the beliefs have different *conceptual constituents*. The belief that H_2O is nearby contains the concept of H_2O as a constituent, while the belief that water is nearby does not. Since the concept of water is distinct from the concept of H_2O, the concepts can figure in different beliefs.[23] This explanation of how the beliefs differ is, of course, consistent with the content principle. But the point I want to underscore now is that it does not imply it. One can avail oneself of this explanation without being committed to the content principle.

The explanation does assume, of course, that the concepts are distinct. That raises the question of concept individuation, that is, the question of the correct nonduplication principle for concepts. The received view is, I think, that the following counterpart of the content principle for beliefs is correct:

> *The Content Principle for Concepts*: No two concepts can be exactly alike in their content.

Given this principle, since one can have the concept of water and lack the concept of H_2O, it follows that the concepts have different contents. And one might argue that since they have different contents, so do the belief that water is present and the belief that H_2O is present. However, Dretske has offered an explanation of why the concepts in question are distinct which does not presuppose the content principle for concepts, though it is consistent with it. The explanation parallels his explanation of why the belief that water is present and the belief that H_2O is present are distinct. The concepts in question are distinct, he says, because they have different conceptual constituents: The concept of H_2O does while the concept of water does not contain, for instance, the concept of hydrogen as a constituent (Dretske 1981, pp. 217–18). There are complex concepts: concepts that contain other concepts as constituents; and the content of a complex concept is a function of the contents of its constituents. The concept of 23 is different from the concept of the cube root of 12,167 since, for example, the latter does and the former does not contain the concept of a cube root as a constituent. And so it is with the concept of fourteen days and the concept of a fortnight: They are distinct since the former does and the latter does not contain, for example, the concept of fourteen as a constituent (cf. ibid., p. 216). Notice that if the content principle is false, then the fact that the concepts are distinct does not imply that the concepts have different contents.

I propose the following nonduplication principle for concept:

> *The Encoded Content Principle for Concepts*: No two concepts can be exactly alike in their content and in the manner in which they encode their content.

This is implied by, but does not imply, the content principle for concepts. Unlike the content principle, it leaves open whether two concepts can have the same content.

To return to the point made at the close of part I, Dretske can maintain that (1)–(3) are inconsistent if he rejects the content principle but maintains the encoded content principle. If (1)–(3) are inconsistent, then a state has, for example, the natural function of indicating that water is present *iff* it has the natural function of indicating that H_2O is present. But this does not imply that the natural indicator function proposal is false. For it may be that when (2) holds, the content that F is present = the content that G is present. If so, then the content that water is present = the content that H_2O is present. This does not, however, imply that the belief that water is present = the belief that H_2O is present, *if* the content principle is false. For then it is possible for two beliefs to have the same content. Moreover, if the encoded content principle is true, then while the beliefs have the same content, their difference may lie in the way that they encode the content in question. The encoded content principle is *consistent* with the claim that if (2) holds, then the content that F is present = the content that G is present. If the encoded content principle is correct, then from the fact that (1)–(3) are inconsistent, it does *not* follow that the indicator function proposal is false.

Dretske's natural indicator function account of content seems best suited to a denotational account of concepts. But whether or not he holds such an account, such an account would require the rejection of the content principles. Thus, suppose that one held a *denotational* account of (say) the contents of natural kind concepts: The content of a natural kind concept is the natural kind it denotes. Then, for example, the concept of water and the concept of H_2O have the same content, since these are natural kind concepts and the kind water is the kind H_2O. However, the concepts are distinct: Someone could have the one concept without having the other. This denotational account of natural kind concepts violates the content principle for concepts. It is, however, *consistent* with the encoded content principle for concepts. The concepts are different because they encode the content differently. The concept of H_2O encodes the content by means of containing a constituent concept which denotes hydrogen, while the concept of water does not so encode the content (cf. Fodor 1987). This difference in the manner of encoding suffices for a difference in concept. This difference in the manner of encoding does involve a denotational difference, but not a difference in what the concepts themselves denote, and so not a difference in their content. Rather, it is a difference in what their constituent concepts denote.

I should note that it is not my concern here to defend a denotational account of any concept. My point has just been that the encoded content principles, unlike the content principles, are consistent with such accounts.

I want now to focus exclusively on the encoded content principles themselves and put aside further discussion of Dretske's account of content. I will appeal to these principles in making a case that the content principles are false. Much of what I say will be contentious. But I would be happy, at this point, to settle for a Dutch Verdict concerning whether the encoded content principles are correct and the content principles incorrect.

Synonomy and Content

Synonyms, you will recall, appear to fail to substitute *salva veritate* in (oblique) that-clauses in belief contexts and propositional attitude contexts in general. One could of course deny linguistic appearances and maintain that there is no failure of *synonyms* to so substitute since expressions in that-clauses mean something different from what they mean outside them. But this seems *very* implausible (cf. Loar 1972, Burge 1978, Davidson 1984, McGinn 1989, and Fodor forthcoming a). "Fortnight" does indeed seem to mean fortnight in, for example, "I mistakenly thought that a fortnight was ten, days." Nevertheless, expressions in such that-clauses are *used* in a way that is different from the way they are used outside such clauses (cf. Loar 1972; Burge 1978; and Fodor forthcoming a). The failure of synonyms to so substitute in that-clauses in belief sentences implies that there is a *semantic* contribution that expressions in such that-clauses make to determining what belief is attributed which they do not make solely by virtue of their meanings. Thus, they make a kind of *dual-contribution* to determining what belief is attributed, one by virtue of their meaning and the other by virtue of something other than their meaning alone.[24]

The idea that expressions in such that-clauses can make some sort of dual contribution to determining what belief is attributed is hardly new (see Castaneda 1967; Loar 1972; Schiffer 1977; Hornsby 1977; Burge 1978; Loar 1981; McGinn 1982, 1989). The point is, however, typically made only for singular terms, but it holds as well for general terms and predicates. Moreover, the typical assumption is that expressions in that-clauses make a dual contribution to determining what belief is attributed *by* making a dual contribution to determining the *content* of the belief attributed. Following Jerry Fodor (forthcoming a), I reject this assumption. The additional contribution is not to determine what content is expressed, but rather to *display* what the content is *coded* into.[25]

That-clauses in belief ascriptions serve two functions. They express the content of a belief and display what the content is coded into. In so doing, they determine what belief is attributed. For, as I keep saying, beliefs are individuated both by their contents and by the manners in which they encode their contents. That-clauses do the first job in virtue of their meanings. They do the second job, in part, in virtue of their constituent structure. The constituent structure of the state must be suitably isomorphic to the constituent structure of the sentence.

Recall Burge's claim that contents are more fine-grained than ordinary linguistic meanings. Burge attempted to justify this claim on the grounds that synonyms fail to substitute *salva veritate* in that-clauses in belief sentences. Now, to be sure, such failures are a test for difference of belief state type. Moreover, they would also be a test for difference of content if the content principle were correct: For, given that principle, no two belief state types can have the same content. But I reject the content principle. Synonymous that-clauses, I claim, express the same belief contents. Thus, for example, the belief that Mary will return in a fortnight and the belief that Mary will return in fourteen days have the same content. The beliefs are, however, distinct. So, the content principle is false. The beliefs differ, not in their contents, but rather in the way they encode their contents. Failure of substitution of terms in that-clauses in belief sentences is not a test for difference of content (cf. Fodor forthcoming a).

Expressions that occur in the context "the concept of ...", likewise, make a dual contribution to determining what concept is described: They express the content of the concept and they display what the content is coded into. Synonymous terms express the same concept content. So, the content principle for concepts is false. But differences in the syntactic structure of synonyms can make for differences in what manner of encoding they display. Thus, while the terms "fortnight" and "fourteen days," for instance, being synonyms, express the same conceptual contents, the concept of a fortnight and the concept of fourteen days are distinct. The difference between them lies in the difference in their constituent structures, not in their contents. As we noted earlier, the concept of fourteen days encodes the content in question, in part, by containing a constituent that has the content fourteen, while the concept of a fortnight does not. So, the concepts are distinct.

On two-factor theories of content, content consists of two factors, one of which is functional role. While I reject two-factor theories of content, it is fair to say that I favor a two-factor theory of beliefs (and concepts). What belief a given belief state is (whether it is, for instance, a belief that Mary will return in fourteen days) depends on two factors: its content and the manner in which it encodes its content.[26] And so it is with concepts: What concept a given concept is (whether it is, for instance, a concept of of fourteen days) likewise depends on two factors: its content and the manner in which it encodes its content. And the latter partly determines its functional role. Here, then, is how the two factors relate: The one which encodes the content contributes to determining functional role. The manner of encoding of a concept contributes to determining its functional role in beliefs. And the manner of encoding of a belief contributes to determining its functional role in mental processes.

These differences in functional role make for psychological differences. So, there can be psychological differences between beliefs (or concepts), due to differences in their conceptual structures, without differences in their contents. Thus, I reject the following fairly widely held supervenience principle:

There can be no psychological difference between two beliefs (concepts) without a difference in their content.

The psychological properties of a belief or concept does not supervene on its content: A belief or concept with the same content can have different psychological properties. Differences in how they encode their contents can make for psychological differences without differences in content.

Content and Rational Explanation

One source of resistance to the encoded content principle for beliefs is, I think, the assumption that if two beliefs have different rationalizing roles, they do so *solely* in virtue of differences in their contents. To be sure, rationalizing explanations are content-based. But that does not imply, however, that beliefs rationalize *solely* in virtue of their contents. Two beliefs with the same content may differ in what they can rationalize because of differences in the manner in which they encode their contents. To think otherwise is to fail to appreciate the dual-contribution of expressions in that-clauses. If, as I have suggested, synonymous that-clauses express the same contents, then beliefs do not rationally explain solely in virtue of their contents: For the belief that P can have different explanatory force from the belief that Q, even when P and Q are synonymous, and so when the beliefs have the same contents. Not just the content expressed by the that-clause, but also the manner of encoding displayed by it are what do the explaining. To be sure, we use that-clauses to attribute to belief states properties in virtue of which they enter into rationalizing relationships with other belief states, with actions, decisions, intentions, and so on. But the properties in question are that of *having a certain content encoded in a certain way*. These are the properties in virtue of which beliefs participate in rationalizing relationships.[27]

Encoding and The Language of Thought Hypothesis

It can be left open for present purposes what the manner of content encoding is. One natural suggestion is that it is linguistic, but there is no *a priori* guarantee that it is.[28] *The encoded principles do not imply that there is a language of thought.* The language of thought hypothesis is an empirical hypothesis about the manner in which the contents of thoughts are encoded in systematic minds. The encoded content principles are intended to be nonempirical. They do not imply that mental representation is linguistic, but rather just that mental representations encode content. It is important to separate the a *priori* issue of whether belief and concept content must be encoded from the empirical issue of what the actual manner of encoding is.

I should note, however, that I sympathize with the view that language users and many nonverbal organisms have "languages of thought." The reason is that there is, I think, compelling evidence that the minds of language users and many sorts of nonverbal organisms are systematic. (By saying that a mind is systematic, I mean that it consists, in part, of a vast range of systematically related cognitive capacities to represent.) And the best explanation of the fact that a mind is systematic is, I think, that its system of mental representation has a combinatorial syntax and semantics (cf. Dretske, 1982, pp. 230–1). In systematic minds, the encoding system will be, in part, linguistic in this sense: It will, like a language, have a combinatorial syntax and semantics.[29]

Mental Synonomy

Suppose, then, that there are languages of thought and that beliefs are constituted, in part, by sentences of the believer's "mentalese" (Fodor 1975). Then, two beliefs involving syntactically different sentences in mentalese may, nevertheless, have the same content. The beliefs will have different causal roles in mental processes in virtue of syntactic differences in their constituent mentalese sentences. Likewise, two concepts with the same content may be different words in mentalese, and so play a different role in mental sentences. It follows that there can be synonymous sentences and synonymous terms in mentalese.

When a complex concept and a simple concept have the same content, this will be a matter of a syntactically structured mentalese expression and a syntactically unstructured mentalese expression having the same meaning and so being synonyms. There seems no reason to deny, however, that two distinct syntactically unstructured mentalese expressions can have the same meaning. This would be a case of two simple concepts having the same content. Of course, if this is the case, then neither concept will be *primitive* for the organism. But not all simple concepts are primitive. A concept is simple *iff* it is not complex; and a concept is complex, you will recall, *iff* it contains another concept as a constituent. The notion of a simple concept is, so to speak, a "syntactic" notion. In contrast, the notion of a primitive concept is a "semantic" notion. A concept is *primitive* for a cognizer *iff* its content is not a function of the contents of other concepts and constitutent structures possessed by the cognizer. It follows, of course, that every primitive concept is simple. A complex concept is invariably nonprimitive since its content will be a function of the contents of its constitutent concepts and its constituent structure. A concept may be simple, however, even though its content is a function of the contents of other concepts the organism possesses.[30] For example, if the organism has the concept of a right-angled equilateral and the concept of a square, then the content of the latter is a function of the contents of the constituents of the former together with the former's constituent structure; so, the latter is not a primitive concept for the organism. It may, however, be a simple concept: It may not contain other concepts as (syntactic) constituents. We see, then, that not all simple concepts are primitive. An organism could not, of course, have two primitive concepts with the same content. But it could have two simple concepts with the same content.

As has often been argued (Fodor 1975; Stich 1983), differences in the syntax of mental symbols can make for psychological differences. Two mental symbols, I claim, can have the same meaning while being syntactically different. So, there can be a psychological difference without a semantic difference between two mental symbols. That is why the supervenience principle cited earlier is false. There can be psychological differences between beliefs (or concepts) without differences in their contents.

This point that the syntactic structure of a mental representation affects its functional role in an organism's cognitive economy is, of course, nowadays a familiar one. But it is often overlooked that nonsyntactic, nonsemantic properties of mental representations can affect functional role also. In particular, abstract structural properties of mental representations that are analogous to orthographic properties can affect their participation in thoughts (e.g., beliefs, desires, etc.); and this, in turn, affects the participation of the thoughts in mental processes.[31] Two syntactically unstructured mentalese synonyms which differ in their "orthographic" properties can function as different coin in the cognitive economy of an organism. And that, in a nutshell, is why an organism can have two simple concepts with the same content.

I will conclude by noting one consequence of this: Even a denotational account of concept content *restricted* to simple concepts would have to reject the content principle for concepts and, in turn, the content principle for beliefs. For two distinct simple concepts might denote the same property or kind, and so have the same content.[32]

Notes

1　This question concerns *belief state types*.
2　Cf. the puzzle about event individuation raised at the beginning of Davidson 1984.
3　But this is not universally held. Jerry Fodor (forthcoming a), for example, has recently rejected this answer. I am deeply indebted to him for opening my eyes to what is wrong with it.
4　The general idea of a nonduplication principle is David Lewis's. I learned

about it from reading Johnathan Bennett (1988), where it is employed in a discussion of event individuation.

5   I will not, however, attempt a general defense of Dretske's proposal; that is, I will not try to argue that the proposal is correct.

6   More precisely, "fortnight" and "period of fourteen consecutive days" are synonyms.

7   Burge cogently replies to Alonzo Church (1954) and to Wilfred Sellars (1955).

8   This project is in the foreground in Dretske (1981) and in the background in Dretske (1988). However, Dretske's account of intentionality is revised and developed in the latter work, and so I will focus on what he says there. For troubles with his earlier naturalized account of intentionality see Loewer (1983) and (1986).

9   I should note that Dretske does not use the term "Brentano's Problem." What he says is: "The entire project can be viewed as an exercise in naturalism – or, if you prefer, materialistic metaphysics. Can you bake a mental cake using only physical yeast and flour? The argument is that you can" (1981, p. xi).

10 I cannot say, exactly, what makes a condition broadly physical. But nothing will turn on this in what follows.

11 Dretske cites a debt to Stampe (1977) and Millikan (1984), among others, for their work on natural functions. I should note, however, that Dretske's, Stampe's, and Millikan's approaches to content differ in various ways that I cannot discuss here. For a critique of the Stampe-type approach, see McLaughlin (1986).

To avert possible misunderstanding, I should also note that Dretske uses the expression "intrinsic function" rather than "natural function." The functions are intrinsic in that they are not relative to the purposes and intentions of cognizer(s). But "natural function" appears in the index of Dretske 1988 and seems a more apt expression than "intrinsic function" since indicator functions are relational.

12 Dretske's explication of the notion of information in 1982 is best viewed as a would-be explication of the notion of natural meaning. But his discussion in 1988 does not depend on that earlier probabilistic account. For problems with the earlier account see Loewer (1983) and (1986).

13 I should note that Dretske allows that there is a second basic way that B can count as having a natural indicator function in O. B might have a control duty in O as a result of O's genetic inheritance; the trait of B's having a control duty might have been selected in O's species because tokens of B in earlier members of the species indicated that F was present, and not because of the indication of any other condition by those tokens. If this is the case, B has, in O, the natural function of indicating that (an) F is present. This is not, however, a process by means of which B is selected for a control duty in O because tokens of B *in O* indicated that F was present. So this, Dretske says, is not a natural process of the sort required by (iii). And (i) and (ii) alone, according to Dretske, do not suffice for b's being a belief (or proto-belief). The reason, according to Dretske, is that an indicator function must be acquired by means of a learning process for the content of the state to be a causally relevant feature of it; and it is, he says, an essential property of beliefs (and proto-beliefs) that their contents are causally relevant features of them. Whether this is indeed an essential feature of beliefs is a controversial

issue that I cannot address here. Likewise, I cannot address here Dretske's explanation of the causal relevance of content.

As Dretske (1988) admits, these two ways of B's counting as having a natural indicator function – in virtue of individual learning history and in virtue of genetic inheritance – are "quite different" (p. 64). Indeed, they seem different enough that it might have been better to use a different term for each, or to have used subscripts, say, "natural indicator function$_L$" to indicate that the relevant backward-looking fact concerns the learning history of an individual organism, and "natural indicator function$_E$" to indicate that the backward-looking fact concerns the evolutionary history of the organism's species. Since natural indicator function$_E$ is not, according to Dretske, relevant to belief or proto-belief I will not discuss it.

14 Dretske (1988) is neutral concerning what rewards are exactly. We can, he says, for present purposes, think of the reward as stimuli, or as response, or even as "pleasure (need or tension reduction) that certain stimuli (or responses) bring to an organism" (p. 100).

15 He also holds that when D is so recruited for a control duty in O its tokens, thereby, count as pure desires for R (1988, pp. 111–15). I restrict myself here, however, to his account of content for beliefs.

16 One group of questions that I will not address concern the important issue of semantic normativity. Kripke (1982) raises skeptical worries about the possibility of a naturalistic account of semantic normativity. I cannot pursue here, however, whether Dretske's account can answer those worries. This, to be sure, is a central issue where the reduction of intentionality is concerned, but my interests in this paper can be pursued without addressing it. I will not, as I said, attempt to settle whether Dretske's indicator function proposal is correct.

17 I include the paranthetical qualification since, while all identities are (arguably) metaphysically necessary, *statements* of identity can be contingent. For example, the statement "blue = my favorite color" is contingent.

18 I should mention two (unrelated) points. First, when (2) holds, the mechanisms of natural selection will not distinguish B's indicating that F is present from B's indicating that G is present either. There can be no selective advantage conferred by the one that is not conferred by the other. Second, I do not think that Dretske has even succeeded in explaining how when F and G are nomologically equivalent, B could, by means of operant learning, acquire a control duty because its tokens indicated that F is present and not also acquire a control duty because its tokens indicated that G is present. But I do not pursue this since there is, so far as I can see, no reason in principle why he could not lay down further contraints so as to distinguish B's having the natural function of indicating that F is present and B's having the natural function of indicating that G is present even when F and G are nomologically equivalent.

19 Dretske (1988) remarks at one point that Berent Enc (1982) has shown "that we can distinguish between the representation of logically *equivalent* situations by appeal to (among other things) the functions of a system" (p. 76). Distinct representations may indeed represent logically equivalent situations, or, indeed, the same situation, the differences between the representations being in their distinct functional roles in a system. I take Enc to have illustrated this. However, if a state naturally functions to represent situation

S, S = S', and if "S = S'" is metaphysically necessary, then it naturally functions to represent situation S'. Enc has not shown that this is false. And this is the point I am stressing.

20 Rather, he offers an explanation of how the indicator functions of states can become interrelated and how a state might change its indicator function. Moreover, his chief concern seems to be explaining how a network of belief states can develop from a system of proto-beliefs. In any case, I lack the space here to discuss his intriguing suggestions in the final section of Dretske (1988). To anticipate a point to be made later, Dretske should offer a two-factor theory of belief states and of concepts. He should not, however, offer a two-factor theory of their contents. More about this below.

21 Fodor (forthcoming a) has recently claimed that we individuate beliefs, in part, by appeal to the vehicle of expression partly constitutive of the belief; and he holds that different vehicles can express the same content. The encoded content principle for beliefs incorporates essentially the same idea. Fodor pointed out to me that the core of the idea can be found in Church (1954): Intentional isomorphism is, in part, a syntactic notion.

22 Concepts are, I think, capacities to token certain sorts of states. To say that a concept is a constituent of a belief is to say that the concept is exercised in the belief. This will typically involve the tokening of a state which is a proper part of the belief state.

23 While this idea is discussed at length in Dretske (1981), it does not appear in Dretske 1988. Dretske (personal correspondence) assures me, however, that he still endorses it. Despite his silence about compositionality in Dretske (1988), he still thinks the notion must be invoked in an account of belief (personal correspondence).

24 There is a worry about failure of substitution of synonyms in that-clauses that should be mentioned explicitly. The worry concerns compositionality: If synonyms fail to substitute *salva veritate* in propositional attitude sentences, then there is a *prima facie* worry that compositionality fails for such sentences. It is this worry, no doubt, that motivates the desperate move of claiming that terms have different meanings in (oblique) that-clauses from their meanings outside such clauses. But the move seems no less desparate for all that. It would be serious indeed if compositionality failed for propositional attitude sentences. But surely there is a better way to save it. I think that failure of substitution of synonyms in that-clauses in belief contexts is compatible with compositionality. For some support for this position, see Burge (1977) and (1978, p. 127). See also footnote 25 below.

25 The idea of displaying is Fodor's; see Fodor (forthcoming a).

The encoded content principles suggest an approach to capturing compositionality. Expressions in that-clause display manners of encoding, and this should be captured in the logical form of belief sentences. I think that an adequate account of displaying would enable us to see why compositionality does not fail in propositional attitude sentences, though I am unable to provide one here.

26 As has often been pointed out, we accept various paraphrases of what someone believes and of what someone said (cf. Ziff 1972; Stich 1983). What paraphrases are acceptable depends, in part, on features of the conversational context. Sometimes a paraphrase is acceptable because it reveals a certain feature of the manner of encoding that is of interest, and sometimes one is

acceptable because it reveals a certain relevant feature of interest of the content (or meaning) which is independent of the manner of encoding. But I lack the space to elaborate on this here.

27 It is, of course, a hotly debated issue whether the property of having a certain content has a causal explanatory role. As I mentioned earlier, Dretske (1988) has attempted to explain how it does. This important issue is, however, independent of the issue over whether the content principles or the encoded content principles are correct. Suffice it to note that Dretske's explanation of the causal role of content is consistent with the encoded content principles.

28 Fodor (forthcoming a) would agree: He leaves open whether the encoding is linguistic.

29 The language of thought hypothesis has recently come under heavy attack by some connectionists who try to explain systematicity without postulating a system of mental representation with a combinatorial syntax and semantics, and constitutent sensitive mental processes. I think the attack is unsuccessful. For replies to it see McLaughlin (1987), Fodor and Pylyshyn (1988), and Fodor and McLaughlin (1990).

30 I thus agree with Dretske (1981) that a concept can be primitive for one organism and nonprimitive for another.

31 The concept that an expression displays thus does not depend *solely* on the constituent structure of the expression, for an expression that lacks a constituent structure can display a concept. I owe thanks to Gary Gates here.

32 I addition to the acknowledgments in earlier notes, I would especially like to thank Fred Adams, Fred Dretske, Jerry Fodor, Gary Gates, Steve Lawrence, Barry Loewer, and Colin McGinn for helpful discussions, and to acknowledge the large debt I owe to Fodor's and Dretske's recent work on content.

References

Bennett, J. 1988: *Events and Their Names*. Indianapolis/Cambridge: Hackett.

Block, N. 1986: Avertisement for a Semantics for Psychology. In *Midwest Studies in Philosophy*, vol. 10, ed. P. French, T. Vehling, and H. Wettstein, Minneapolis: University of Minnesota Press.

Burge, T. 1977: Self-Reference and Translation. In *Translation and Meaning*, ed. M. Guenthner-Reutter and F. Guenthener, London: Duckworth.

—— 1978: Belief and Synonymy. *Journal of Philosophy*, 75, 3, pp. 119–38.

Castaneda, H. N. 1967: Indicators and Quasi-Indicators. *American Philosophical Quarterly*, 4.

Church, A. 1954: Intentional Isomorphism and Identity of Belief. *Philosophical Studies*, 5, 5.

Davidson, D. 1985: On Saying That. Reprinted in *Essays on Truth and Interpretation*, Oxford: Clareudon Press.

Dretske, F. 1981. *Knowledge and the Flow of Information*. Cambridge, Mass.: MIT Press/Bradford Books.

—— 1988. *Explaining Behavior: Reasons in a World of Causes*. Cambridge, Mass.: MIT Press/Bradford Books.

Enc, B. 1982: Intentional States of Mechanical Devices. *Mind*, 91, pp. 161–82.

Field, H. 1977: Logic, Meaning, and Conceptual Role. *Journal of Philosophy*, 69.

—— 1978: "Mental Representation" *Erkenntnis*, 13, pp. 9–61.

Fodor, J. 1975: *The Language of Thought*. New York: Crowell.

—— 1984: Semantics, Wisconsin Style. *Synthese*, 59.

—— 1987: *Psychosemantics*. Cambridge; Mass.: MIT Press.

—— Forthcoming a. Belief Individuation and the Substitution Argument. *Minnesota Studies in Philosophy of Science*.

—— Forthcoming b. A Theory of Content Part I.

—— Forthcoming c. A Theory of Content Part II.

Fodor, J. and Pylyshyn, Z. 1988: Connectionism and Cognitive Architecture: A Critical Analysis. *Cognition*, 28, pp. 3–71.

Fodor, J. and McLaughlin, B. P. 1990: Connectionism and the Systematicity Problem: Why Smolensky's Solution Fails. *Cognition*, 35, pp. 183–204.

Grice, H. P. 1957: Meaning. *Philosophical Review*, 66, pp. 377–88.

Hornsby, J. 1977: Singular Terms in the Context of Propositional Attitude. *Mind*, 86.

Kripke, S. 1982: *Wittgenstein on Rules and Private Language*. Oxford: Basil Blackwell.

LePore, E. and Loewer, B. 1986: Dual Aspect Semantics. In *New Directions in Semantics*, ed. Ernest LePore, New York: Academic Press.

Loar, B. 1972. Reference and Propositional Attitudes. *Philosophical Review*, 80, pp. 43–62.

Loar, B. 1981. *Mind and Meaning*. Cambridge: Cambridge University Press.

Loewer, B. 1983: Information and Belief. *Behavioral and Brain Sciences*, 5.

—— 1986. From Information to Intentionality. *Synthese*, 2, pp. 287–317.

Mates, Benson. 1952: Synonymity. In *Semantics and the Philosophy of Language*, ed. Leonard Linksy, Urbana, University of Illinois Press.

Millikan, R. 1984: *Language, Thought and Other Biological Categories*. Cambridge, Mass.: MIT Press.

McGinn, C. 1982: The Structure of Content. In *Thought and Object*, ed. A. Woodfield, Oxford: Clarendon Press.

—— 1989: *Mental Content*, Basil Blackwell.

McLaughlin, B. P. 1987: What is Wrong With Correlational Psychosemantics. *Synthese*, 2, pp. 271–86.

—— 1987: Tye on Connectionism. Spindel Conference, *Southern Journal of Philosophy*, pp. 185–93.

Schiffer, S. 1977: Naming and Knowing. In *Midwest Studies in Philosophy*, vol. 2, ed. P. French et al., Minneapolis: University of Minnesota Press.

Sellars, W. 1955: Putnam on Synonymity and Belief. *Analysis*, 15, 5, pp. 117–20.

Stampe, D. 1977: Toward a Causal Theory of Linguistic Representation. In *Midwest Studies in Philosophy*, vol. 2, ed. P. French, et al., Minneapolis: University of Minnesota Press.

Stitch, S. 1983: *From Folk Psychology to Cognitive Science*. Cambridge, Mass.: MIT Press.

Ziff, P. 1972: What is Said. In *Semantics of Natural Languages*, ed. D. Davidson and G. Harman, Boston: Reidel.

10
Dretske's Replies

Preface

There is more here than I could possibly digest, let alone answer. I know the contributors will be disappointed. I am sure they will feel that I misinterpreted or deliberately ignored some of their most inspired criticism. I know I deliberately ignored things. That is the advantage a respondent enjoys and, believe me, I enjoyed it. In particular, I chose *not* to comment on the alternative ideas that were sometimes developed. I had my hands full defending my own views. Besides, I thought, the best way to handle proffered alternatives was to show that alternatives were not really necessary. In this case, a good defense seemed like the best offense.

But however inadequate they may regard the product, I assure the contributors that their efforts were not wasted – at least not *on me*. However little *they* may learn from reading what follows, *I* learned an enormous amount by writing it. To them, and their incisive essays, I am grateful. They have somehow managed to teach me, in only the way that a friendly but persistent critic can, what I really think and why.

Perception: Heil

When I finished writing the first draft of *Seeing and Knowing* in 1966, I thought seriously of scrapping the chapter on nonepistemic seeing. It wasn't that I thought it was wrong. Quite the contrary. It sounded just right to me. Details aside, it still does. The trouble was that it started sounding *too* obvious. Too trivial. Would anyone – *could* anyone (once they thought about it a few minutes) – really disagree with any of this? Why spend 70 pages defending something no one would attack?

What finally convinced me, despite these doubts, to keep the chapter is that, with very few exceptions,[1] philosophers had refused to acknowledge that seeing was *not* knowing, that it was *not* believing, that seeing a physical object and knowing or believing something about it – that it was a physical object – were quite different things. Or, if everyone *had* recognized this and merely failed to mention it because (as I feared) it was too obvious, there had been a conspicuous failure to appreciate the fundamental significance of this point for both epistemology and the philosophy of perception. Conclusions were being reached about what we could and couldn't see from premises about what we could or couldn't know. And vice versa. Shopworn objections to knowing objective reality were being treated as objections or obstacles to *seeing* objective reality. Because it was hard to know what lay behind the appearances, it was hard to see beyond the appearances. Thus was ignorance of X being confused with a kind of blindness of X. Furthermore, conceptual differences (in the way we conceived what we saw) were being confused with differences in what we saw. These arguments often surfaced in the philosophy of science. As though a cat, lacking *our* concept of a cockroach, and therefore unable to think of it – or see it – *as* a cockroach, couldn't *see* a cockroach scuttling across the kitchen floor. As though the early Babylonians, lacking our concept of a star or a planet, couldn't see the same stars and planets we see merely because they had different beliefs about them.

Our experience *of* the world, the *sensory* dimension of our mental life, was thereby being confused with cognitive phenomena, with possession and deployment of *concepts*. But surely – or so it seemed to me – the having of sensations, our sensory experience of the world, however much it might (in normal adults) culminate in knowledge, did not itself require the possession of the concepts required for this knowledge.

So, despite my apprehensions, I kept the chapter on nonepistemic seeing. To my surprise, it provoked the most debate. This *still* surprises me. It is quite true, as John Heil points out, that I am committed to something called sense experience. I should have thought that, as philosophical commitments go, this one involved a tolerable level of risk. After all, there was a time, not so long ago, when philosophers thought that sense experience (at least one's own) was virtually the *only* thing one could be sure of. But the pendulum swings. And now, I am told, the burden of proof falls on *me* to justify talking about such exotica.

Very well. I'm perfectly prepared to accept this challenge as long as we understand that what I'm being asked to do is to show that seeing an object is something that a human being, or an animal for that matter, can be described as doing *without* thereby being described as believing (consciously or not) anything about the object seen – that seeing X is not constituted by, nor does it require, the having of beliefs about X. Seeing X is a relation between seer and seen that involves some quite different, some nonepistemic, response to X. Seeing the bug is, in this sense, like stepping on it. Whether we have – whether we *always* have – beliefs about the bugs we see (or step on) is *not* the issue. If bugs emitted a deafening roar when molested, we would doubtless notice their presence when we stepped on them. This would be no reason to advance a doxastic or cognitive theory of *stepping on*.

Heil, in an otherwise excellent essay, says that according to me *all* seeing is like the first experience of someone, blind from birth, who gains his sight. The idea seems to be that such a person would be so "awestruck" (Heil's word) by the experience of seeing a pale blue wall that he wouldn't know what to believe. Hence, he might not have *any* beliefs. Therefore, he might, in Dretske's sense, see the pale blue wall nonepistemically. He also suggests that I have a notion of seeing that "requires" there to be cases in which an object is seen without any beliefs whatsoever.

These are uncharacteristic lapses. Heil knows that the claim is, and has always been, not that simple seeing of X occurs *only* (or, indeed, *ever*) when one has *no* beliefs about X, but that its occurrence is *compatible* with no such beliefs. So, yes, the awestruck man Heil describes sees a blue wall. He sees it nonepistemically. But, in the *same* nonepistemic way, and much more commonly, a normally sighted person sees a blue wall when he, not at all awestruck, sees the wall and sees how badly it clashes with the curtains. To describe an unusual, a comparatively rare, way of seeing blue walls as what, if Dretske is right, *all* seeing is like is unfair. It is as bad as saying that because I think stepping on things is noncognitive (you can step on X without knowing it is X you are stepping on – without, in fact, knowing you are stepping on something), stepping on something is *always* like walking in your sleep.

What, exactly, is wrong with the idea of sense experience? Why do cognitivists (as I shall call them) always have to drag knowledge and belief into the act? Why does seeing a bug have to be the arousal (by the bug, presumably) of a *doxastic* (belief) or *cognitive* (knowledge) condition? One reason, I suspect, is that cognitivists like Heil think (or think people like me think) that if visual experience (of colors, say) doesn't amount to having *beliefs* about colors – so that seeing a blue wall in good light is believing that the wall (or something) is blue – then there is nothing left for the experience of blue to be but a little bluish expanse in the head. There is ample evidence in Heil's paper for this interpretation.

I do not, of course, think our experience of an object, the kind of experience that helps constitute our seeing objects, has the properties that the objects themselves have. When a stick, placed in water, looks bent, there is no reason to suppose that there is something, in the experience itself, that *is* bent. The experience of blue needn't itself be blue (though I don't see why it *can't* be blue). I do not, as Heil suggests, want to transfer into the head all the properties that objects outside the head appear to have. Why should anyone (today) want to do anything so silly? Do beliefs about the color blue have to be blue? Must the belief that the stick is bent be bent? If not, why should experience of blue (bent sticks) need to be blue (or bent)?

What we need in the case of sense experience is not little colored shapes (muffled sounds, etc.) in the head, but a stage in the processing of sensory information *about* these properties in which such information is made available to cognitive centers for conceptual utilization – for the fixation of belief. We know that *more* information gets in, and becomes available to the cognitive mechanisms, than ever is, or ever can be, used. We know this not only through careful experimentation, but through the fact that learning (concept learning) enables us to exploit more of this information. So there is, in most conscious experiences of the world, this surplus of sensory information – usable but unused information about what is going on around us. So what is wrong in calling this pool of information, as psychologists are wont to do, the sensory information store (SIS), or, as you and I are wont to do, sensory experience? On this account of things, our experience *of* blue, of extendedness, of shape and orientation is just the occurrence, in us, of elements (in a larger pool of information) bearing (or purporting to bear) information about color, extension, shape and orientation. Depending on our interests, purposes, attention, and learning, these elements can be, but *need not* be (and often *are not*), cognitively processed in any further way. They are like books in a library waiting to be checked out. The information – more of it than can be used by any single patron – is made available. Whether or not it is ever *used* depends on the interests and needs of the individual.

How else is one to account for the obvious differences between what we see and what we know (or believe)? What, after all, is the difference between seeing 50 stars on a flag (all clearly visible, none being occluded by folds in the cloth or other objects) and seeing 49 stars? Are we (those who believe our perception of things has to do not with our beliefs about, but with our experience of, the things around us) being asked to believe that this perceptual difference is a difference in what the person who sees the stars believes about the stars she sees? This seems incredible since we can easily imagine circumstances in which people seeing different numbers of stars believe exactly the same thing – e.g., that they see a lot of stars. We could, I suppose, drag in unconscious beliefs: Tom (who sees 50 stars) believes he sees 50 while Tim (who sees only 49) believes he sees 49; or, if this strains credulity (making everyone, at the unconscious level, an *idiot savant*), we might try saying that Tom acquires, almost instantly, and without being conscious of it, 50 separate beliefs (one for each star he sees) while Tim acquires only 49 such beliefs. If this last maneuver is tolerated, we could, of course, defend a doxastic account of almost anything – including stepping on things. Nobody steps on a bug without acquiring a belief that he has stepped on it – the belief often being unconscious. When treading on anthills one unconsciously acquires an enormous number of beliefs, one for each ant one steps on.

Heil, quite rightly, dismisses this foolishness as *ad hoc* and implausible. He suggests, instead, that we supplement a doxastic account of perception with a causal account of the objects of perception. The objects of perception – what we see – are given by causal factors not (necessarily) reflected in the beliefs we form about what we see. So, it seems, Tom could see 50 stars while Tim sees only 49 (thus Tom sees at least one thing Tim doesn't – let us, for convenience, call it star #50) because, though they do not differ in what they believe about what they see (both

believing only that they are seeing a lot of stars), Tom causally interacts
(Heil's language) "in a certain way" with 50 stars (and, specifically, with
star #50), while Tim interacts with only 49 (and not at all with star #50).

Unless I am missing something, this is a way of saying that Tom sees
star #50, while Tim does not, because – *whatever* they happen to believe
– Tom is causally interacting *in a certain way* with star #50 and Tim isn't.
It is important, of course, to know what this "certain way" is in which
one must interact with X in order to see X. One can, obviously, interact
with a great many things (even through the eyes) without seeing them.
And, as I argued in *Seeing and Knowing*, even when the things one
interacts with are *parts* of the thing one sees, one needn't see them. One
doesn't see *all* the bricks in a wall just because *every* brick is reflecting
light into one's eyes (thus making it true that one is causally interacting
with each brick). As Heil observes, this would be a fallacy of division;
one doesn't hear *each* drop of water hitting the beach just because one
hears the wave hitting the beach and the wave is made up of millions of
drops). So the question for Heil is this: *how* must one be causally
interacting with a star (and, in particular, star #50) in order to see it?
Obviously this is not a *cognitive* interaction since we have already said
that Tom and Tim are the same in this respect. So what is it? What does
star #50 have to cause in us for us to see it? How does Tom, who sees
star #50, differ from Tim who doesn't?

That is a question that the concept of sense experience is designed to
answer. In *Seeing and Knowing* I spoke about the way things looked. I no
longer like this way of talking, preferring instead the sort of information-
theoretic idiom I alluded to above (seeing X is a certain stage in the
processing of sensory information about X) – but it will do well enough to
make the present point. Tom sees star #50, while Tim does not, because
it *looks* some way to Tom, not to Tim. Since there are 49 other stars that
are contributing to the way things look to Tom, Tom sees a total of 50
stars. Tim sees a total of 49 stars. The difference in what they see comes
down to a difference in the way things look to them. The fact that they
can't *tell* (i.e., *know* without counting) that there exists this difference in
the way things look to them is irrelevant. It only shows that the sense of
"looks" is itself nonepistemic, *not* to be confused with "looks *like*" or
"looks *as if*."

Heil asks whether this sense experience is – or must be – conscious. He
is thinking about blind-sight, the ability some people apparently have of
seeing what is in front of them – in their blind field – while totally lacking
visual experience. This is, I admit, a puzzling phenomenon, but I think
we must be very careful before drawing conclusions from it. I think
conscious experience *is* necessary to nonepistemic seeing, to seeing the
objects in front of you. If blind sighters do not have conscious visual
experience, they do not see the objects in front of them. This, in fact, is
why they think they are blind: they don't have any conscious visual
experience.

This is not to say, however, that one needs conscious visual experience to see *what* is in front of one. For "seeing what is in front of you" can be, and typically is, used to describe an epistemic perceptual act – a seeing *that* it (what is in front of you) is so-and-so (for some suitable value of "so-and-so"). I can see what is in front of me by looking, not in front of me, but at the descriptive card on my right (the card tells me it is a Manet, not, as I thought, a Monet). I don't have to see *the object* in front of me (the Manet) to see *what* object is in front of me (that it is a Manet). And I see no reason to suppose that epistemic perception (seeing what, where, when, that) requires visual experience (my use of the verb in this sentence being a case in point). So I am happy to admit that blind sighters can see *what* it is in their blind field while totally lacking visual experiences. What remains to be shown is that they can actually see, not only *what* objects are in front of them (or *where* these objects are), but the objects themselves.

Knowledge: Sanford and Cohen

In *Seeing and Knowing* I compared a skeptic to someone who doubts that a foreigner – someone from Uganda, say – could, as he claims, have reached Times Square by walking. The disbelief, I said, was premature. There is no special problem – even for Ugandans – about walking to Times Square. Not if they walk there *from* Central Park. Perhaps one can't walk to Times Square from Uganda, but that doesn't prevent a Ugandan from walking to Times Square. Describing someone as having walked somewhere reveals very little about what they did. The words themselves don't tell you whether it was an easy stroll, an exhausting hike, or an impossible journey. This being so, skepticism is misplaced until one learns *how much* walking, and over what kind of terrain, it took to get there.

I used this analogy to illustrate an important aspect of perceptual knowledge claims. Reports about what one has seen to be the case reveal *nothing* about where one *came from* in acquiring that knowledge. They are descriptions of *where* one arrived and *how* one arrived, but not how far one had to travel to get there. They are, therefore, silent about the magnitude of the epistemic achievement. Saying, as skeptics are wont to say, *before* they learn where we came from, *before* understanding what we are claiming to have *done*, that we cannot know (by seeing) the ordinary things we say we know (by seeing) is like dismissing, *before* learning where he came *from*, the Ugandan's claim to have walked to Times Square.

David Sanford, in his witty and challenging essay, correctly identifies these early ideas on the *incremental* character of perceptual knowledge as an important source for my later views about relevant alternatives. It is no objection to a person's having *seen* that something was so to point out that there are obstacles to his knowing this which are visually insurmountable. Whether or not that is relevant depends on whether the person is supposed to have surmounted those obstacles visually. The words we use to describe what people have seen to be the case normally don't tell you. The fact that your cousin, when nervous, looks just like my aunt, when bored, or just like some cleverly made, but completely emotionless, robot does not prevent me from *seeing* that your cousin is nervous.

Thus emerges the idea of a visually irrelevant alternative: something incompatible with what one knows (by seeing) to be the case but which one cannot know (by seeing) to be not the case. Seeing that your cousin is nervous is seeing something to be so that excludes the possibility of its being my bored aunt (or an emotionless robot) but the exclusion is not, or *need* not, be visual: I needn't be able to visually discriminate between your nervous cousin and my bored aunt (or a robot that is neither).

Since possibilities are excluded by what one has seen to be the case that are not *visually* excludable, perceptual knowledge is not *closed* under known logical entailment. I can see that P, know that P entails Q, and not be able to see whether or not Q is the case.

It is, however, one thing to make these claims for the *perceptual* verbs, verbs that describe *how* we know what we know, and quite another thing to claim this for knowledge itself, for verbs that describe, merely, *what* we know. It may well be true that in seeing that a person is nervous, certain alternatives (its being an emotionless robot) need not be excludable on *visual* grounds. Nonetheless, if seeing that P implies knowing that P, as I assume it does, then, it seems, these alternatives must *somehow* be excluded. The impossibility of walking on water may not be relevant to whether our Ugandan did what he said he did – walked to Times Square – but if he began his journey in Uganda, then he must have *somehow* got across the water – if not by walking, then by flying or by boat. Hence, whatever problems there might be in traversing large bodies of water *become* problems for walking to Times Square. For if Ugandans can't get across the water, they cannot get *to* any place *from which* they can walk to Times Square. By the same token, if one can *see* things to be so for which there are alternative possibilities one cannot *visually* exclude, one must, nonetheless, be able somehow to exclude these alternatives. Otherwise one doesn't have the knowledge that the perceptual report describes one as having. One cannot *reach* the place (the knowledge that P) the perceptual report describes one as having reached by seeing.

I think, therefore, that although an appreciation of the incremental nature of perceptual knowledge is suggestive, and though it naturally leads one into thinking of knowledge in a more "contextually sensitive" way, a theory (such as the one in *Seeing and Knowing*) whose primary concern is with the knowledge acquisition process (*how* we know what we know) cannot be extended in any automatic way to the product of this process (*what* we know). For even if certain alternatives are irrelevant to S's *seeing* that P, even if such perceptual claims are viewed as ruling out only selected (visual) competitors (to P), remaining alternatives, those *not* ruled out visually, may yet be relevant to one's *knowing* that P.

Still, though quick generalizations are not available, there is every reason to suppose that the concept of knowledge exhibits the same contextual relativity, the same sensitivity to a range of understood contrasts, as the verbs that describe the way we reached that knowledge. If describing someone as having seen, or learned, or discovered, that something was so doesn't really tell you much about *what* he learned, discovered or saw in reaching this knowledge, then perhaps this is because describing him as knowing this doesn't tell you much at all about what, exactly, is known. If situations can easily be imagined in which someone can see that water is frozen without being able to distinguish what he sees from unfrozen non-water, then why can't someone know this without being able to distinguish the condition he knows to obtain from a variety of other conditions incompatible with it?

We know, after all, that describing two objects as empty doesn't say much about the contents of either. In describing them both as empty we do, of course, describe them both as in the same state or condition – a state of total depletion. But knowing that something is in a state of total depeletion doesn't tell you much. Depletion of *what*? We don't know what it *takes* to be in this condition until we know what these objects are and what they are being used for. After all, two objects can both be empty and, yet, there be enough stuff in one to fill 20 of the other. Think of one as a classroom and the other as a box used to hold folding chairs. Student (in search of a classroom) reporting back to a teacher: "Room 342 is empty; let's hold class there; it has enough chairs for all of us." Is this really *false* because the room contains enough chairs to fill 20 boxes?

The same is true of knowledge. Two people, both of whom know that P, may have had to overcome much different obstacles in reaching this state. They are, to be sure, in the same epistemic state – the condition of knowing that P – but we don't really know what it takes to be in this state until we know something, not only about the circumstances and intended application of this knowledge, but perhaps also (but more of this in a moment) about the intentions and assumptions of those who describe them as being in this condition. Describing X as empty says *something* about X (that there is nothing of the relevant kind in it), but to know *what* it says, to know what is relevant to its being in this condition, one has to know not only that X is *a room* (and not a box), but something about the purposes and interests of those who use and occupy the room. Knowledge is like this.

Such, at least, is the general orientation I reached over the years. Both David Sanford and Stuart Cohen share this general point of view. We agree that the way to proceed (as Sanford puts it) is to expose less flank to skeptical attack by reducing the scope of knowledge claims. We disagree – at least it isn't clear that we always agree – about important details, about *how* to expose less flank and (perhaps) *how much* flank needs to be exposed, but it is a pleasure (not to say a relief) to find oneself discussing issues *at this level* of detail with two acute critics.

Sanford politely suggests that some machinery (propositional "allomorphs") I introduced for the purpose of streamlining the theory of relevant alternatives had (*had*, I think, is the correct tense to use here), at best, a "decorative function." The appearance of scientific rigor and precision was misleading. The arrows didn't point anywhere; the ordering and metric were completely phony. The essential points can be put more economically and directly, he says, by simple lists that convey what he calls the horizontal and vertical contrasts. Everything that needs to be done can be done without the glitz.

I must, regretfully, agree. Like everyone else, I dearly love my own toys, but these toys, besides not being much fun, get in the way of more serious business. So let them retire to that twilight-hued obscurity from which Sanford dragged them.

We do, however, need to attend to the serious business. We need, first, to understand better *claims* to knowledge, what the speaker is *saying* is known. This involves, among other things, understanding the presuppositional structure (of the speaker and his listeners) that determines what sort of thing is being *said* to be known. Here, of course, I think contrastive phenomena are relevant. But aside from better understanding what we are *saying* when we describe someone as knowing something, we also need to understand the way contextual factors – factors in the knower's (not necessarily the speaker's) situation – operate to modify what is relevant to one's knowing what one is described as knowing.

Sanford and Cohen have their own preferred ways of talking about these matters. Sanford speaks of *scope* and what one knows in some *proper* way. Cohen distinguishes between various *kinds* of contextual sensitivity and endorses an *indexical* account of the concept of knowledge. These may all seem to be different ways of getting at the same basic idea, the idea of salvaging our common wisdom about what and when we know while simultaneously exposing less flank to the philosophical skeptic. In some respects I think this is right. We are all pulling in the same direction. Nonetheless, there are important differences, differences that, in the final analysis, change what it is we know and when we know it. Let me say why this is so and why I still prefer to say all this (minus the glitz, of course) in my own way.

According to Sanford, if S knows P in a *proper* way, then every possible alternative to P is a relevant alternative. If Q is known to be incompatible with P, then knowledge of P requires knowledge that Q is false. Proper knowledge is therefore closed under known implication: you must, when you know something in this proper way, know everything you know to be entailed by what you know.[2]

So proper knowledge doesn't come cheap. It's the high grade stuff after which skeptics hanker. It is also, at least in the way Sanford conceives it, fairly abundant – abundant enough to satisfy the popular demand for wide distribution. Everybody has it – some of it, anyway – and, generally speaking, they have it when they think (and say) they know. The trouble, of course, is that what we common folk think (and say) we know isn't what we really know – at least not what we *properly* know. What we think and say we know is P. What we *properly* know is that *if* certain conditions (call them C) obtain, then P. What we properly know is something conditional in nature, the antecedent of which defines a range of conditions (the *relevant* alternatives) from which our evidence selects P. In knowing that the fellow sitting at the bar is Fred Dretske, what Sanford *properly* knows is that *if* it is a nondisguised philosopher attending the convention, *if* this is the range of possibilities the (perceptual) evidence is called upon to choose between, then this evidence is adequate to the task: it singles out, from this range of options, Dretske as the one at the bar. The fact that the fellow at the bar *might* be someone disguised to look like Dretske is not even an alternative possibility, let alone a *relevant* alternative possibility, to this (proper) knowledge claim.

Sanford concedes that this approach to a theory of knowledge doesn't promise everything. There is still *much* that we do not properly know – in fact, many of the things the skeptic says we don't know. Still, though it doesn't promise everything, it does promise something. "It shows how a great many of our ordinary attributions of knowledge, first person, second person or third person, are immune from standard skeptical challenge." It shows this *if* we understand our ordinary attributions of knowledge (of P) as, in fact, tacit attributions of proper knowledge of something quite different: if C then P. Immunity is secured, yes, but for a much less desirable commodity.

This is Sanford's way of doing what Palle Yourgrau (1983) describes as the exportation of pragmatic context into semantic content, an effort to make contextual factors on which knowledge depends into an explicit part of what is known. Conditional knowledge of the unconditioned becomes unconditional knowledge of a conditional. One goes from

(1) If C (or in context C), S knows that P

to

(2) S knows that if C then P

where C is understood to be, or to imply, some range of relevant alternatives. It is unclear whether or not Sanford accepts some general forms of argument that exports context into content. It is nevertheless useful to consider the plausibility of such forms together with Sanford's proposals concerning proper knowledge.

Suppose S's evidence, E, is such that if C is the range of alternatives among which S must discriminate on the basis of E, then this evidence is good enough to select P as the certain choice. That is, if C, then E makes P evidentially certain. It does not follow, however, that E makes it evidentially certain that if C, then P. Making something evidentially certain is a relation on which we cannot perform logical exportation. From the fact that in conditions C, E will cause (or be the effect of) P, for example, we cannot conclude that E is therefore the cause (or effect) of some conditional state of affairs (if C then P). From the fact that if they are using Morse Code, this sequence of dots and dashes means P, we cannot infer (without equivocating on the word "means") that this sequence of dots and dashes means that if they are using Morse Code, then P. In the sense in which, *if* they are using Morse Code, it means P, it may not, in fact, mean *anything* (certainly not that *if* they are using Morse Code, P). Or, to use a more suggestive illustration (given what I say in *Knowledge and the Flow of Information* about channel conditions), we cannot infer from

(3)   In conditions C, E carries the information that P

that

(4)   E carries the information that if C, then P.

If things are working normally in my automobile, the red light doesn't come on unless my oil pressure is low. This is the kind of information the light was designed to carry and, when things are working right, the kind of information it *does* carry. This doesn't mean, however, that the light carries information about its function, about what *kind* of gauge it is – the information, namely, that when things are working right, it registers engine oil pressure. E and P can co-vary in conditions C (hence, E carrying information about P *in* conditions C) without E co-varying with (and, hence, carrying information about) the circumstances described by the conditional: if C then P. If I rewire things to make the light indicate something about battery fluid level, the light (when it comes on) will, in this altered situation, convey information about the battery fluid level without indicating (by its coming on) that the situation has been altered in this – or, indeed, in *any* – way. The light, depending on the way it is connected, indicates (by coming on) different things (P_1, P_2, ...) in different conditions (C_1, C_2, ...), but we cannot infer that, therefore, it indicates (certainly not by coming on) that these conditional facts – if C_1 then P_1, if C_2 then P_2, ... – are true. The light doesn't blink on and off in any way that co-varies with these conditional facts.

The failure of all these arguments reinforces my skepticism about the idea that by importing context into content we can exchange imperfect knowledge of P for some more perfect knowledge of something else. Unless some way can be found of executing this maneuver, we will be unable to exchange our conditional knowledge of P (conditional on our being in circumstances C) for some unconditional knowledge of something else (e.g., if C then P).

This, in turn, means that we must live with the failure of closure. We cannot reinstate it for *proper* knowledge. As long as context is kept out of content, as long as we understand that our knowledge of P is conditional on C, that what we know, what we *really* know, in conditions C is not *if* C then P, but P itself, then there will remain (in most instances at least) alternatives to what we know (P) that we do not know to be false. The fact that were C, unknown to us, *not* the case, we would not know that P does not make our knowledge of P any the less real or useful, of course. The truth of what we believe, and the confidence with which we believe it – factors on which the *usefulness* of knowledge depends – remain intact. Conditionalizing knowledge merely means, among other things, that normally we will not (perhaps cannot) know *that* we know or *when* we know.

Though this approach does not, in Sanford's words, promise everything, though it leaves much that we cannot know, it does promise something. Perhaps we cannot know the exotic things that the skeptic says we cannot know – that we are not being tricked by cunning demons or misled by extraordinary circumstances. Still, we can relinquish this knowledge with the assurance that the baby isn't going out with the bathwater. Everyday knowledge – the things we know *if* we are not being tricked by cunning demons or misled by extraordinary circumstances – remains secure. Unlike the approach (I interpret) Sanford as advocating, what remains secure, furthermore, is exactly what we ordinarily think and say we know. Not only is ordinary knowledge preserved against skeptical assault, ordinary beliefs about *what is known* are likewise preserved. We end up knowing, *really* knowing, not some conditionalized version of what we think and say we know, but exactly what we think and say we know. This is not a benefit to be lightly dismissed.

But this leaves us with an important question about the background context, the context on which knowledge allegedly depends. If certain conditions exist, conditions I do not know to exist, I can (according to the present account) know P. In conditions C, but not outside conditions C, I can know P *without* knowing I am in conditions C (without even knowing that *if* C, then P). This set of background conditions can change from case to case. That, at least, is the theory: that a knowledge of P is relative to a set of variable background conditions. What, then, determines membership in this privileged class of background conditions – "privileged" because it is their mere existence, the fact that they obtain, and not a knowledge or reasonable belief that they obtain, that makes knowledge possible?

This brings me to the very important distinction Stewart Cohen raises. In regarding knowledge, or (better) attributions of knowledge, as context sensitive, is this to be understood as the context of the knower or the context of the speaker: the attributee or the attributor? To illustrate, suppose, to modify Sanford's example slightly, that Stewart (not David) says that David knows that Fred is in the room. Is the truth of Stewart's claim relative to David's (the knower's) special circumstances (to *his* purposes and intentions, and the sorts of alternatives *he* takes himself to be in a position to exclude)? Or are they relative to Stewart's circumstances – to the kinds of conditions that he, Stewart, takes (or assumes his listeners take) to be pertinent? Or both? Cohen speaks of the latter as *indexicality*, the former as the relativity of knowledge to extra-evidential circumstances. These are, he says, quite different things, and they should be carefully distinguished. What, he asks, did *I* mean when I insisted that knowledge was only *relationally* or relatively absolute? Was it the circumstances of the attributor or the circumstances of the attributee (or both) to which I was relativizing knowledge?

I am grateful to Cohen for raising this issue. Though now, in being forced to think about it in a systematic way, I feel that I always had only one thing in mind, I confess to not always being alert to the differences. It is easy to get muddled when thinking about examples in which the speaker and knower are the same. When this occurs, as it often did in the examples I considered, it is difficult to know (or to even appreciate the fact that it is important to know) whether a given circumstance (on which the knowledge is said to depend) merits this status in virtue of its relation to the person as knower or as speaker.

Let me, therefore, try to give a careful answer to this question. Though Cohen is attracted by an indexical account, I find the costs of this approach prohibitively high. Someone with very high standards, someone who considers almost any alternative relevant – a skeptic, for example – will, I think, speak falsely if he denies that you and I, in perfectly ordinary circumstances, know the things we take ourselves to know. The alternatives we must exclude in order to know are not, in other words, the alternative the *attributor* (or, in this case, the denier) of knowledge takes to be relevant. Skepticism, as a doctrine about what ordinary people know, cannot be *made* true by being put into the mouth of a skeptic. Treating knowledge as indexical in the way Cohen does seems to have, or to come dangerously close to having, exactly this result. For this reason (among others) I reject it.

What *is* relative to the attributor and the circumstances of utterance (the context of utterance, if you will) is what the knower is *said* to know. This is what contrastive focusing is all about. But this doesn't make the concept of knowledge indexical. We can easily imagine contexts in which saying that David knows that Fred is at the bar says little more than that David knows that Fred isn't (yet) *under* the bar, that he can, as it were, distinguish between upright and prostrate people (or, perhaps, merely upright and prostrate *Fred*). Nothing much (perhaps nothing *at all*) is being said about David's ability to identify Fred among the philosophers attending the convention. Maybe David was just introduced to Fred, has had him under continuous surveillance since the introduction, and now knows (and *says* he knows – perhaps for the benefit of an anxious wife) that Fred is (still) at the bar. A hotel filled with Fred clones would not interfere with David's ability to do what he is *here* described as doing – seeing that Fred is (still) at the bar. The possibility that there is another philosopher – Marvin Shaw, for example – who looks just like Fred, is an irrelevant alternative to what David is here being said (by David or someone else) to know. The irrelevance of this alternative derives, it is true, from the circumstances of the speaker, but this is only because the circumstances of the speaker affect what the speaker is *saying* David knows. It is *not* because it affects what it *takes* for David to know what he is said to know. The fact that the circumstances of the speaker can affect what the speaker is *saying* someone (himself or another) knows, though it is obviously important to understanding whether we know what we are said to know (since if affects what we are said to know), is *not* relevant to understanding the concept of knowledge itself – what it takes to know what we are said to know.

Therefore, though I think an understanding of attributor circumstances is important in the total effort to neutralize skeptical arguments (since only by understanding them, and the way they affect what we are being *said* to know, can we appreciate how *little* we are often being said to know), I do *not* think these circumstances are relevant to the attributee's possession of the knowledge he is said to possess. Once we get clear about *what* knowledge is being attributed, speaker circumstances (contrastive phenomena, etc.) are no longer relevant.[3] Knowledge is not relative to the circumstances of attribution, is not (therefore) indexical, just because these circumstances are relevant to evaluating whether people know what they are commonly said to know.

Compare words like "empty" and "flat" – words that Cohen (correctly) says I use as a model (with thanks to Peter Unger) for relationally absolute concepts. Cohen argues that these words are plausibly interpreted as indexical. What is relevant to whether something is empty or flat depends, he says, on *the speaker*'s interests, purposes and standards. Whether the road is flat or not depends on the standards deployed by speaker and listener (are they from Kansas or Colorado?), not on where the road they are describing is located (Kansas or Colorado). Since I maintain that a refrigerator may be described as empty to someone looking for something to eat, but not (truly) described as empty to someone looking for spare refrigerator parts, Cohen concludes that I favor an indexical account of knowledge, an account in which the truth of knowledge claims depends, in part at least, on the interests, purposes and standards of those who attribute the knowledge.

One must, however, proceed with caution in using the words "empty" and "flat" as models for knowledge. This is especially so when the issue is, as it is here, the *kind* of sensitivity to context exhibited by our attributions of knowledge. For though there is a clear distinction to be drawn between attributor and attributee in the case of knowledge (even when the attributor *is* the attributee), and hence a reasonably clear difference between the context associated with each, this is not so clear when one is describing rooms as empty and roads as flat. When I describe a refrigerator as empty, I am clearly the attributor, but who or what is the attributee? Surely not the refrigerator since it doesn't have interests, purposes or standards in terms of which to define relevance. When I (to use an earlier example) describe a student (looking for a room in which to hold class) as finding an empty room (a room that is, despite being empty, full of chairs), is this false if *I*, the speaker, have a consuming interest in chairs rather than people? Aren't I, as speaker, and unless I signal a shift, constrained to adopt the viewpoint of the people whom I am describing, the people who have a purpose and interest in *using* the room?

Though the matter is complex, it seems to me that the only relevance *the speaker* has to the truth of claims about rooms (or refrigerators) being empty, or roads and surfaces being flat, is as someone who *shares*, or is assumed to share, in the standard uses and applications of the objects being described. It is this background of standard or intended *use* to which the claim is relative, and the speaker's context is relevant to the truth of what is said only in so far as it can be presumed to reflect or indicate what this background is. A speaker who brings a novel or unusual viewpoint to the situation being described, a standard *other than* that of the people he is describing, is expected to indicate that difference in order to avoid misunderstanding. If I'm interested in the location of extra chairs and the person I'm describing is interested in the rooms in which to hold class, I can say, if I like, that they found the room empty *of people* but full *of chairs*. Without this, though, it is the standards of the users (*their* intentions and purposes) that prevail. Despite my interest in chairs, it would be false, not just misleading, to say that they held their class in a room that wasn't empty.

Whether the room is empty or not may depend on the speaker, then, but not *qua speaker*, but, rather, *qua* representative of some standard user group which defines, by its use, the objects of relevance. Giants may (as Cohen says) have their own standards of flatness; even our roughest roads are flat and smooth to them. But in describing a giant as finding our roads thus, I describe the roads from the point of view of potential users – either *us* ("our roughest roads") or the giant ("smooth and flat"). I see no reason to think that the speaker's context adds an *extra* dimension of relativity beyond that of assumed, or standard, or implied *users* of the roads in question.

If this is so, words such as "flat" and "empty" though context sensitive, are not indexical. They are relationally absolute, but the standards to which they are relative are the standards implied by the use to which they are being put or, if no particular use is indicated, by the normal use to which such things are put. If an extraordinary or unusual use is in question (someone looking in the refrigerator not for food, but for spare parts), then this, if not otherwise obvious, must somehow be indicated. A simple modifier will usually do: the refrigerator, though empty *of food*, has plenty of useful *hardware* (brackets, screws, hinges) in it.

I think this is true for such notions as *flat* and *empty*. But even if it isn't, it *is* true – or so I think – for knowledge. Knowledge is relative, yes, but relative to the extra-evidential circumstances *of the knower* and those who, like the knower, have some stake in what is true on the matter in question. Knowledge is context sensitive, according to this view of things, but it is not indexical. If two people disagree about what is known, they have a genuine disagreement. They can't both be right.

Cohen, I confess, has good reason to wonder about my views on this. I think, though, that my heart and (less frequently) my head were always in the right place. I waffled at times. At other times I was simply confused about the difference between the context of attributor and attributee. But there is, I think, a consistent thread throughout. When I spoke, for instance, of a concept's sensitivity to the interests and purposes of people applying it, I *meant* (even if the words I was using didn't *mean*) the interests and purposes of those who were *using* the objects (refrigerators, rooms, roads) to which the concept was applied. And when I said that relevant alternatives (to knowledge) were responsive to the interests, purposes, and values of those with a stake in the communication process, I *meant* something quite different by the words "communication process" than the process occurring between speaker (describing someone as knowing) and listener. That *is* a communication process, yes, but when the speaker is describing someone as knowing something, there is another "communication" process of interest – the process by means of which information reaches the knower about the condition known to exist. It was *that* process (indeed, *all* processes in which information is transmitted) I meant to be relativizing to extra-evidential circumstances. The relevant interests, purposes, and values, then, were not those of the speaker (*qua* speaker), but those of the knower and those with a stake in whether he or she got the information on which the attributed knowledge depends.

Cohen observes that it is not very original to relativize knowledge to the extra-evidential circumstances of the knower. In so far as knowledge requires truth, the difference between a person who knows that P, and someone who doesn't, may be simply that P is true in the first case, not in the second. They can have exactly the same evidence. Hence, as long as the evidence required for knowledge (of P) *permits* the falsity of P, knowledge of P will depend on extra-evidential circumstances (i.e., P).

This is true, of course. What I have always taken this to show is that the evidence required for knowledge did *not* permit the falsity of what is known. If the evidence needed to know P is such that you can have this evidence for P without knowing P – merely because, as chance would have it, P is not true – then *of course* knowledge of P is going to depend on the extra-evidential circumstances of the knower, on whether he is in circumstances in which what he believes happens to be true. This, though, has always struck me as an implausible account of the evidential requirement for knowledge. It makes knowledge a matter of luck, believing something that *happens* to be true – "happens" to be true because one's evidence, the evidence that lets you "know" it to be true, is perfectly consistent with its *not* being true.

What is required, of course, is to relativize knowledge (so as to expose less flank to the skeptic) while retaining a secure connection between one's evidence and the truth, a secure *enough* connection to make it (in Unger's words) not at all accidental that one is right. What we want, or what I have always wanted, in order to avoid the paradoxical results described above, was a conception of the evidence required for knowledge which made it *conclusive* for P, evidence that (in the required sense) qualified as *information* that P, evidence that (to use Nozick's terms) *tracks* the condition P, and, yet, evidence that (in order to expose less flank to skepticism) makes the knowledge so obtained *relative to* extra-evidential conditions of which one may be ignorant. *That* is a result not so easy to get. How can you make the evidence conclusive (thus securing an absolute conception of knowledge) while, at the same time, admitting that there are possibilities it does not exclude (thus making it *relationally* absolute)? A theory embodying relevant alternatives, with the consequent denial of closure, is, I think, the only way.

Behavior: Adams and Horgan

Behavior is, for me, of secondary importance. Of primary interest is the mind. But we can't understand the mind until we understand what the mind is supposed to do. One of the things the mind, in the form of belief and desire, is supposed to do is to guide and motivate the behavior of its possessor. Thus our talk about the mind, of what a person thinks and wants, should (if the mind is doing its job) help us understand that person's behavior – *why* (say) they jumped up and suddenly headed for the kitchen. If the person went there to get a beer, then we can better understand the nature of both belief and desire – and, in this respect, the mind – if we can understand just *how* this belief (that there is a beer in the fridge) and this desire (for a beer) explains their trip to the kitchen. To do so, however, requires that we *first* understand what we are seeking to explain – that trip to the kitchen, the person's behavior.

For this reason I devote a separate section of this reply to the topic of behavior. Despite the absence of direct criticism on this topic from contributors to this volume, much of what they say about other matters – in particular my views about the way beliefs and desires explain behavior and, hence, my views about the *nature* of belief and desire – requires, for its proper evaluation, some preliminary skirmishing in this area.

Behavior, at least those behaviors whose descriptions imply the occurrence of bodily movement, are distinct from the bodily movements they necessarily involve. Moving your finger is not to be identified with your finger's movement. It is, rather, some internal event's *causing* your finger to move – a process, a *causal* process, having an event (the finger movement) as its product. And walking to the fridge, a more complex piece of behavior, is not to be identified with the movements that get you to the fridge. Or so I argued, at great length, in *Explaining Behavior*.

This is, as Adams observes, a *component* view of behavior: the reasons – the beliefs and desires that help to explain the behavior – are actual *parts* of the behavior. Another part of the behavior is the result – often some bodily movement – that the behavior requires for its occurrence (finger movement in the case of moving your finger). This means that (*contra* Davidson) reasons do not *cause* behavior. Nonetheless, the fact that we believe this and desire that, facts about the intentional or semantic properties of these internal states, explain why these internal states *cause* the movements (or bring about the results) they do. Given the identification of behavior with the causing of such movements, we thereby secure an explanation of why the behavior occurs.

Adams also suggests that I don't need this view of behavior. "The job of content [what we believe and what we desire] is to explain why we get *one product rather than another*", and this, he says, can be done without identifying behavior with a process having bodily movements as its product.

Perhaps he is right about this. Perhaps the difference between explaining behavior and explaining the bodily movements such behavior involves *can* be put in terms of a difference in our explanatory "set." There is, to be sure, a difference between explaining why the light *came on* (understood contrast: instead of remaining off) by mentioning the fact that S flipped the switch, and explaining why *the light* (rather than something else) came on. In the second explanation, in contrast to the first, we are no longer taking existing wiring connections for granted. We are, in fact, asking why things got wired that way, why things got arranged so that the switch controls *this* light rather than *some other light* (or, perhaps, no light at all). We are asking, not for the cause of this light's going on, but why the cause of this light's going on (the switch) *causes* this light (rather than some other light or, perhaps, no light at all) to go on.

So Adams may be right. One doesn't *have* to put it my way in order to capture the essential difference between explaining behavior and explaining bodily movements. So one doesn't *need* my view of behavior to provide, as it were, an explanatory role for reasons. Asking why S moved his finger, as opposed to asking why his finger moved, may be merely asking for a different kind of explanation of why the finger moved. One is still looking for a *causal* explanation of finger movement, but a causal explanation of this movement *with*, as it were, *a different set of contrasting alternatives*. The biologist (explaining finger movement) wants to know why the finger *moved* rather than remaining stationary; the psychologist, including the folk psychologist, on the other hand, wants to know why *the finger* (rather than the ear, the tongue, the toes, or perhaps nothing at all) moved. Why did the (internal) cause of finger movement have *that* result rather than some other result or no result at all?

This is, I think, an interesting and important point, and I am grateful to Adams for pointing it out. It is always nice to know that one's conclusion (in this case, a conclusion about the way reasons explain behavior) can be held up in ways other than the particular way one chose to support it. The whole structure is much more stable when individual supports become dispensable. Nonetheless, I still prefer to put it my own way, and the reason I do is because this conception of behavior (as a process having bodily movement as its product) does (among other things) explain *why* there is this systematic shift in explanatory interest when we turn from bodily movement to behavior. The shift occurs because when our concern is with behavior, with why we moved our finger (rather than why our finger moved), we are no longer interested in what made (caused) the finger (to) move, but with the causal arrangement, the process, *in which* this finger is made to move. What is more natural than to suppose that this shift in explanatory interest occurs *because* there has been a change in the character of what we are explaining – a change from explaining a movement to explaining a process having movements as its product? You don't *have* to say this, but why not?

Aside from this important benefit, thinking of behavior as a causal process also gives one a more plausible account of the spatio-temporal aspects of behavior – why, for instance, scoring a goal (in hockey) is not something that occurs *before* the puck enters the net (or, even worse on some accounts, *before* one even swings the stick). This, of course, needs argument, something I will not (again) take the time to give.

Terry Horgan gives an admirably clear account of my motivation for not having actions (behavior *explained* by reasons) *caused* by reasons. Nonetheless, he finds that this conception of behavior (wherein reasons are a *part*, and therefore not a cause, of the behavior they help explain) offends our pre-theoretic understanding of the "because" in rationalizing explanations. If a woman at the cash register reaches into her purse because she thinks that's where her money is, a philosophically untutored view of this process, according to Horgan, is that the woman's belief and desire *cause* her to reach there. I don't believe it. That doesn't sound to me like a *pre*-theoretic intuition at all. It sounds to me like a post-Davidsonian dogma. If there are any genuinely pre-theoretic intuitions floating around, it strikes me that they are better described by saying that the woman's belief that her money is in her purse (along with her desire to pay the check) *explains* her reaching into her purse. Perhaps we can even go so far as to say that these reasons, somehow, *causally* explain her behavior. But, surely, pre-theoretic intuitions are not so finely tuned as to distinguish between the woman's belief and desire causing her to reach into her purse (reasons causing behavior) and the belief and desire causing whatever movements are needed to reach there (reasons causing movements). The latter option is a way of having reasons, in virtue of their content, explain – yes, even *causally* explain – behavior without having them *cause* behavior. Behavior is explained (by reasons) by letting reasons explain why those movements constituting behavior are being caused (by the reasons). I doubt whether pre-theoretic intutions tell us that the "because" of rationalizing explanations *cannot* be preserved in *this* way.

I think it is important to understand the way reasons – what we believe and desire – can causally explain behavior *without*, at the same time, being the *cause* of behavior. It is important from the point of view of understanding the structure of voluntary behavior, of free action, how we can freely and rationally do A (because we believe this and want that) even though we are (as we often are) caused to believe this and want that by external events over which we have no control. If our beliefs and desires, the beliefs and desires that explain why we do what we do, were the causes of our behavior, then whatever caused us to have these beliefs and desires would be the cause – at one remove, so to speak – of our actions. Anything that caused the woman to believe her money was in her purse (e.g., seeing it there this morning) would automatically become a cause of her reaching into her purse. By causing you to believe there is a beer in the fridge (by telling you) I would thereby *cause* you (and, in this sense, *make* you) go to the fridge if, indeed, you go there, in a perfectly rational and voluntary way, because you think there is a beer there. The trick to avoiding this result – a result that is disastrous for a proper understanding of the *autonomy* of intentional behavior – is to understand how reasons, *qua* reasons, can explain behavior without, at the same time, causing it. We are not made to do the things we do by the events that make us want and believe what we do *even when* we do what we do *because* we believe and desire what we do.

Horgan also thinks my account of the way reasons explain behavior robs reasons of their "here-and-now" explanatory relevance. I go to the refrigerator in order to get a beer. My thirst (for a beer) and my belief that there is still a beer there explain my here-and-now trip to the fridge. On my account, though, reasons (as structuring causes of behavior) only explain why my nervous system (in the past) got configured this way, why the causal process (that *is* the behavior) came to have *these* movements (the ones that get me to the refrigerator), rather than other movements or no movements at all, as its product. Hence, according to Horgan, my account of the way reasons explain behavior leaves my *present* trip to the fridge unaccounted for in terms of *present* active causes.

Token behaviors (S moving his finger here-and-now) consist of token Cs causing token Ms (finger movements). If you want to know why this (token) C is causing this (token) M, why S is here-and-now moving his finger, it seems to me quite reasonable to explain this by explaining why things got arranged so that token Cs would, if and when they occurred, produce token Ms. Why does *this* pressure on the door button cause *this* ringing of the bell. Well, because the button is (was?) wired to the bell. That is why this button push causes this ringing and why, in fact, when things are working right, each and every button push is followed by a corresponding ring. The doorbell system *behaves* that way, *every* day, including today (here-and-now), because that is the way it was installed and wired. The behavior of buttons and bells is, in this respect, no different than the stereotyped behavior of animals (including humans): we often behave the way we do because of something that happened yesterday or, perhaps, many years ago.

Horgan won't be satisfied with this. He wants content to be presently active, working (somehow) as a *triggering* cause of the behavior it explains. I am quite happy to acknowledge triggering causes of behavior. There is surely *something* that makes me move my finger *now*, something the touches off the sequence of events comprising this behavior. Perhaps it is some event in my environment – the arrival of my accomplice, say – that (through some perceptual process) arouses in me the belief that it is

time to move my finger. I have no quarrel with this. I am, furthermore,
quite happy to admit that the beliefs and desires that explain *why* I move
my finger *trigger* (act as here-and-now cause of) a sequence of events
culminating in finger movement. They, here-and-now, cause my finger to
move. Reasons are causes, yes, but they are *not* causes of the behavior
they explain. They are, rather, causes – here-and-now causes – of the
movements that (partially) constitute this behavior.

This, apparently, isn't enough for Horgan. I don't see why. He claims
to have virtually unshakeable intuitions that the belief that explains why
I, here-and-now, move my finger is the cause, not merely of my finger
movement, but of my moving it. These are, indeed, convenient intuitions.
They are, in effect, intuitions that I am wrong – lock, stock, and barrel –
about the relationship between movement and its causes, on the one
hand, and behavior and its explanation on the other. Maybe I am. But
I think the intuitions, unshakeable though they may be, should be but-
tressed by an argument.

One final point before leaving behavior, a point raised by Adams in his
discussion of the way behavior might be individuated and explained in
twin-earth situations. Since behavior is the production – the causing – of
some result, M, a difference in the result implies a difference in the
behavior. When the result is quite remote, as it is when we speak of
someone turning on the light (something that requires the light actually to
go on) or scoring a goal (the puck must actually enter the net) we can
imagine two individuals, as similar as we please, doing quite different
things. Tom is scoring a goal, Tim – his clone – though operating in
exactly the same (type of) circumstances, and moving in exactly the same
way, is not. Why? Because Tim's puck doesn't go in. Or time expires
before it goes in. Tom is a hero. Tim isn't.

We wouldn't, of course, expect to explain *this* behavioral difference
(though it is a perfectly respectable difference in behavior) in terms of
what the actors believe and want. They believe and want exactly the same
thing – or so we may suppose. At least they want and believe the same
thing if we ignore *de re* differences in the expression of their beliefs and
desires (Tom wants *this* puck to go in, Tim wants *that* puck to go in, and
this ≠ that). But not every difference in behavior will be explained by the
agent's reasons. There is no reason it should be. Some of the differences
in what people do will be explained by the differences in the circumstances in which they do things.

Learning: Adams, Dennett, Cummins, and Horgan

Dan Dennett wants to know why I make a fuss about learning. It is, he
says, only *one* of the ways of coordinating meaning with causal roles. It is
only *one* of the ways of making a syntactic engine *appear* to be a semantic
engine. Besides some irrelevant possibilities (cosmic coincidence and
divine intervention) that both Dennett and I choose to ignore, there are

the three cousins: (1) natural selection, (2) learning, and (3) deliberate design. Each is a process in which meanings and causal roles can be, and often are, coordinated. An element that means *M* is made to cause something appropriate to its meaning. As a result, there is a correspondence between what a thing *means* and what a thing *does*, a correspondence that (by making assumptions of appropriateness – i.e., by adopting the right stance) we can exploit in order to use meanings to predict effects. The illusion is thereby created that things behave the way they do (have the effects they do) because they mean what they do. Thus is created the further illusion that minds, repositories of meaning, enjoy an existence and an efficacy independently of our predictive and explanatory attitudes.

I agree with Dennett that each of these processes is a way of aligning meaning with causal role. If that was *all* I was looking for, there would be no reason to make a special fuss about learning. That, however, isn't all I'm looking for. I am, I fear, even more reactionary than Dennett feared. I am looking for a genuine semantic engine, one whose behavior – some of it anyway – is fueled by meaning, one who behaves the way it does because it *thinks* what it does. Dennett and a great many other philosophers don't think this is possible. Meanings are inert. They are impotent. The idea of a causally efficacious meaning is a mechanical impossibility. The best that can be done with them is to *attach* them to structures that already have, or can be given (by design, selection, or learning), a causal efficacy appropriate to their associated meaning. The best we can get, then, are syntactic engines that, with the help of design (in the case of artifacts like computers), learning and evolution (in the case of living organisms) masquerade as *agents* – objects that do things because of what they think, want, and intend.

I disagree. We can do better. One of the reasons I am interested in the learning process is because I think that is where we see meanings – at least the extrinsic relations that underlie meaning – doing some real work in shaping behavior. It is here, and in no other place, that elements with meaning not only acquire an appropriate causal role (they do this, I admit, in natural selection and design also), but acquire it precisely because they mean what they do. It is here, then, as in no other place, that we find a convincing model of belief: a structure causing what it does (its possessor thereby *behaving* the way she does) because it, the internal structure, means what it does.

Before trying to defend this view against the objections of Dennett, Cummins, and Horgan, let me try to say, in a very general way, why I think learning *should be* important. This isn't an argument that it *is* important. Its just a fact that I find suggestive – a clue, if you will – on which others (those who don't find learning of any special significance) might well ponder.

Why does the mind – or at least the most prominent citizens of the mind (belief, desire, intention, purpose, etc.) – only help to explain behavior that is in some way a product of individual learning? Beliefs and desires, intentions, and purposes, explain *voluntary* behavior (indeed, one might *define* voluntary behavior as behavior that beliefs and desires explain, behavior that we do *for reasons*), and voluntary behavior is precisely the behavior we have learned to do or can, at least, learn *not* to do. Is this some kind of remarkable coincidence? Could it turn out that some animals (plants?) are blessed with minds – a rich, interconnected network of beliefs and desires – but, because they are incapable of learning, because all their behavior is genetically programmed – never *do* anything that is explicable in terms of what they want and believe?

Why, in other words, are beliefs and desires (and all the other content-bearing internal states that function as *reasons for* doing something) conveniently located in (and, it seems, *only* in) animals capable of learning? Why, furthermore, do these reasons only begin to appear *when* the animal starts exhibiting behavior that is in some way the product of learning? Very young infants, even when they get what they want (food or attention) by sucking and crying, do not suck and cry *because* they think it will get them what they want. There are, often enough, reasons *why* they behave this way (they are thirsty, hungry, or in pain), but these are not *the baby's reasons* for behaving this way. There are not – not *yet* anyway – *rational* explanations for this behavior. That comes later, after learning has occurred. Then, as we all know, they start yelling *because* it will get them the attention they desire.

Since minds conveniently appear on the evolutionary and developmental scene when, and only when, learning occurs, when there appears the kind of behavior (voluntary or purposive behavior) that minds are invoked to explain, the suspicion is irresistible that the elements of these explanations – the beliefs and desires we invoke to explain voluntary behavior – have their origin in precisely those transactions (the learning experiences) that gives rise to the behavior needing explanation. Beliefs and desires, internal states with meaning, emerge *as* internal states with meaning, *as* mental states, in the learning process wherein is created the conditions that make possible the kind of behavior that internal states with meaning are needed to explain.

Such, at least, is how I read the clues – the remarkable "correspondence" in living things between those that have a mind and those capable of exhibiting the kind of behavior – *voluntary* behavior – that is in some way the product of learning.

Robert Cummins is not impressed by this clue. Quite the contrary. He criticizes my emphasis on learning as the source of mental content because, he says, it cannot explain unlearned behaviors in terms of innate knowledge.[4] Since cognitive science, according to Cummins, claims that some learning is based on innate knowledge, any theory (such as mine) that denies this (by denying that there are innate beliefs) is in serious trouble. I assume he thinks philosophical skepticism, because it denies *all* knowledge, is similarly refuted. Who said philosophy was hard?

As soon as Cummins has an argument that what cognitive science says is *true*, and true, moreover, in a sense of the word knowledge for which belief of the relevant kind is necessary, he will have an argument that what I say is false. In the meantime, I remain persuaded that learning is the key to the explanatory efficacy of internal states with content, those beliefs, desires, purposes, expectations, intentions, plans, fears, and values that we invoke to explain why we do the things we do. Unless one uses the word knowledge for *any* pre-existing structure that helps to explain the behaviors and capacities of a system (in which case the point about innate knowledge is irrelevant since my thesis is one about belief, internal structures with propositional content or meaning), why should one want to invoke knowledge – let alone *innate* knowledge – to explain unlearned behaviors at all? These are precisely the behaviors and capacities we don't *need* reasons (in the sense of beliefs and desires) to explain. Should we also postulate innate knowledge to explain why birds fly south in the winter or why trees shed their leaves in autumn?

Cummins has a tendency to let cognitive science set the philosophical agenda. Anything that doesn't contribute to what he sees as the scientific business at hand is contemptuously dismissed as "ordinary language philosophy" or "folk-wisdom journalism." So he and I are, most of the time, at cross purposes. I'm interested in what beliefs are and how, if at all, they are supposed to explain behavior. Cummins doesn't think cognitive scientists are interested in this question. So (p. 114) he feels justified in ignoring my problem and, as he says, following "serious science" in not caring.

Well, whether or not Cummins cares, or cognitive scientists care, *I* care. So let me, following the clue described above, pick up the trail where I left it: why learning – as opposed to deliberate design and natural selection – is special.

Assume, for the moment, that beliefs are internal states with meaning, the meaning in question being *what* we believe. This is not meant to be a substantive point; it is merely a terminological device enabling me to describe *what* people believe and desire, *what* they intend and fear, as *meanings*. The ordinary view of the mind, and in particular of belief, is that some of our behavior (voluntary behavior) is the result, in part, of what we believe. I go to the fridge because I think there is a beer there (and, of course, because I *want* a beer). If this ordinary view of the mind is even roughly correct, then, we have internal states that cause what they do because they mean what they do. A belief *is* an internal state whose causal role (in the production of output) is determined by its meaning.

Assume, also, that the meaning of a belief (just as the meaning of a word) is an extrinsic property of an internal state of the believer. Assume, in other words, that "meanings ain't in the head" (Putnam 1975). I, myself, favor an information-based theory of meaning wherein the meaning of (primitive) conceptual elements is the information they have the job of carrying (their indicative function). Without going into details (but see Kim's excellent summary), this makes the meaning of an element depend on its relations – specifically, its correlations – with the environmental conditions about which it is supposed to carry information.

On this view meanings are extrinsic. But I don't want to insist on this view of meaning. At least not here. Take your choice. There are a variety of theories – functional, causal, historical – all of which make meaning a function of an element's extrinsic relations to other things. Just as the marks and sounds composing our written and spoken language can have, or be given, quite different meanings without changing the intrinsic properties of the marks and sounds themselves, so the same (*intrinsically* the same) heads can harbor quite different meanings. This much, surely, is plausible. *If* there is something in the head that means there is beer in the fridge, it is, surely, nothing *intrinsic* to the brain – its electrical-chemical profile, for instance – that makes it mean this.

Given these assumptions – assumptions that are, I assume, widely enough shared to make their implications of some general interest – the job of understanding how beliefs *could* do the job they are supposed to do, how they could (together with desires, etc.) explain the behavior of the animals in which they occur, is the job of meeting what Cummins (p. 102) calls Stich's Challenge, the task of understanding how an element's extrinsic properties could help to explain the behavior of the system in which that element occurs. If we let M stand for the extrinsic relations from which an element derives its meaning, and E the range of effects this element has, the problem – in its most general form – is to understand how the fact that X has M can explain why X causes E.

In *Explaining Behavior*, and several articles, I tried to show how this is not only possible, but how it actually occurs in discrimination learning. The cases I talk about are extremely simple and idealized, but that isn't the point. The point, at least the *philosophical* point, is to show how semantic engines are possible, how the fact that X means M (in some plausible sense of "means") can actually explain why the animal in which X occurs behaves the way it does. I needn't repeat the analysis here. That isn't necessary. Contributors to this volume have done an admirable job of summarizing the main points. In answer to Dennett's query, however, I do want to amplify some of the points I made in the book to show why natural selection and deliberate design do *not* do the job that needs to be done.

In talking about artifacts I have always prefered talking about such simple devices as thermostats. Others prefer talking about computers. Since the issues are basically the same, and since I don't understand computers all that well, I will stick with thermostats. Its easier for me to see exactly what is causing what and why. Furthermore, as a bonus, we avoid a lot of the jargon from the information sciences (e.g., computation, data structures, storing values for variables) that really obscure the essential issues (in talking about data structures, for instance, are we talking meanings or the physical events that *have* these meanings?)

So consider, once gain, this simple instance of design.

We want certain things (furnace regulation), have certain purposes (automatic control of room temperature) and beliefs (that a certain bi-metal strip is both a good thermometer and, properly arranged, a workable electrical switch). As a result, we *do* certain things: we design and install devices incorporating bi-metal strips into electric circuits for our furnaces. The explanation of why these thermostats are there, doing what they are doing, why there is this correspondence between a piece of metal's meaning (that it is getting too cold in the room) and its causal properties (turning the furnace on *when* it gets too cold in the room), is that it was put there and wired that way. And the explanation for why it was put there and wired that way is because we (or some engineer) thought it would further his (our) purposes – the purpose of providing automatic control of room temperature. Aside from the kind of meaning involved (natural versus conventional)[5] we do the same thing when we build a device to automatically add numbers for us.

It is important to realize that the fact that the bi-metal strip (its degree of curvature) means (in the indicational sense of means) something about temperature is a fact about the strip that is powerless to alter the strip's causal role *except through an intentional intermediary* (the designer) who knows (or at least believes) that the strip *has* this (natural) meaning. Even if we supposed that these thermometers occurred naturally – growing on trees like apples, say – they would not, left to themselves, and leaving aside the cosmic accidents and miracles that both Dennett and I prefer to ignore, spontaneously arrange themselves into furnace switches (i.e., thermostats). We need *designers*, and we need designers because there are no other mechanisms – mechanisms other than intentional systems in which meanings are *already* operative – to institute the required correspondence between meaning and causal role. But this no more demonstrates the causal or explanatory power of meaning than does the fact that meaningful words can affect the world in some way appropriate to their meaning *if* their causal influence is transmitted *through* someone who already *understands* (and can, therefore, discriminate between) meanings. What we want are meanings, not meanings-cum-understanders-of-meaning, doing the work.

To get a philosophically interesting case, one that we can use as a model for belief, a case where meaning *itself* does some genuine explanatory work, we have to get understanders-of-meaning out of the causal circuit, the circuit from X's meaning M to X's causing E. For an understander-of-meaning is precisely an object on which meanings, and differences in meaning, have an effect. How is this possible? Design is not one of the solutions to our problem. It is, in fact, part of the problem.

Adams puts the point correctly when he observes that the intentionality we are looking for, and that this account tries to provide, is *intrinsic* (or, as some people prefer to call it, *original*) intentionality because, although meaning is derived from a structure's extrinsic relations to other things, none of these extrinsic relations is (as they are with artifacts like computers) itself semantic. If we want to build a genuine semantic engine, what we have to find is a case where these extrinsic relations *themselves* – and not merely some interpreter, understander or appreciator of them – have a role in the explanation of engine performance.

The difference between a computer and a person, then, is not *merely* that the meanings have been aligned with causally efficacious structures in different ways: design in the case of the computer, learning and natural selection in the case of a person. For, as Adams also notes (note 26, p. 155) the fact that they have been aligned in these different ways gives the person, and not the computer, *access* to these meanings. This is not the kind of access Dennett (rightly) ridicules as an inner homuncular "appreciation" or "understanding" of what one's internal states mean. We can all agree that if meanings really are extrinsic, *nothing* in a system, *including* the mind-brain in a person, can get outside the system of which it is a part to find out what its internal states mean (*how* they are related to the external conditions on which their meaning depends). If meaning is extrinsic to the system, *nothing* inside the system has access to its own meanings in *this* sense. Dennett (1978) puts this point convincingly, and I entirely agree with it. There is, however, another sense of access that, if I am right, a learner has that an artifact (one whose meanings have been coordinated with its causal role by deliberate design) never has: the behavior of the learner – some of it anyway, including what the learner *says* his internal states mean – *depends on what these internal states mean* in a way a computer's behavior – including what it "says" about its own internal states – doesn't.[6] *We*, but not the computer, have access to the meaning of the computer's internal states because what these states mean changes what *we* do (including what we, as designers and programmers, do *to* the computer) but not (except, indirectly, through us) what the computer does.

What, then, about Dennett's first cousin: natural selection? Suppose X means M, and X is selected for job E (as a cause of E) *because* it means M. In order to have an instance which differs from deliberate design, we must suppose that the selection of X is done in some natural way (if this were *artificial* selection, then X's selection would be the result of someone's *belief* about what X meant, and we would merely have another – albeit special – case of deliberate design). If this is an evolutionary process (and not some fortuitous accident), we must suppose that today's organisms, those whose internal X causes E, have an internal X which causes E, *not* because *their* internal X (either type or individual tokens) mean M (they may not mean M), but because a corresponding X in their ancestors meant M. The coordination between M and E (by structures of type X) in remote ancestors led to today's organisms being so constituted, genetically, that structures of type X in them, whatever it means, will produce E. What explains the coordination between M and E in *this* animal – indeed, in *any* animal – is not the fact that there is anything in the animal that means M (in today's possibly altered environment there may not *be* anything in the animal that has this meaning), but genetic programming. Doing E in conditions M is a reflex, an instinct, a form of behavior that is involuntary, genetically fixed, and unmodifiable by learning. It will, therefore, persist whatever its internal cause happens to mean (if anything) about environmental conditions (M). What explains why the

X in *this* animal causes A, then, is not *its* meaning, but the meaning of corresponding Xs in remote ancestors.[7]

This, then, is *not* a case where the meaning of an organism's internal states makes a difference, a causal difference, to what *that* organism does. It may, after many generations, and given the right selectional pressures, make a difference to what *some descendant* does in some reflexive or instinctive way, but that, obviously, is a different matter. This is not, therefore, an adequate model of *belief*. We have, to be sure, the extrinsic properties of structures (the information they carry) making a difference in the world. They do not, however, make the *right* difference to qualify as a belief. Nothing, on this account of things, turns out to be a semantic engine, something whose *own* behavior is driven by the meanings of *its* internal states. All we get is an explanation, via natural selection, of why there are, today, so many syntactic engines of a certain kind – the kind in which something that means M causes E. The syntactic engines in which an element that meant M happened to be, as part of its heritable constitution, a cause of E, were more successful in reproductive competition.

All of us come equipped with various internal indicators of important internal and external conditions relating to pressure, temperature, proximity and orientation of objects, movement, and so on. Such indicators were doubtless developed and pressed into service (in the regulation of bodily activities) by processes of natural selection. All this is, in a way, basic biology (if not sociobiology), a description of the way control systems evolve so as to become better adapted to the external conditions in which they must initiate and guide need-satisfying behavior. Dennett, gave a good account of this evolutionary process, including what he described as intra-cerebral evolution (i.e., learning) 20 years ago in *Content and Consciousness*. He seems annoyed that I don't realize how much of what I'm trying to do has already been done – that the holy grail for which I've been looking has already been found. It has been on a shelf – lo, these many years – somewhere in Boston.

I don't want to downplay Dennett's contributions in this area. I, in fact, learned a lot from his exciting and ground-breaking book. But one of the things I didn't learn – and I can't imagine Dennett (given his views on these matters) thinking I *could* have learned – was the way beliefs, internal states with meaning, explain behavior in virtue of what they mean. *That* is the grail for which I have been looking and unless I mistake the thrust of Dennett's writings the past 20 years – including *Content and Consciousness* – this is something Dennett has made a career out of denying *could* be found. There are, he will be the first to insist, *no* semantic engines – in Boston or anywhere else.

A learning-based account of the origin and explanatory role of meaning has implications, very clear implications, about *when* belief-desire explanations of behavior are possible. Cummins, Dennett, and Horgan describe a few. They agree that one of the more undesirable implications is that you can't tell the true believers from the fakes without a scorecard – in this case, a *biography*. Whether a piece of behavior is voluntary behavior, intentional behavior, a genuine action – whether, in other words, it is explicable in terms of the meanings of the actor's internal states – depends on the history of the actor, on the way the internal cause of movement came to be a cause of movement.

Cummins (p. 107) describes this as a "disturbing" feature that my account shares with Ruth Millikan's theory, and he goes on to observe that, on this conception of things, most of Artificial Intelligence (since it assumes one can *give* artificial systems whatever it is natural systems have acquired through learning) is based on a conceptual error. Horgan (p. 87), adapting Steve Stich's (1983) Replacement Argument, invites one to imagine a Frankenstein creature (assembled my Martians) who looks and behaves just like one of us but lacks the relevant learning history. One's intuitive judgment about the mental lives of such creatures, he says, is strong and unequivocal: despite the lack of learning, they *are* true believers. Dennett puts a slightly different spin on this criticism, but he, too, doubts the necessity of a learning *history* in order to assume (presumably with as much validity as the assumption of this stance ever has) the intentional stance. How much traffic with the world, he asks rhetorically (pp. 87–8), is *enough* to ensure that genuine meaning has been established? He doesn't like the question, but if he is forced to give an answer, it is clear his answer is "None."

I have individual quarrels with these criticisms, but let me be brief (and probably, therefore, unfair) so that I can get to the general issue. Dennett seems to be using some version of the Sorites Argument: if you can't say exactly *when* a poor man ceases to be poor as you continue to give him pennies, then there really is no principled distinction between rich people and poor people. If you can't say exactly *how much* learning (selection) is needed to generate meanings (adaptations), then ...? Then what? Then there are no meanings (adaptations)? Then meanings (adapations) don't depend on learning (selection)?

I've never understood this kind of criticism. Fodor (1984) uses a similar criticism against my (1981) learning-based account of concept formation: does someone, he asks rhetorically, blow a whistle when the learning period ends and the application of concepts begins in earnest? No they don't. There are no sharp boundaries here. But that would only be a criticism if there *were* sharp boundaries in the phenomenon being modeled. Do whistles blow to mark the difference between someone's acquiring, but not yet having, a concept and their full possession of that concept? Do whistles blow to tell us exactly *when* we can start explaining a child's behavior (crawling toward the kitchen) by saying the child *thinks* the dog is in the kitchen? Is there some way of saying *how much* traffic with the world (kitchens, dogs, and the like) the child must have in order for us to understand its behavior this way. If not, why should it be a criticism of a theory about how these internal meanings (for *dog*, *kitchen*, etc.) get developed, or how they function in rational explanations of behavior, that it provides no way of saying exactly when such meanings are established?

Cummins, once again, invokes the weight of cognitive science to arbitrate philosophical disagreement, and Horgan, once again, invokes everyman's clear and distinct intuitions. I come out wrong each time. But then I could name a dozen quite respectable philosophical theories (not to mention scientific theories) that would (would have) come out wrong if we used *these* yardsticks.

I would like to leave the matter here, and refer interested readers to Ruth Millikan's (1989) bold response to the same criticism, but the matter is too important to shrug off. So let me try to say a bit more. One of Fred Adams's examples is useful here. There is a genuine difference between an object whose *function* it is to hold papers on his desk and one, of equal size and mass, doing the same thing, *without* having that function. The fact that one cannot tell (without knowing some history) that an object *has* that function is irrelevant: "replacement of one structure by another that is molecule for molecule physically identical is never," Adams points out, "sufficient for having the same function" (p. 151) And the fact that one cannot say, on a historical view of functions, precisely *when* something gets its function is, Dennett notwithstanding, no objection to its having that function nor to its function depending on its history. I see no reason for not saying the same thing about meanings.

Since some will doubtless object to Adams' example on the grounds that an object's function as a paperweight depends, not (necessarily) on its history, but merely on how we, its users, currently *regard* it, let me use the kind of botanical example I used in *Explaining Behavior*. Two plants, as similar as you like in physical constitution, can *behave* in exactly the same way (both changing color, say, at exactly the same time in their growing season) without their doing so for the same reasons. One is doing so in order to, for the purpose of, attracting different pollinators. The other is doing so for a different reason. It is, let us say, a Martian variety that changes color in order to repel (Martian) beetles. This teleological language is obviously to be cashed out in terms of the evolutionary history of these plants. We can imagine still a third plant, indistinguishable from the other two, which changes color for no reason at all – the change being a side effect of another change that has adaptive significance or (the botanical analogue of Horgan's Frankenstein monster) that was intended and designed by the botanists who created it. If cognitive scientists think, or if Cummins thinks they think, this is impossible because we can *give* an artifical plant – one we create in the laboratory – anything a natural plant could have acquired as a result of its history; or if ordinary folk have, or if Horgan thinks they have, strong and unequivocal intuitions that this is impossible, I find this only mildly interesting. I remain *more* interested in arguments that plants can't differ in this way or, failing that, arguments that our doing things for reasons – because of what we believe and desire – isn't (in its dependence on our history) analogous to why plants behave the way they do.

Given developments in the philosophy of mind over the past 30 years, I find it surprising that anyone would any longer be moved by the Replacement Argument – the argument, namely, that if two organisms are intrinsically the same, the same in all nonrelational aspects, then they must be psychologically identical and, therefore, do things for the same reasons. Putnam's and Burge's examples haven't convinced *everyone*, of course, but they have convinced many that meaning does not supervene on the biological substrate, that *what* you and I believe can differ even if you and I don't differ (in any intrinsic way). Biological twins can differ psychologically. I think anyone attracted (as I am) to a causal or an information-theoretic account of meaning (or, indeed, any nonsolipsistic account of meaning) is driven to exactly the same conclusion. Since physically identical signals (structures, events) can differ in the information they carry, can differ in their causal (including historical) antecedents, one would naturally expect explanations couched in terms of meaning or information to be no respecter of properties that supervene on what is inside the skull or skin (the structures that *carry* information or *have* meaning). When dealing with the information in, or the meaning of, brain structures, the skin is certainly not a significant boundary.

Given this background, and assuming reasons have to do with the meanings of internal states, and assuming (with common sense) that animals sometimes do things for reasons, one is driven, inescapably, to the view that physically identical systems can behave the way they do for much different reasons. As far as I can see, then, this possibility should no longer constitute an objection to any theory of meaning. It is almost a part – though, admittedly, not always a clearly understood part – of the growing orthodoxy.

If one accepts these background ideas (it is clear that Dennett, Horgan, and Cummins differ substantially among themselves over how much of this background they would accept), then the only real question is whether we should follow common sense and accept the idea that we do things *for* reasons, *because* we want this and believe that. This, though, has to do, not with the view that meanings derive from learning (the topic of this part), but the explanatory power of such learning-derived meanings – the topic of the next section.

Explanation and Meaning: Kim, Horgan, Cummins, and Dennett

Sometimes you think you understand a problem – even think you have a solution to it – without realizing that the problem is, in fact, several problems and what you have is (at best) a solution to only one of them. Jaegwon Kim and Terry Horgan distinguish at least three problems relating to the explanatory role of meaning. They not only make relevant and useful distinctions, they point out exactly where I belong – or where my theory commits me to belonging – on each of the different questions they pose. I can only nod, appreciatively, at their thoroughness, fairness, and accuracy.

But they also – together with Cummins and Dennett – worry about just how, on my account, meaning *could* explain behavior. How can the meaning of an element, a meaning that derives from its *history* (the learning episodes from which it derived its indicative function), explain current, ongoing, behavior? Each of the four authors comes at this question in a slightly different way, but they each see it as a problem. So I want to spend some time responding to it. First, though, let me acknowledge the helpful clarifications of Kim and Horgan.

I can do no better than agree with Kim (pp. 60–1) and Horgan (p. 83) when they conclude that my distinction between behavior and bodily movement – the distinction underlying what Kim calls the dual-explanandum approach – was designed, not to help solve the exclusion problem (it doesn't help here), but what Horgan calls the Soprano Problem (p. 73) and Kim describes as Syntacticalism (p. 54). By distinguishing behavior from bodily movements one can see how meanings can figure in the causal explanation of behavior without in any way threatening the hegemony of neurobiology in providing causal explanations for bodily activities. Psychology, including folk psychology, adverts to the extrinsic properties – the meanings – of internal states to explain behavior; neurobiology restricts itself to the intrinsic properties of these same internal states to explain the bodily movements that (in part) constitute such behavior. What keeps psychology from collapsing into speculative biology is their different explanatory projects.

As far as the Explanatory Exclusion Problem I am, as Horgan puts it, a compatibilist. I don't see any tension between giving both a mental explanation of behavior (one in terms of meanings) and a physical explanation of behavior because, as Kim rightly observes, I am a reductionist on meanings. I think meanings *are* physical: in giving a psychological explanation of behavior, an explanation in terms of what S's internal states *mean*, one is merely giving a very special kind of physical explanation, an explanation in terms of the *extrinsic* (physical) properties of S's internal states. Since a structure's meaning is derived from its indicator function, from what information it has the job of carrying, and since both information and function are (or so I argue) physically constituted, facts about what something means are just special kinds of physical facts.

Kim correctly points out that the reduction base is *not* the internal biology of organisms whose internal states have meaning (p. 60). What makes psychological meaning a special kind of thing, what gives it its mental character (and, at the same time, makes its explanatory role so puzzling), is the fact that the meaning of a system's internal states is constituted by properties that, though physical, are *extrinsic* to the system whose behavior they help explain. I am a reductionist about meaning, yes, but a *wide* reductionist. Meanings supervene, not on biology, but on a much larger network of relationships – including the history of those elements that have meaning – into which systems enter. Minds are brains whose extrinsic properties, including their history, helps to explain the behavior of their possessor.

All this is set out with wonderful clarity by Kim (pp. 60–1). I can do no better than refer the reader to his account. Before leaving the matter, however, I want to register dissent from a point that Horgan makes about explanatory exclusion. I am, as he says, a compatibilist on this matter, but I am so for more than the reason just given. Psychological explanations are not only compatible with the physical explantions to which (on my account) they reduce, they are also compatible with physical explantions to which they do not reduce. If we explain S's behavior by describing S's reasons for behaving this way, the beliefs and desires that moved him to action, this does not exclude other possible explanations, explanations that in no way mention (or imply the existence of) reasons for the same behavior. The fact that X means M can figure in a *legitimate* explanation of why B occurred without it being *necessary* to mention this fact (that X means M) in *every* true explanation of B.

This is merely the (by now) familiar point that explanation is an epistemological business that is responsive to an audience or intended audience. What belongs in an explanation is partly a function of what the audience already knows, what they are trying to find out, what gap in understanding one is trying to fill. As a result, there are no privileged explanations, no explanations you *have* to give no matter what your audience's interests, purposes, or understanding. The fact that a La-Placean demon (p. 83) might explain why I went to the fridge without mentioning my desires and beliefs shows absolutely nothing about whether I went there in order to get a beer. It might only show something about the demon's intended audience.

In *Explaining Behavior* I describe a thermostat that behaves in a bizzare way: it opens the garage door every time it gets chilly in the room. If a visitor wanted to know *why* the device behaved in this odd way, a normal response would be to describe the prank played by (or, perhaps, the incompetence of) the electrician who installed it. Assuming (by the form of their question) the visitor is asking a question about the behavior of the thermostat, why *it* is opening the garage door, what they are (normally) looking for is what I called a *structuring* cause of the thermostat's behavior: why are the events (whatever, exactly, they are) inside the thermostat, events that normally cause the furnace to ignite, causing, instead, the garage door to open? Telling them about the mischievous (or incompetent) electrician will answer their question.

But you don't *have* to give this explanation. You don't *have* to mention the electrician or the things that happened *yesterday*. Depending on the interests and knowledge of one's audience, one could explain the device's behavior by simply saying that there are wires leading from the thermostat to a motor that opens the garage door, that these wires are supplied with electricity, that changes in room temperature cause a metal strip in the thermostat to bend, closing an electrical circuit, energizing the motor, etc., etc. With the right audience, an audience that doesn't know enough about thermostats and how they work to understand how thermostats *could* open garage doors, this may be the *right* way to explain the thermostat's behavior. The thermostat opens the garage door because, you see, there are these wires that lead from the thermostat to the garage

... By giving an elaborate description (perhaps even a schematic diagram) of the electrical wiring of the house, a listener is brought to understand how events occurring in the thermostat cause the garage door to move – hence, *why* the thermostat opens the garage door when it gets cold in the room. The fact that this is a proper explanation of the thermostat's behavior in some contexts, an explanation that sticks to *present* facts about the wiring and ignores what went on yesterday (when the electrician wired things this way), does not show that the electrician's activities yesterday *don't* explain today's behavior of the thermostat.

For the same reason explanations in terms of an agent's reasons are not privileged. Just as we did with the thermostat, we (or a LaPlacean demon) might explain why I went to the kitchen by mentioning only my present neurological condition. Fred went to the kitchen because, you see, he was "wired" in this way ... By giving a description of the current state of my nervous system (or maybe just a schematic) one is brought to see *how* events of type C occurring in my right temporal lobe bring about limb movements of type M, movements that (in the circumstances I am in) bring me from the living room sofa to the refrigerator in the kitchen. Hence, one is brought to understand *why* I went to the fridge in the kind of conditions that trigger event C. If one isn't interested in how or why the nervous system got wired this way, maybe this is the best explanation. Even if it is, this doesn't mean I didn't go to the fridge *because* I wanted a beer and thought I could get one there.[8]

It is important to notice that you can, in one sense (a sense relevant to the way reasons explain behavior) understand why a device (thermostat or human being) is behaving the way it does *today* without knowing what events are triggering today's behavior. One need not know what triggered today's behavior to know *why* the thermostat behaved that way today. Normally, of course, the thermostat's behavior will be triggered by a drop in room temperature. But – who knows? – maybe this time the device, through some kind of interference, misrepresented a drop in room temperature. In this case the sequence of events culminating in the rising of the garage door was not triggered by a drop in room temperature. Still, despite ignorance of the trigger, one knows why the thermostat responded (to whatever it responded to) by opening the garage door. It did this because the electrician changed the wiring yesterday. There is nothing unusual about this kind of structuring explanation. What is a bit unusual, I suppose, is the suggestion that explanations of human behavior in terms of what we believe and desire *are* of this form.

It may appear, however, that explanations in terms of reasons constitute action at a (temporal) distance. It looks that way only if one doesn't understand the nature of behavior and the character of structuring causes. One explains why the process occurs, why tokens of event type C (including *today*'s token) cause tokens of event type M (resulting in tokens of behavior of type B), by explaining why things were organized in such a way that tokens of event type C would – if and when they occurred – produce tokens of event type M. If this reconfiguration took place yesterday, then yesterday's events explain why today's token behavior occurs. *Not*, mind you, why today's events, the events (C and M) constituting this behavior, occur, but why these events are related (causally) the way they are – hence, why a token behavior occurs.

Dennett complains (pp. 125–6) that on this account of things there are still no *locally* potent meanings: the fact that *this* (i.e., today's) token of C means (or indicates) F does not explain why *it* causes M. It is, rather, the fact that previous tokenings of C, those that occurred during learning, meant (or indicated) F that explains why this (present) token of C causes M. Hence, he says, learning is no better than natural selection in its demonstration of the efficacy of meaning. It is always – both in learning and in natural selection – the meaning or indicational properties of earlier instances of the structure type that figure in the explanation of why present tokens of this type behave the way they do (have the effects they do).

Cummins' third objection (p. 106) is basically the same:[9] on my learning-based account, it isn't *current* meaning that explains current behavior. It doesn't, he says, make any difference what *this* token of C means (or indicates): once the causal structure (the result of learning) is in place the C to M connection is guaranteed regardless of what current tokens of C mean or indicate.[10] Horgan, in an objection discussed earlier (under "Behavior") registers what I think is a similar complaint when he insists that reasons should be here-and-now structuring causes rather than (as they are on my account) merely *past*-structuring causes. And Kim, making careful and needed distinctions between types and tokens (p. 62), is puzzled by how a causal structure in place (as a result of learning) long before time *t*, a structure wherein tokens of C, when they occur, will produce M, can be exlained by the fact that *this* token of C, one occurring *at t*, has a certain meaning. What explains the recruitment of C as a cause of M is, he correctly observes, the past history of instantiations of these properties. So how, he asks, is the fact that the present token of C has a certain meaning supposed to explain *its* causing M (i.e., *current* behavior)?

When four astute critics all point, accusingly, in the same direction, its time to take a closer look. Most of the trouble lies, I think, in my (deliberate) choice to reduce the number of abbreviatory symbols and to avoid the stylistically cumbersome practice of always marking – in some explicit way – the difference between types and tokens. I ran a risk, but I thought context and the general drift of my argument would make things clear enough. Apparently not. I am grateful to Kim, therefore, for introducing some needed discipline into the discussion of this issue. I will try to respond to these criticisms on this point by using Kim's notation: C will always be some token occurrence of physical type N; N is the type of physical condition whose correlation with condition (type) F makes tokens of N indicate (carry the information that) F (when they do so)[11] and whose relationship with M (established through learning) makes tokens of N (when circumstances – motivational and otherwise – a♦ right) cause M.

A particular piece of behavior – my going to the kitchen yesterday afternoon at 3:00 p.m. or the thermostat opening the garage door just now – is a C causing M. When C has a meaning, when it represents (say) F, it does so because it is a token of type N, and this type, in virtue of its indicator (informational) properties (its correlation with F), was recruited for control duties (as a cause, say, of movements of type M) because it was an indicator of F. By saying that it – this structure *type* – was recruited as a cause of M because of what it indicated about F, I simply mean that as learning progresses later tokens of N (later Cs) cause M and the explanation, or part of the explanation, of their causing M is the fact that earlier tokens of N (earlier Cs) indicated F. When this is true, the later Cs, *whether or not they indicate F*, represent F. They represent F because they (in virtue of being tokens of type N) have the function of indicating F. They have the function of indicating F because they are of a type (N) that has this function. The needle on a gauge pointing at "0," this token condition, means that there is nothing left because it is a token of a type of condition (pointing at "0") whose function (in this case assigned function) it is to indicate that nothing is left.

With this much in place, the reply to Dennett,[12] Horgan, and Cummins (I'm not sure about Kim) can be put thus: the fact that C (a particular local instance of type N) represents F (has this content property) is, on this account of meaning, a fact about earlier tokens of N. It is, if you will, an *historical* fact about the role of N in the causal re-organization of the system in which its tokens occur. It is the fact that earlier tokens of N – because of what *they* (not C) indicated, because *they* successfully indicated F – shaped the causal role of subsequent tokens of N (including, of course, C). To say that C means F is to say that earlier tokens of this type carried the information that F and the fact that they carried this information was responsible for the recruitment of N (hence, C) as a control structure, as a cause of bodily movements (*which* bodily movements depending on the total motivational-cognitive state of the organism).

To attribute a meaning to a token internal state is, on this account of meaning (and belief), to describe the *source* of its causal efficacy. It is to say that C gets the meaning or content F because *past* Cs (past tokens of the same type), by carrying the information that F, gave C its functional role in the regulation and direction of output.

According to this view, then, meanings are locally potent (as Cummins says, definitionally) because, given the nature of meaning, local meanings, the fact that *this* C means F, is, in reality, a fact about the kind of information that restructured control circuits so as to give C a voice in determining output. Why is the system behaving this way? Why (on this account of behavior) is C causing M? Because C means F – a fact which, on this account of meaning, describes, in terms of their indicator properties, why Cs were given this job.

The key to this analysis is an understanding of how two pieces interlock. There is, first, the fact that behavior is a process wherein C, a token of physical type N, causes M. The fact that it is a process makes it susceptible, therefore, to causal explanations of *both* the triggering and structuring kind. Second, there is the fact that meaning is something C has in virtue of being of a type previous tokens of which had (in virtue of their indicator properties) certain organizational effects on system output. The first fact makes behavior the sort of thing that can be explained by the sort of thing the second fact tells us meanings are. Structuring explanations are exactly the kind of explanations meanings (on a learning-based account of meaning) can provide. Indeed, if meanings are to provide structuring explanations of current behavior, meanings *must* be the sort of historical property a thing has in virtue of what occurred *before*, perhaps long before, the behavior to be explained. So these pieces fit together in a particularly intimate way. Furthermore, the second fact, the fact that C has a meaning in virtue of the work of previous tokens (of the type of which it is a token) is what makes meanings effective *even when* they are false – even when there is misrepresentation. Meanings are effective even when false, even when C *fails* to indicate what it is supposed to indicate, because the fact that C means F derives its explanatory power from past tokens *doing* (i.e., indicating F) what it is C's function to do, what C is *supposed to be doing*.

Kim (p. 66) offers me an answer to the difficulty he describes, an answer he describes as "not altogether implausible" which is close to the answer I have just given. This answer is, I think, to be found in chapters 3 and 4 of *Explaining Behavior*, but I admit it would be easier to find if I had adopted Kim's device of making the type-token distinction in a more systematic way.

To put this in a more general light, the idea is that the sort of meaning attaching to psychological states (particularly belief) is a historical property: to say that S believes F is to say that there is some C inside S that means (non-naturally) F, and this, in turn, is to say something about the way *past* Cs – in virtue of what *they* meant (natural meaning) ·· changed the way the system was causally organized. Present meanings explain present behavior, but only because both meaning and behavior (at least the structuring explanations of behavior) are backward looking phenomena.

Cummins is right, then, when he says (p. 106) that it is natural meaning that explains behavior, the natural meaning (indicator properties) of *past* tokens of N explain *present* behavior, why this C is causing M. But he is wrong when he goes on to conclude that this shows that the non-natural meaning of C, the current token of N, does *not* explain the same behavior. For the meaning, the non-natural meaning, of the present C *is*, on this view of non-natural meaning, whatever natural meaning (information) in past Cs explains the present causal arrangements. The fact that this makes the non-natural meaning, the content, of C relevant in some *definitional* way to the explanation of behavior is, it seems to me, a

bonus. It is not, as Cummins suggests, a problem. This is exactly what w
want beliefs to be: maps which, by definition, are our means of steering.

Belief and Belief Content: McLaughlin

I don't know how to improve on McLaughlin's treatment of belief content. So I won't try. What I hope to do, instead, is show why it is so easy for me to agree.

McLaughlin argues that a naturalistic account of belief must reject the content principle (no difference in belief without a difference in content) and accept the *encoded* content principle (beliefs can differ in the way they encode the same content). If content is understood in one way, I agree. This, in fact, and as McLaughlin notes, is the view I adopted in *Knowledge and the Flow of Information*. I there distinguished *semantic* content (roughly the kind of information the belief structure was developed to carry) from *cognitive* structure. Cognitive structure has to do with the way semantic content is conceptually embodied, the way it is (so to speak) assembled out of representationally simpler elements. Belief content, I argued, is *conceptualized* semantic content. Two beliefs can, therefore, have the same (semantic) content, differing only in the way they encode (conceptually partition) this content. So if we are talking about semantic content, I agree with McLaughlin: the *encoded* content principle is the right principle. Two beliefs can have the same (semantic) content and differ only in the way they encode that content.

McLaughlin, however, thinks there is some difficulty for naturalistic accounts of belief in accepting this result. He poses a dilemma to dramatize the problem. How can a naturalistic account of belief or representation have B (some internal state) represent F and not represent G when F and G are necessarily the same (the way a fortnight is necessarily the same as fourteen days)? Since any structure that carries the information (or indicates) that Mary will return in a fortnight necessarily carries the information (indicates) that she will return in fourteen days, how can a theory of belief that analyzes belief content in terms of the information-carrying (indicational) function of structures distinguish the belief that Mary will return in a fortnight and the belief that she will return in fourteen days? Belief content, it seems, must be something *more* than indicational (information-carrying) function. Or, to put it yet another way, though information is an intentional commodity, it doesn't cut the intentional pie finely enough to capture the idea of belief content. For that we have to *distinguish* conditions (like a fortnight and fourteen days) that are informationally indistinguishable.

I think the analysis of belief begun in *Knowledge and the Flow of Information* and extended in *Explaining Behavior* leads more naturally to this result than McLaughlin realizes. In fact, if I'm not mistaken, it yields exactly the result for which he argues so carefully and convincingly. Let me illustrate with a simple example. The example involves (what I call) assigned functions, functions that depend, in one way or another, on the information gathering purposes and needs of conscious agents. It is not, therefore, quite what I need to make a case about belief, a form of representation that depends on *natural* functions. It will help, nonetheless, to illustrate a point.

Many cars come equipped with a tachometer, a device whose purpose it is to indicate how fast the engine is running. In my terms, then, since it has the function of indicating, say, engine revolutions per minute (rpm), it *represents* engine revolutions per minute (rpm). In cars equipped with automatic transmissions, there is also something to indicate which gear (neutral, reverse, first, second, etc.) the car is in. Since it, too, has an indicator function, it, too, is a representation. Both indicators, for example, can *misrepresent* what it is their function to indicate. It turns out that under normal operating conditions, these two indicators, taken together, indicate *how fast the car is going* (vehicle speed). If the car is in third gear, say, and the tachometer registers 3,000 rpm, then the car is (must be) going 45 mph. The joint registration of these two indicators (call this composite state B) indicates exactly what the speedometer indicates – how fast the car is going. A bad case of indicator (informational) redundancy. In point of fact, any two of these devices (taken together) indicate what the third indicates. If all we were interested in was having something inside the car to indicate engine rpm, car speed, and gear, we could eliminate one of the devices. Informationally speaking, two do everything that the three do.

But though we have indicational redundancy, we do not have *representational* redundancy. Two of these indicators, taken together, do *not* represent what the third represents. It is not the function of the tachometer and the gear indicator (either singly or jointly) to indicate vehicle speed – although if we removed the speedometer, it might *become* their (added) function to represent car speed. Although they indicate vehicle speed, they do not *represent* vehicle speed – *not* if the representational content is identified (as I identify it) with what it is the *function* of something to indicate. Not everything that indicates speed (e.g., vibration in steering column) has the *function* of indicating (i.e., represents) speed. It is the speedometer's function to indicate car speed. That it what *it* represents.

So we have, in the car, a condition B (composite registration of tachometer and gear indicator) that represents engine rpm (G) *and* gear (H) – and, therefore, represents the combined state of the engine and transmission, G + H, but does not represent car speed (F) even though nothing *can* indicate (carry information about) the one without indicating (carrying information about) about the other. These two states, B + G and F, are informationally indistinguishable in the sense that nothing *can* carry the information that B + H without carrying the information that F.[13] Nevertheless, though we cannot separate the information that F from the information that G + H, we *can* clearly distinguish, in terms of their information-carrying *functions*, one way of carrying this information from the other. The speedometer has the function of carrying information, about car speed, the tachometer and gear indicator, though necessarily carrying this same information (coded as B + H), do not have this function. If we removed the speedometer from the car, there would no longer be anything that *represented* car speed although there would remain (in the tachometer and gear indicator) an indication of car speed. If we wish to say that the tachometer and gear indicator have the function of carrying information about car speed (since they have the function of carrying information about conditions which necessarily embody information about car speed), then we must say that they have the function of carrying this information coded in a certain way (as G + H) while the speedometer has the function of encoding the same piece of information in a "simple" (*representationally* simple) form, F. The speedometer, as it were, does not resolve this information into the same (indeed, into *any*) representational or conceptual pieces. Hence, on a theory (such as that in *Explaining Behavior*) that views representation in terms of indicational function, it is possible to have a B represent one thing (e.g., B + H) and not represent another (e.g., F) even though B cannot indicate the one without indicating the other.

Similarly, on this account of belief (as internal representation), believing that Mary will return in fourteen days is to token internal structures that, when things are working right, jointly carry the information that she will return in a fort-night. The composite structure, however, carries this information *in a certain way*. It encodes information about a fortnight in structures having the function of indicating something about NUMBER (i.e., fourteen) and DAY. There is no reason information about a fortnight *has* to be encoded in structures having *these* indicational functions anymore than information about car speed has to be coded in terms of engine rpm and gear. And when it isn't, the identification of a fortnight with fourteen days (the belief that a fortnight *is* fourteen days), though informationally barren (having an information content of zero) will be representationally (and, hence, *cognitively*) significant.

The question, of course, is how far we can go with this model. Are there comparable situations that develop in living systems when the functions defining representational (belief) content are *natural* functions, functions derived from learning. Though McLaughlin expresses doubt, I see no reason to think this impossible – or even improbable. On the contrary, it seems to me that the brain's informational needs are best served by the kind of redundancy witnessed here. Things can acquire indicational functions – hence, acquire a representational status – when there are other elements which, because they (in combination) indicate the very same thing, could have been recruited for the very same job. This (as we just saw) happens (indeed, it is deliberately made to happen) in artifacts like cars. It happens in language. Why not in brains? If so, the encoded content principle is just what one would expect on a naturalistic theory of belief, one that identified what is believed with what it was the function (acquired through learning) of a structure to indicate.

Notes

1 At the time I wrote *Seeing and Knowing*, I was only aware of Warnock (1954) and Chisholm (1957).

2 It is important that the denial of closure be understood as the denial that you know everything you know to be implied by *what* you know, *not* everything that is implied by *that* you know. The latter is, or *should* be, uncontroversial. It is simply the denial of the KK thesis: that knowing P implies knowing that you know P. That you know P is implied by *that* you know P, but not by P itself – by *what* you know.

3 This was David Sanford's point in the quotation he gives from his earlier paper. Contrastive focusing will help make explicit what is claimed to be known, but it will not help to supply a theoretical account of knowledge itself. Though he now "repudiates" these earlier remarks, he does not do so, he says, because they are false.

4 What he actually says (p. 106) is that learning itself (some of it) is unlearned behavior explained in terms of unlearned knowledge. I do not know what it means to say that learning *is* unlearned behavior. Perhaps he means learning is (or is a manifestation of) an unlearned capacity to learn.

5 There is nothing in the computer that means that 42 is the square root of 1,764 the way the degree of curvature of the metal strip in a thermost means that the room temperature is 42.

6 This is access in the sense that Dennett himself recognizes when he says (1978, p. 258) that the job of getting information interpreted correctly is "getting this information into functional position to govern the behavioral repertoire of the whole organism." If Dennett means what I mean by the word information, and if he intends to be taken literally in speaking of giving information a functional role, then we are in complete agreement: systems operate with *interpreted* information (*meanings*) – hence, in this sense, they have *access* to the meaning of their internal states – when the *information* embodied in these states (not just the states that embody it) is given a causal role in the governance of behavior. Unfortunately, though, I don't think Dennett means what I mean by the word information. And even if he did, he would certainly not want to be taken literally in speaking of the functional role of information. Dennett and I use the same words, but we don't always speak the same language.

7 I return to Dennett's charge that all this shows is that meanings are not *locally* potent in evolution, a potency they also lack (he says) in learning, in the next section.

8 I hope it is clear that my analogy with electricians and thermostats is meant to be only an analogy. Though thermostats do things – sometimes strange things – and we give explanations for why they do these things, these explanations for the behavior of artifacts are much different, of course, than our explanations (in terms of reasons) for the deliberate behavior of human beings. No resemblance between internal states with meaning (beliefs and desires), the sort of thing that explains *our* (voluntary) behavior, and electricians with prankish intentions (the sort of thing that, in our analogy, explains a thermostat's behavior) is intended.

9 Cummins also makes the point (his second objection, p. 106) that it isn't a structure's meaning (in the relevant sense) but its indicational properties (its

natural meaning) that explains the behavior. This is, I think, an independe
criticism and I return to it below.

10　It is misleading to speak of the C to M connection being established (much less guaranteed) by learning. The sort of learning from which an internal state (C) acquires its meaning, its indicator *function*, will always involve some behavior (C → M) since it is in the promotion of this behavior that C acquires its indicator function, but C's function is *not* to cause M. C has an *indicator* function, the function of indicating whatever condition explains its recruitment (during learning) as a cause of M. What C causes *after* learning, *after* it has a meaning, however, depends on what *other* beliefs and desires it co-occurs with.

11　They don't always do so, of course, as the possibility of misrepresentation shows.

12　I earlier (section entitled "Learning") tried to respond to Dennett's claim that the respects in which meanings were causally efficacious were the same in natural selection as in learning (and, hence, that learning was nothing special). Here I address merely that part of his objection that he shares with Horgan and Cummins.

13　The information that F (car speed) and information that B + G (engine rpm + gear) are not informationally indistinguishable (there is not an *equivalence* of informational contents) since there are various combinations of engine rpm and gear that can result in a given car speed. But I do not think this fact detracts from the illustration. The point is that a structure can be made to represent one thing, not another, even though it cannot be made to carry the one piece of information without the other.

References

Chisholm, R. 1957: *Perceiving*. Ithaca, N.Y.: Cornell University Press.

Dennett, D. 1978: Current Issues in the Philosophy of Mind. *American Philosophical Quarterly*, 15.

Fodor, J. 1984: Semantics Wisconsin Style. *Synthese*, 59, pp. 1–20.

Millikan, R. 1989: In Defense of Proper Functions, *Philosophy of Science*, 56, 2, pp. 288–302.

Putnam, H. 1975: The Meaning of Meaning. In *Language, Mind and Knowledge*, vol. 7, *Minnesota Studies in the Philosophy of Science*, ed. K. Gunderson, Minneapolis: University of Minnesota Press.

Stich, S. 1983: *From Folk Psychology to Cognitive Science*. Cambridge, Mass.: MIT Press/Bradford Books.

Warnock, G. 1954: Seeing. *Aristotelian Society Proceedings*, 55, pp. 201–18.

Yourgrau, P. 1983: Knowledge and Relevant Alternatives, *Synthese*, 55, pp. 175–90.

Bibliography of Fred Dretske's Publications

Bibliography of Fred Dretske's Publications

Seeing and Knowing, 1969, University of Chicago Press and Routledge and Kegan Paul. Midway Reprint Edition (University of Chicago Press), 1988.

Knowledge and the Flow of Information, 1981, Cambridge, Mass.: MIT Press Bradford Book, (published by Basil Blackwell in England). Spanish Edition: *Conocimiento E Informacion*, 1987, Biblioteca Cientifica Salvat, Barcelona. Chapter 6, "Sensations and Perception," reprinted in *Perceptual Knowledge*, ed. Jonathan Dancy, Oxford: Oxford University Press, 1988.

Explaining Behavior: Reasons in a World of Causes, 1988, MIT Press Bradford Books.

Articles

"Particulars and the Relational Theory of Time," *Philosophical Review*, 50, 4 (October 1961).

"Moving Backward in Time," *Philosophical Review*, 71, 1 (January 1962).

"Observational Terms," *Philosophical Review*, 73, 1 (January 1964).

"Particular Reidentification," *Philosophy of Science*, 31, 1 (April 1964).

"Counting to Infinity," *Analysis*, supplementary volume (January 1965).

"Reasons and Falsification," *Philosophical Quarterly* (January 1965).

"Can Events Move?" *Mind* (October 1967).

"Ziring Ziderata," *Mind* (October 1967).

"Reasons and Consequences," *Analysis* (April 1968).

"Seeing and Justification," and "Reply to Hugly," in *Perception and Personal Identity*, ed. Norman S. Care and Robert H. Grimm, Case Western University Press, 1968.

"Epistemic Operators," *Journal of Philosophy* (December, 1970).

"Conclusive Reasons," *Australasian Journal of Philosophy*, (May 1971). Reprinted in *Essays on Knowledge and Justification*, ed. George Pappas and Marshall Swain Cornell University Press, Ithaca and London, 1978; and translated into German in *Analytische Philosophie Der Erkenntnis*, ed. Peter Beiri, Athenaum, 1987.

"Reasons, Knowledge and Probability," *Philosophy of Science* (June 1971).

"Perception from an Epistemological Point of View," *Journal of Philosophy* (October 1971).

"Casual Irregularity" (with Aaron Snyder), *Philosophy of Science* (March 1972).

"Contrastive Statements," *Philosophical Review* (October 1972).

"Perception and Other Minds," *Nous* (March 1973).

"Causal Sufficiency; A Reply to Beauchamp" (with Aaron Snyder), *Philosophy of Science* (June 1973).

"The Content of Knowledge," *Forms of Representation*, ed. Bruce Freed et al., North Holland; Amsterdam, 1975.

"Explanation in Linguistics," in *Explaining Linguistic Phenomena*, ed. David Cohen, Halsted Press, John Wiley and Sons, New York, 1974.

"Perception," *Collier's Encyclopedia*, Macmillan Publishing Company, New York, 1974.

"Causal Theories of Reference," *Journal of Philosophy*, 74, 10 (October 1977).

"Laws of Nature," *Philosophy of Science*, 44, 2 (June 1977).

"Referring to Events," *Midwest Studies in Philosophy*, vol. 2, ed. II Peter French, Ted Uehling, and Howard Wettstein, University of Minnesota Press; Minneapolis, 1977.

Replies to Mary Hesse ("Truth and the Growth of Scientific Knowledge") and Dudley Shapere ("The Influence of Knowledge on the Description of Facts"), *Proceedings: Philosophy of Science Association*, vol. 2, 1977.

"Reply to Niiniluoto," *Philosophy of Science*, 45, 3 (September 1978).

"The Role of the Percept in Visual Cognition," *Minnesota Studies in the Philosophy of Science: Perception and Cognition*, vol. 9, ed. Wade Savage, University of Minnesota Press, Minneapolis, Minn. 1978.

"Chisholm on Perceptual Knowledge," *Grazer Philosophische Studien*, vol. 7/8, 1979.

"Simple Seeing," *Body, Mind and Method: Essays in Honor of Virgil Aldrich*, ed. D. F. Gustafson and B. L. Tapscott, D. Reidel, Dordrecht-Holland, 1979.

"Meaning and Information," *Concept Formation and Explanation of Behavior*, ed. Robert Hannaford, Ripon College Studies in the Liberal Arts, vol. 4, Ripon, Wis. 1980.

"The Intentionality of Cognitive States," *Midwest Studies in Philosophy*, vol. 5, ed. Peter French, Theodore Uehling, Howard Wettstein, University of Minnesota Press, Minneapolis, Minn. 1980.

"The Pragmatic Dimension of Knowledge," *Philosophical Studies*, 40, 3 (November 1981).

"A Cognitive Cuel-de-Sac," *Mind*, 91, 361 (January 1982).

"The Informational Character of Representations," commentary on H. L. Roitblat's "The Meaning of Representation in Animal Memory," in *The Behavioral and Brain Sciences*, 5, 3 (September 1982).

"Precis of *Knowledge and the Flow of Information*," for multiple book review in *Behavioral and Brain Sciences*, 6, 1 (March 1983), pp. 55–63. Reprinted in *Naturalized Epistemology*, ed. Hilary Kornblith Cambridge, Mass., Bradford Books/MIT Press; 1985.

"Why Information?" response to commentators, *Behavioral and Brain Sciences*, 6, 1 (March 1983), pp. 82–9.

"The Epistemology of Belief," *Synthese*, 55, 1 (April 1983). Reprinted in *Doubting: Contemporary Perspectives on Scepticism*, ed. Glenn Ross and Michael Roth, Kluwer Academic Publishing Co., 1990.

"Lost Knowledge" (with Palle Yourgrau), *Journal of Philosophy*, 80, 6 (June 1983).

Abstract of "Seeing through Pictures," (reply to Ken Walton), *Nous* 81, 1 (1984).

"Causal Theories of Knowledge (with Berent Enc), *Midwest Studies in Philo-

sophy, ed. P. French, T. Uehling and H. Wettstein, University of Minnesota Press; Minneapolis, Minn. 1984.

"Constraints and Meaning," commentary on Barwise and Perry, *Situations and Attitudes*, in *Linguistics and Philosophy*, 1985.

"Mentality and Machines" (Presidential Address, APA Western Division), *Proceedings and Addresses of the American Philosophical Association*, 59, 1 (September 1985). Translated into Hebrew and appearing in *The Philosophical Machine*, ed. Avron Polakow; reprinted in *Philosophy, Mind and Cognitive Inquiry*, ed. James Fetzer, Kluwer.

"Aspects of Cognitive Representation," in *Problems in the Representation of Knowledge and Belief*, ed. Myles Brand and Mike Harnish, University of Arizona Press; Tucson, 1986.

"Misrepresentation," in *Belief*, ed. Radu Bogdan, Oxford, Oxford University Press, 1986. Reprinted in *Mind and Cognition: A Reader*, ed. William Lycan, Oxford, Basil Blackwell, 1990.

"Stalking Intentionality" (comments on Ken Sayre), *Behavioral and Brain Sciences*, 9, 1 (March 1986).

"The Explanatory Role of Content," in *Contents of Thought: Proceedings of the 1985 Oberlin Colloquium in Philosophy*. University of Arizona Press, Tucson: 1988.

"Bogdan on Information," *Mind and Language*, 3, 2 (Summer, 1988).

"The Stance Stance," *Behavioral and Brain Sciences*, 11, 3 (September 1988) (comments on Dennett).

"Reasons and Causes," *Philosophical Perspectives*, vol. 3, *Philosophy of Mind and Action Theory*, ed. James Tomberlin, Atascadero, Ca., Ridgeview Publishing Company, 1989.

"The Need to Know," in *Theory of Knowledge: The State of the Art*, ed. Keith Lehrer and Marjorie Clary, University of Arizona Press, Tucson, 1989.

"Dretske's Replies," in *Dretske and His Critics*, ed. Brian McLaughlin, Oxford, Basil Blackwell, 1990.

"Precis" (of *Explaining Behavior*) and "Reply to Reviewers" (Stich, Millikan, Tuomela, Stampe, Bratman), *Philosophy and Phenomenological Research*, 50, 40 (June 1990).

"Seeing, Believing and Knowing," chapter 5 in *An Invitation to Cognitive Science*, vol. 2, *Visual Cognition and Action*, ed. Dan Osherson, Stephen Kosslyn and John Hollerbach, Cambridge, Mass., MIT Press, 1990.

"Does Meaning Matter?" paper delivered conference on information theoretic epistemology and cemantics, Mexico City, August 1988, published in *Information, Semantics and Epistemology*, ed. Enrique Villanueva, Oxford, Basil Blackwell, 1990, also forthcoming in Spanish.

"Putting Information to Work," in *Information Language, and Cognition: Vancouver Studies in Cognitive Science*, ed. Philip Handson, Vancouver B.C.; University of British Columbia Press, 1990.

Index